Achieve the Honorable

ACHIEVE THE HONORABLE

A MISSOURI CONGRESSMAN'S JOURNEY FROM WARM SPRINGS TO WASHINGTON

—

IKE SKELTON

The State Historical Society of Missouri / *Columbia*
Southern Illinois University Press / *Carbondale*

16 15 14 13   4 3 2 1

Library of Congress Cataloging-in-Publication Data
Skelton, Isaac Newton.
Achieve the honorable : a Missouri congressman's
journey from Warm Springs to Washington / Ike
Skelton.
     pages cm
Includes bibliographical references and index.
ISBN 978-0-8093-3283-0 (cloth : alk. paper)
ISBN 0-8093-3283-3 (cloth : alk. paper)
ISBN 978-0-8093-3284-7 (ebook)
ISBN 0-8093-3284-1 (ebook) (print)
1. Skelton, Isaac Newton. 2. Legislators—United
States—Biography. 3. United States. Congress.
House—Biography. 4. Missouri—Politics and
government—1951– I. Title.
E840.8.S5495A3 2013
328.73'092—dc23
[B]   2013006668

Printed on recycled paper. ♻
The paper used in this publication meets the minimum requirements of American National Standard
for Information Sciences—Permanence of Paper for
Printed Library Materials, ANSI Z39.48-1992. ∞

Admonition at Wentworth Military Academy, Lexington, Missouri, alma mater of Ike Skelton. Courtesy of Wentworth Military Academy

*I have had a lifelong love affair with the state of Missouri.
This memoir is dedicated to my home state
and its wonderful people.*

With prayerful thought,
I believe each of us can be
inspired to achieve
honorable goals

*Ike Skelton's sermon at St. James United Methodist Church,
Kansas City, Missouri, July 3, 2005*

CONTENTS

A NOTE

The events of thirty-four years in Congress, much less those of a lifetime before and after, would take many volumes to properly tell. What follows are the highlights, those events and observations that burn brightest in memory. To anyone whose story I did not tell, or who hoped to see a particular subject covered that I left out, I apologize. But stop me sometime and I'll tell you all about it.

Also, it may seem as you read this book that everyone I ever met became a good friend. Thumper in the movie *Bambi* gave some advice, "If you can't say something nice, don't say nothing at all." I like that advice and have tried to live it in these pages.

ACKNOWLEDGMENTS

My life, my work in public office, and indeed whatever success I have enjoyed through the years are attributable to the efforts of many other people. This is also true of this memoir. I want to take this opportunity to particularly acknowledge some people who have been especially important in helping me share these memories.

First and foremost are two of the most important women in my life—my wife, Patty, and my late wife, Susie; my sons Ike V, Jim, and Page and their wives and children; my longtime Chief of Staff Bob Hagedorn and former Chief of Staff Jack Pollard; Deputy Chief of Staff Whitney Frost; former Press Secretary Lara Battles; my veteran research guru and advising wordsmith, Michael Rowan; Professor Richard H. Kohn of the University of North Carolina at Chapel Hill, one of the nation's most respected military historians; Dr. Archie Barrett, a former Air Force officer who soared to still greater heights as a critical staff player and deep thinker advising the House Armed Services Committee; my cousin Dr. Earl F. Skelton of Georgetown University and his dear wife, Francesca, who provided invaluable Skelton family historical research; and past colleagues in public service too numerous to name for their ideas, comments, memories, and participation in the events I recount in these pages. God bless them all.

Special thanks go to my friend and former Armed Services Committee staffer J. J. Gertler, who reviewed the manuscript and suggested many helpful revisions. I can attest that if you ever need an unfamiliar religious service translated from Armenian to Latin to Italian to English, he's your man.

And I want to thank my initial collaborator on this memoir, Scott Charton, with whom I spent many pleasurable days reviewing my life and its ups and downs. We first met more than two decades ago when Scott covered Missouri politics as a veteran Associated Press correspondent. A student of history, Scott has coaxed from me so many memories of my life and helped me organize those memories into this narrative. Scott is a superb journalist and a trusted friend to whom I remain grateful.

Finally, I must thank the people of Missouri for so many precious memories and the opportunity to represent them for thirty-four years in Congress. I am eternally grateful to call Missouri home, and to call so many Missourians my friends and neighbors. God bless Missouri, and God bless America, land that I love.

ACHIEVE THE HONORABLE

A Wreck in Iraq

CONGRESSMEN AREN'T SUPPOSED to be upside down.

Now, it's no secret that through the years, congressmen have been found in a number of unusual positions. And that's true of political positions as well as physical ones. But whether you're a Republican, Democrat, or neither, and whatever you may think of our country, Washington, or the Congress, I think we can all agree that legislators generally function best with their heads at least on a level with their feet.

My name is Ike Skelton, and I am proud to be an American, a Missourian, a Democrat, and a resolute optimist. I've believed all my life that challenges are best met not with rancor or rhetoric, but with grit and good cheer. I can tell you, though, that this attitude is hard to maintain when you are upside down in a ditch in Iraq.

As a boy in Lexington, Missouri, I had dreamed of serving my country and seeing the world. Both dreams had come true, although not always in the way I had imagined.

When my friends and fellow Missourians permitted me to represent them in Congress, I chose to pursue my lifelong interest in military service by joining the House Armed Services Committee. Throughout my time there, including from 2007 to 2011 as the committee chairman, I made it a point to spend the Thanksgiving or Christmas holidays, and often both, with U.S. troops in the field. Although I could not wear the nation's uniform (for reasons I'll discuss later), breaking bread and sharing fellowship is something I could do to express my own appreciation to the men and women who stand guard and risk everything for America every hour of the day.

But how on earth did I wind up in a ditch? On Saturday, November 26, 2005, some colleagues and I had just wrapped up a Thanksgiving tour of operations briefings, personal inspections, and visits with troops around Iraq. We were loaded into a military vehicle that was heavily armored but box-shaped like an ice cream truck, and we were rushing down the middle of a narrow two-lane road to the Baghdad airport.

That may sound like an odd way to travel, but it's how the U.S. military moved official civilian visitors in that strife-riven country—commanding the road, helicopters swirling overhead, rolling swiftly in a secure procession to get to the destination in no-nonsense fashion while minimizing exposure to threats.

But as darkness fell that particular Saturday evening, not everyone seemed to know or care for the unusual rules of that road. A water-tank truck with an Iraqi driver coming from the opposite direction did not yield to us, and the sergeant driving our truck swerved to avoid a head-on crash. Our truck went into a ditch and overturned.

On earlier trips, the military had moved congressional delegations in armored SUVs, usually black Chevy Suburbans. To increase protection against hazards peculiar to Iraq—roadside bombs, rocket-propelled grenades, and the like—they had since created a more sophisticated, better-protected truck. But the design omitted one of the key safeguards against more prosaic road hazards—seat belts. So when the truck began to roll, we were tossed around the hard-edged metal passenger compartment like socks in a dryer. My Georgia colleague, Jim Marshall, grabbed me to slow my fall as the truck went over, and I was somewhat cushioned by landing against an unfortunate lieutenant colonel who was next to the door.

Thankfully, Jim Marshall was unhurt. But Pennsylvania Congressman Tim Murphy and I were hurting indeed. We'd both landed on our necks, and I had struck something sharp with my back. Tim was also bloodied from a cut over one eye. Out of concern for possible spinal damage, we had to be lifted out the back window of the toppled truck. Guards with machine guns created a secure perimeter. I was placed on a stretcher. Ambulances quickly appeared, and I was loaded into one and sped to the Army hospital in Baghdad.

At the hospital, medics took off my belt and combat boots and then sliced my pants right off to begin medical treatment. My belt and boots never turned up again, but I got to keep my slivered pants. My back and neck were hurting like the devil, but I believed I would be OK—and I knew my pain was small potatoes compared to what so many American troops had been through.

Tim Murphy and I were put into a hospital room with a six-year-old Iraqi boy who was moaning in pain. He had been shot by insurgents, who killed his mother and father in the same attack. That kept matters in perspective for me. And I was proud to see that the excellent standard of care was the same for a six-year-old Iraqi as for an American congressman, soldier, or any other patient.

After several hours of treatment at the Baghdad hospital, I was rolled on a gurney to a helicopter, which flew us to a C-17 medical evacuation plane where I joined a group of wounded troops for the flight to the military hospital in Landstuhl, Germany.

I was pretty helpless, not a condition I care for, and the pain showed little interest in leaving me. I realized one key thing: the often abstract idea of America's young men and women in uniform standing up for us had turned very real. I had always cared deeply for them and had devoted my professional career to them, but suddenly they were my protectors and caregivers in a quite personal way. I owe them my deepest thanks for their fast actions that day. (And I still apologize to the lieutenant colonel who cushioned my fall.)

I recovered for four days in Germany, at that same U.S. hospital where our injured troops receive excellent care every day. One day, I received a call expressing get-well wishes from President George W. Bush. Marine General James Jones, the Supreme Allied Commander of NATO (and later President Barack Obama's national security adviser), drove over to see me. But one of the most thoughtful and welcome hospital visits was from a Lexington native, Navy Captain Randy Jackson. It was particularly uplifting to see a face from back home in Missouri.

The hospital staff was spectacular and made it easy for me to stay on the bright side. I expressed appreciation to one of the nurses for the standard of care, and she replied, "Don't think you're getting anything special—we treat everyone like this." I believe it. The hospital staff and medical experts are really professional, and I was glad to be able to stop in again in 2009 to thank them once more for taking care of me.

But the truck wreck in Iraq wasn't the first time I relied on the help and caring of others to overcome a life-threatening challenge, nor was it the first time I lay in a hospital bed, thinking about the uncertainties of the future. I had been there before, as a boy back in Missouri.

ROOTS

LET ME START with some context. Although everybody knows me as Ike, my full name is Isaac Newton Skelton IV, and yes, I've heard about every falling-apple joke there is. The Skeltons can track the family back to 1750, to a John Skelton in what is modern Page County, Virginia. We can't go back further than that yet—our family genealogist, my cousin Dr. Earl Skelton, notes there is a Skelton, England, but he cannot prove a connection.

We also believe there is a family connection to Bathurst Skelton, a classmate of Thomas Jefferson at the College of William and Mary, who successfully competed in romance against Mr. Jefferson, winning the hand in marriage of the mutual object of their affection, Martha Wayles. After Bathurst's death, his widow and Thomas Jefferson did marry, and she was said to be the great love of the future president, who was terribly bereaved for a long time after her death.

John Skelton had six sons. Everyone knows the wonderful comedian Red Skelton, who has passed on after a career as a television pioneer. He was from the Indiana branch of the Skeltons, and though we are unsure of any relation, Indiana is where some of John Skelton's sons settled. When I was a new congressman, Red Skelton paid a visit to Capitol Hill, and I took my sons out of school to meet him. He was very courteous, and it was a treat for the boys.

John Skelton's youngest son was Isaac, who was the first of our line with that name. Isaac had a son named Washington Mason Skelton, a Confederate soldier who fought in Virginia, in what is now West Virginia. Washington Mason Skelton came to Missouri to be with his sister, and by 1869 they lived in Waverly, Missouri, just east of Lexington.

Evidently, Washington Mason Skelton liked to drink a bit, but he reformed and became a deacon in the Baptist Church at Waverly. He had served as a private in Ashby's Brigade of Stonewall Jackson's army, and he fought in the battle of Romney, Virginia. Washington Mason Skelton outlived three wives and died in 1920 while residing at the old Confederate Veterans Home in Higginsville, Missouri, at the age of ninety-six years, six months, and six days.

His son, Isaac Newton Skelton II, was my grandfather. I never knew him because he was struck by a train and killed in 1908, when my father was seven years old. My father worked from that time on, and he considered Washington Mason Skelton to be his father figure. My great-grandfather imbued my father with his love of history in general and the Confederacy's history in specific, and my father instilled this love of history in me at a very young age. It was not difficult, since he was a great natural storyteller.

Although my maternal grandfather didn't carry the name Skelton, he had an enormous positive influence over me. He was John T. Boone, known to all as "Brother Boone," a minister in the Disciples of Christ. A native of Tennessee, he came to Missouri and pastored churches in Joplin, Jefferson City, and St. Louis. It was during his time in St. Louis that he married the church organist, a pretty native of Foristell, Missouri, named Elizabeth Blattner. They moved to Jacksonville, Florida, where for the next forty-five years he led congregations of two churches, was active in Masonic bodies, and was beloved by local residents.

Brother Boone was known as the "Marrying Parson," because couples wanting to tie the knot flocked to his parlor for a very special ceremony he wrote, in which he emphasized faith and fidelity.* As a small boy, I got to watch in wonderment as my grandfather performed the weddings—and Brother Boone was always the first to kiss the bride and wish the newlyweds Godspeed. There were other neat advantages in being Brother Boone's grandson. For example, he preached funerals and allowed me to ride with him in the hearse. Now that was an experience a nine-year-old boy won't forget.

He was a very warm person, but he was also very much a disciplinarian, which didn't hurt me at all. That school year, I attended the third grade in Jacksonville because my mother, Carolyn Boone Skelton, was there on her annual visit to her parents. At the time she was pregnant with my little brother and had been advised by her doctor against making the long trip back to Missouri.

I loved that year in Florida and made some great friendships. And I got to spend a lot of fun time with my grandmother's sister, Aunt Sally, who spoiled me terribly. Every Saturday, she and I would go on the bus into Jacksonville and have lunch at Morrison's Cafeteria, where she would always eat a carrot salad. Then by prearrangement we would go to a movie, and afterward go by the Kress five-and-ten-cent store where I might buy a toy—a model airplane or such—before we got on the bus to come back. Every Saturday we did that. She just spoiled me rotten. She was a lovely lady. By tradition then, relatives lived with relatives. They don't do that today.

Most of the time we went to see Gene Autry movies, because Aunt Sally liked his singing. In 1939, she took me to see *The Wizard of Oz* at the Arcade Theater and *Gone with the Wind* at the Florida Theatre in Jacksonville. I had never thought about how *Gone with the Wind* would be received by a Southern audience.

---

* Brother Boone used a distinctive wedding service, a copy of which is reproduced in Appendix E at the back of the book.

One night I came in late from school after playing with some other boys, and Aunt Sally had been out looking for me. My grandfather was very unhappy—it turned out they had been quite worried while I was ignoring the clock—and he sent me to bed without supper. I let him know I thought it was seriously bad that I hadn't gotten to eat. He thought I was sassing him so he gave me a whipping, which he also would from time to time administer to his own boys. It was a common part of child rearing then, and it was most effective, because such a loving and kind man was letting me know I was not doing the right thing, and was in fact spoiled.

That is the Blattner side of my family. During a 2008 congressional trip that took us through Edinburgh, Scotland, the hotel general manager greeted us. He introduced himself as William Blattner, and I told him that Blattner was my grandmother's maiden name. "Is she from Switzerland?" he asked. I replied, "No, but her parents were." And I called the hotel manager "Cousin Willie," and we became pals.

My mother eventually delivered my little brother, John Skelton, and later another brother, Jim Skelton. Jim works with his wife at an insurance business in Warrensburg, Missouri, and John is a retired banker in Florida.

This is my family, and I am proud to carry their name.

A SOUND FROM THE SKY

LEXINGTON, MISSOURI, IS home. Nestled atop a bluff along the Missouri River and surrounded by forests and farmland, Lexington is a town of stately homes with a commercial district along Main Street. By most measures, it's a small town, although I don't remember it ever lacking in any particular. We had the best of all worlds. If we wanted to do something in a big city, Kansas City was an hour away. But we had everything in Lexington we needed. I've never called anywhere else home; I was born on December 20, 1931, in a house on one block of Franklin Avenue, lived through my school years in a house on another block of Franklin Avenue, and today my house is on still another block of Franklin.

And it was right there on Franklin Avenue in the autumn of 1943 that an unfamiliar noise rumbling from the wide blue skies stopped me right in my tracks and made me look up. The hypnotic hum was coming from a big Army transport plane towing a sleek glider, flying from north to south over the winding Missouri River toward the Sedalia Army Air Corps Base a few dozen miles away. The sound was as thrilling to an eleven-year-old boy as it must have been to hear the American Revolution's storied opening fusillade.

That moment lives bright in memory as a tangible realization of World War II, a faraway fight made familiar to me by the young men in uniform who came home on leave; the newspaper headlines, movie newsreels, and radio reports; the whispers of concerned grown-ups and the patriotic speeches of politicians; the food and fuel ration books and drives to collect scrap metal and sell war bonds.

On some Lexington homes there were blue stars hanging in the windows, proud testament to a family member on active duty. A gold star similarly displayed meant a family member had made the ultimate sacrifice, and such symbols were revered. The war was real, but it was a world away from my carefree Lexington boyhood.

The sound and sight of that massive transport plane with its winged shadow in tow packed a personal, even exotic, impression about America's military might in World War II. For me, it was a reaffirmation, even at age eleven, that my future would be in uniform. Eventually my ambitions gained focus: I would attend West Point, learn to be a soldier, and carry on a proud family tradition of military service.

My father, Isaac Newton Skelton III, was too young to serve in World War I without his mother's permission, which she wasn't about to give. So he misrepresented his age to get into the Navy, eventually serving as a coal-shoveling fireman and sailor-in-charge of the ship captain's gig on the World War I–vintage battleship called *Missouri.* After leaving the Navy, he built a career in the law. He was my pole star—a role model not just as a fine lawyer but also as a man who believed in causes and ideas bigger than himself. He also became a pilot in 1940 and passed his interest in aviation on to me—which was, in part, why those Army airplanes were so mesmerizing.

My exposure to Dad's legal work came at about this same time, when I slipped into a chair reserved for lawyers right in front of the bench to watch him argue a case before a jury. As I observed the action, I very unceremoniously sipped on a bottle of orange soda pop. My father noticed my lack of decorum out of the corner of his eye, and suffice it to say that after court I received a lesson in proper courtroom deportment that I never forgot.

Being a small-town lawyer is a bit different from being a partner in a four-story firm. We were reasonably well off—not rich, but OK. I remember my father letting clients pay him with items like guns, tools, homemade canned goods, or whatever they could spare.

Growing up on Franklin Avenue in Lexington was a pleasurable experience. All the neighbors were friendly and put up with young cowboys and Indians running through their yards. My best friend, Don Savio, lived three houses down from my home, and my good friend Kent Wingate lived just across the side street. In the guise of Hopalong Cassidy and his sidekicks Lucky and Windy, we dispatched many imaginary outlaws.

Our youthful imaginations were also inspired by knowing Lexington was filled with the romance of history. Lexington had been a principal point of departure for the Oregon Trail, where trappers, miners, settlers, and probably more than a few ne'er-do-wells provisioned their wagons for the long trip west. Many of them dealt with the traders and freight forwarders William Russell, Alexander Majors, and William Waddell. Later, those three Lexingtonians formed the Pony Express, and although it lasted but a year, that service symbolized innovation and derring-do in ways that inspire boys even today.

My mother, Carolyn Boone Skelton, a most determined lady and an ardent churchgoer, was very attentive and encouraging to her three sons. She was very active in the Boy Scouts booster club, so it's no wonder all three of us became Eagle Scouts. She was also a better publicity agent than anyone in Hollywood or on Madison Avenue, persistently instigating hometown news items about my every accomplishment. She was very active in the church and in the Democratic Women's Group. She also promoted my love of history, simply by being a tangible connection to it.

How so? Well, in 1782 the Revolutionary War was still on, despite the fact that Washington had defeated Cornwallis the previous year at Yorktown. British soldiers and an Indian group, mostly Shawnees, under the leadership of the infamous Simon Girty attacked Bryan's Station in northwestern Kentucky in August 1782.

Bryan's Station was a stockade, but the British and Indian group was unable to break into it, and they consequently decided to leave. However, when the fort's reinforcements arrived under a Colonel John Todd and a Lieutenant Colonel Daniel Boone, they decided to follow the attackers.

Daniel Boone suggested that they wait for additional reinforcements because there were a lot of British and Indian forces lying in potential ambush, but the others chose to go on. Boone, a veteran tracker and pathfinder, warned that the opposing forces were trying to hide their larger numbers by walking in one another's footprints, and he warned of a looming ambush.

Still they kept moving, reaching a place called Blue Licks, by the Licking River. That's when Daniel Boone spotted a number of Indians atop a ridge. But that didn't slow down Captain Hugh McGary, who charged up the hill on horseback and challenged, "Them that ain't cowards follow me!" In the ambush that followed, 70 of the 187 American volunteers in the Kentucky frontier militia were killed.

Daniel's son, Israel, was shot and fell at Daniel's feet. Daniel Boone saw that Israel's wound was mortal and the great man fled, which made him feel guilty for the rest of his life.

Daniel's nephew, Squire Boone, was shot in the hip. Someone put him on a horse and led the horse out of the bloody battle. Eventually, Squire Boone recovered, and he went on to a life of spiritual service as a Baptist minister in Kentucky. Squire had a son named Thomas, who begat a son named James, who had a son named John. And John, the great-grandson of Squire Boone, had a daughter named Carolyn Boone, who was my mother.

So, you see? History matters. If a British soldier or a Shawnee fighter had been a more accurate shot, Squire Boone might not have survived and I wouldn't be here to relate the story.

My mother was a complex person and my father rather more straightforward, but together, my parents provided the inspiration, discipline, and encouragement a boy needs to succeed.

More inspiration came from books. As a boy, I loved reading military history, and I still savor reliving through books the clash of battle, the shrewdness of strategy, the courage of the combatants, the victories and failures of warriors. This is true whether the book is Douglas Southall Freeman's singular biography of Confederate General Robert E. Lee, or the *Personal Memoirs* of Union General Ulysses S. Grant, written in the post-presidential years as he was dying.

But in terms of family pride, no book in Lexington's old public library had an account rivaling my dad's personal military history.

As the big and small planes disappeared in tandem on the western Missouri horizon that day in 1943, I was proud to dream of following in the footsteps of my eager-to-serve father and my wise battlefield heroes who came alive in history books.

I couldn't know at the time that plans were already being laid for the D-Day invasion the following summer, when brave men would steer those silent gliders into harm's way, part of a host of courageous sacrifices to free Europe from tyranny. All I knew was that my boyhood ambitions and dreams were as big as the Missouri skies. But never in my wildest dreams did I think I would someday help make important decisions regarding our military forces.

I suppose I should have at least allowed for the possibility—eight other Lexingtonians had served in Congress, a record few small towns can match. That history and my interests came together during my thirty-four years in Congress, as for most of that time I was a member of the House Armed Services Committee. My early interest in military history was an invaluable complement to my work, particularly after I had the honor to be elected as the committee's chairman for the last four years of my tenure.

The opportunity for me to serve on the Armed Services Committee benefited Missouri in many ways, including the delivery of the B-2 stealth bomber, at the time the world's most advanced aircraft, to its permanent home at Whiteman Air Force Base—formerly the Sedalia Army Air Corps Base where the transport and glider that I spotted in 1943 were bound.

But as the planes flew out of sight, all that was in the future. And the chance at such a future seemed remote; my grades in elementary school didn't exactly match my lofty dreams. Sports, Boy Scouts, music, movies, and girls were far more interesting. But I was fortunate to have an excellent military school right in my hometown. Wentworth Military Academy had been part of Lexington since 1880, and I enrolled there for my freshman year of high school. Driven by my military dreams, I started studying hard, improved my grades, and played trombone in the school's band. As far as I was concerned, my next steps were West Point and Army glory.

Then on November 9, 1946, the Wentworth school band boarded a bus for Columbia to participate in Band Day at a University of Missouri football game. The trip would figure in a crushing personal setback that would change my big dreams forever, but also set me on a challenging new course in life.

POLIO AND WARM SPRINGS

IN MY TEENS, I worked as a line boy at the Lexington Airport, right across the river in Ray County. Vernon Van Camp, the airport manager, was a tough taskmaster, and he seemed determined to teach me how to work hard. I was petrified, and I couldn't do very much right. One day it was dark and cloudy outside, maybe even raining, and I was to wash three airplanes in the dark, dirt-floored hangar. So I washed those three airplanes from wingtip to wingtip and nose to tail. Then the sun came out and he rolled them outside, and there were soap streaks all over all three airplanes. Guess who had to wash them all again?

One Saturday in 1944, a Culver Cadet airplane landed at Lexington. When the pilot stepped out, I saw the uniform of the Women's Ferry Command. There weren't too many female private pilots back then, so to meet a female pilot was a rarity. She was transporting the Cadet across country from the West Coast to be used as a drone to pull targets in the East. The right side of the cockpit, where a passenger would usually sit, was filled with a huge radio set used to control the plane from the ground. In those days, radios were heavy. This one was so heavy, compared to the small plane, that the pilot tried three times to take off and each time had to cut the engine. It didn't help that there were telephone wires at the end of the runway. On the third try, she got over the wires by ten feet.

Despite Mr. Van Camp's training in work ethic, my first year at Wentworth Military Academy turned out to be scholastically uninspiring, although I worked hard and enjoyed all things military. I made the rifle team and was one of the freshman cadets who could take rifles apart and correctly reassemble them. Each of us was issued a 1903 Springfield bolt-action rifle, and we were admonished never to forget the rifle number. The same was true my second year when we were issued M1 Garand semi-automatic rifles. Again, we were admonished never to forget the rifle number. I did not forget. As per the instructions: the number of my '03 Springfield was 3819965, and the number of my M1 was 4018591.

Starting my second year, I was determined to improve my grades in order to make it to West Point. My sophomore year was barely under way when I boarded a Wentworth bus for Columbia to perform with our band at halftime of the University of Missouri football game, just a few weeks before Thanksgiving in 1946. My throat was a bit sore, so I brought along a little bottle of Listerine. We put on a dandy show, but I was really tired after we packed away our instruments. I stopped at a clothing store in downtown Columbia where my father had worked during college in the 1920s and had a nice visit with a lady who had worked with him. Then I went to a room our band had rented in Columbia's old Daniel Boone Hotel, flopped onto a bed, and passed out in inexplicable exhaustion.

I was awakened to board the school bus for home, and then I must have slept all the way back to Lexington. I only remember trudging the few blocks from Wentworth back to my house at 1615 Franklin Avenue, making it up the stairs—my parents were asleep—and getting into the shower.

I passed out in the bathtub, later awakening with the cold water rushing over me. I tried to reach up with my left arm to turn off the shower, but I couldn't do it. My arm simply wouldn't work. In my grogginess, I couldn't understand what was happening to me. Finally, I was able to shut off the water with my right hand, struggle out of the shower, and pass out on my bed. I was utterly spent and in a mental fog.

The next morning, Sunday, November 10, 1946, one of my parents must have come into the room, found me passed out, realized my incapacity, and called the doctor. The next thing I remember, I was being carried out my front door on a stretcher to a waiting ambulance.

They carried me past my next-door neighbor, newspaper editor Harry Booth, who told me not to worry—that I would be OK. The ambulance took me to Kansas City General Hospital, where area polio patients were admitted.

I was examined and later heard my worried parents conferring in the corridor outside. I cannot remember which parent came in to tell me—one distraught parent didn't want to tell me I had polio and sent the other one in, but my comment was simply, "I know that."

Now that poliomyelitis has almost been eradicated, it's difficult to put into words just how widespread the fear of the disease was. Polio was spread mainly through contaminated food or water, but contact with another infected person could also pass the virus on. Polio epidemics were big news, and they were frequent. Back then, entire schools and summer camps would be closed if one youngster was suspected of having the virus. Part of the fear was from uncertainty—if you contracted polio, the range of possible effects varied depending on where the virus chose to settle. An infection could be mild, with fairly few effects, and pass. Or it could return and cause great damage. If it paralyzed your lungs or heart, polio could kill you. Some of those whose lungs were affected could breathe only with the assistance of an iron lung, a pressure chamber that you lay in with just your head sticking out.

I was comparatively lucky. Yes, my arms were useless and my neck and shoulders seemed heavy and frozen. But my lungs and legs still worked, although I was drained of energy.

To this day, I have no idea how I got polio. I learned most polio cases were contracted in the heat of summer, but I got it in early November. I was fourteen years old, going to high school, living a pretty austere life at home, walking to and from school, and contemplating boxing, football, and playing Glenn Miller arrangements as the second trombone with the Wentworth Cavaliers dance band.

It's odd, the things you remember so clearly that might seem trivial, like the words to those old songs, while the details of significant moments cannot be recalled so well, such as my deeply worried parents' reluctance to break the news to me that my military dreams were probably dashed forever by illness.

When I realized there was no way I could make it to West Point, I think I must have felt sorry for myself. But I remember being on a gurney, being taken down to the room I shared with another polio patient, rolling past a series of patients in the iron lungs, hearing the constant whooshing of the mechanical "breathing." I didn't realize the full impact of what had happened to me until that moment. The iron lungs were the very symbol of paralyzed incapacity. Even though I wasn't in one, my heart sank.

I stayed in Kansas City General Hospital for two weeks before transferring in late November to St. Luke's Hospital, also in Kansas City. It was at St. Luke's that I marked my fifteenth birthday, on December 20, 1946. After my parents had left for the evening, the nurses, each carrying a lighted candle, walked through the quiet hospital halls singing "Silent Night." I remember vividly lying in that hospital bed, weeping and feeling very sorry for myself. There is no question that it was the lowest point of my life.

I had had an operation the previous summer to lower my too-high arches, and my surgeon had been Dr. Frank Dickson, whose Dickson-Dively Clinic in Kansas City had an excellent national reputation. As a polio patient, I was again under the care of Dr. Dickson and in the same St. Luke's ward with its wonderful, caring nurses. Everyone was very kind to me, though my progress, such as it was, came incrementally and with great frustration. The one bright spot was that I was never in an iron lung.

Eventually, I was allowed to venture on short outings away from the grounds, always wearing my hospital-imposed "airplane splints," which forced my arms out from my sides in a sort of hybrid position between a crucifixion stance and a jumping jack. The splints were supposed to keep the paralyzed muscles from atrophying. I even wore the splints to watch the biggest hit of 1947, *The Jolson Story*, at a downtown Kansas City movie theater.

At the time, I didn't know my father was working to get me admitted as a patient at Warm Springs in Georgia, famous as the place where President

Franklin Roosevelt had been treated for his polio, and which had become a destination for polio patients from around the world. There was always great demand for admission at Warm Springs, and the wonderful foundation there paid less regard to a patient's ability to pay than to how its treatment might be of special help while expanding the body of knowledge in the battle against polio, which culminated with Dr. Jonas Salk's breakthrough vaccine in 1954.

Franklin Delano Roosevelt was born into wealth. He enjoyed an early adulthood of privilege and robust health, and he had high ambitions for a life of accomplishment and leadership in public service and politics. But in August 1921, while vacationing on Canada's Campobello Island, the future president fell ill and eventually was beset by paralysis of his upper and lower extremities and other symptoms of polio. His mind, spirit, and generous heart were still vital, and Mr. Roosevelt refused to surrender.

He was invited to soak in the supposedly healing—or at least helpful—spring waters of an old, run-down rural Georgia resort called the Meriwether Inn. Mr. Roosevelt was convinced the hydrotherapy was beneficial, making paralytics feel more buoyant in the water and better able to work their limbs. In 1926, he used a considerable portion of his personal fortune to purchase the old resort and began upgrading it into a foundation welcoming polio patients. It became a place of hope for the hopeless, welcoming the previously unwelcomed.

It has never been fully clear to me how I received admission to Warm Springs, but my father tirelessly called on friends who in turn called on their friends and even strangers. The local chapter of the March of Dimes was supportive, and so, too, was a Higginsville feed mill owner named Hubert Edwards who had connections far beyond his Lafayette County hometown. I heard that there were direct intercessions to President Roosevelt's widow, Eleanor, on my behalf. And I know that President Truman was aware of my situation, because he sent a letter of encouragement. (Harry Truman later played a significant role in my political life, but that's getting ahead of the story.)

However he achieved it, my persistent father got me in as a patient at Warm Springs. In April 1947, two years to the month after President Roosevelt's death, we drove down to Georgia. We spent the night in a dilapidated motel on Pine Mountain and then drove into Warm Springs the next day. As soon as I arrived, they took off my airplane splints, and I never saw them again. It was not a treatment that they believed in, which was smart on their part—although I have to admit that judgment is based on how I hated the splints. They made me stand out, they were awkward, and I doubted they did any good.

That was the beginning of my Warm Springs experience, which formed the basis for my optimistic approach to life and, in some ways, my whole personality. Wentworth, West Point, my big dreams—they were all in the past. I wasn't even in school. But I completed classes in Latin and geometry at Warm Springs, which kept me somewhat on pace with my class back home.

At the time of my arrival in Warm Springs, the state of Georgia was preparing to take over the Little White House, FDR's retreat at Warm Springs, to be preserved and operated in tribute to the beloved president, and I had the opportunity to go inside in the days before it opened to the public. It seemed as though nothing had been disturbed. President Roosevelt's bed, pillow, and linens were there, and the stone fireplace, and his shelves of books, and the wide back terrace with a majestic view of the sloping valley beyond. The newspaper from April 12, 1945, the day President Roosevelt died, was still on the table. It struck me that a magnificent man had lived quite simply in this cottage among the extended family he loved at Warm Springs. In a real sense, we felt a part of President Roosevelt's lasting legacy in that humble cabin.

I had three roommates at Warm Springs: Jim Roetto from Monett, Missouri, who later became a physical therapist; Peter Hanson, a Harvard student who went through Union Theological Seminary, then became a Methodist minister and a schoolteacher; and Glen Moore, a former football player from Minnesota who later went into insurance. In my mind's eye, I can still see my Warm Springs roommates as they were wheeled off to their physical therapy treatments. I think of a friend with leg braces and crutches trying to conquer the artificial steps on the walking court, where those affected in the legs learned to walk again. I think, too, of hydrotherapy treatments in the pools with patients lying on tables slightly submerged below the waterline, enabling, we hoped, even the slightest movement—and encouragement.

And there was a good education to be had. I had not done well in first-year Latin at Wentworth, so I took it again under another instructor, and then I got polio. Warm Springs had a Latin teacher, a Mrs. Shipley. That was a disaster. Then they changed Latin teachers to an absolutely good-looking twenty-three-year-old recent college graduate and my grade went up to a B+. Language study was suddenly fun.

To be sure, life at Warm Springs wasn't always that serious. After all, we were teenagers, and through side-by-side wheelchair encounters I fell madly in love with various girls, rendezvousing behind "Bush 13" to hold hands. "Bush 13" was not so much a place as a youthful state of mind, an escape with a girl to whisper about a future we just knew would be bright and full of promise. Years later when I had become a congressman, I served as a banquet speaker at Warm Springs and noted that before me was a dining room table where one object of my teenaged love gave me the "let's just be friends" speech, so it was occasionally a place of a type of heartbreak beyond the frustrations of rehabilitation and therapy.

There were hijinks, such as our rush to the surgery floor on Monday afternoons to question recently operated-on pals while they were still under the effects of the anesthesia, sodium pentothal, commonly known as "truth serum." This was an early and hilarious exercise of my skills in prosecutorial questioning—hilarious, that is, until it happened to me.

We performed for one another, with no worries about cruel mocking by outsiders. My roommate Peter and I sang out our own parody of Danny Kaye's version of "Minnie the Moocher" to the assembled patients. I also sang in the Warm Springs chapel choir, not because I had a good voice but because my roommate Peter Hanson was the choir director—and because one of the choristers was a very pretty fellow patient from Avon Park, Florida, Lynn Longbottom (now Rice.) Over time, Lynn and I became good friends.

Warm Springs had first-class medical and physical therapy staffs, but I can say without any doubt that positive spirit and old-fashioned faith pervaded the place and empowered us as much as the evolving science did. The inspiration of the Warm Springs polio experience endures in the lives of hundreds of patients who passed through the institution's gates. There was magic at Warm Springs that moved us to leave for better lives and to forever embody the can-do attitude exemplified by Franklin Roosevelt, with whom we all shared a kinship of determination.

We were centered on going back to school, restarting interrupted lives, and building a future for ourselves back home. Despite the extreme physical hardships of some patients, we were not allowed to have self-pity. It is hard for those who were not at Warm Springs to understand, but being there was like a college experience, and I emerged with lifelong friends and memories from our fraternity of hope.

It was as if Franklin Roosevelt were there cheering on each patient through treatments, therapy, and surgery. I never got to meet President Roosevelt, but like so many of my generation, I felt I knew him intimately through his magnetic radio voice and forceful presence in newsreels and newspaper photographs alongside world leaders. However, I did personally experience and treasure the courtly friendliness of President Roosevelt's good friend and Warm Springs's highly respected registrar, Fred Botts. Looking back on the yellowing personal notes Mr. Botts signed to my parents in Missouri, there is a combination of matter-of-factness about my condition and prospects with a tactful gentility and tender compassion rarely seen in any generation. A polio survivor himself, Mr. Botts was handpicked by President Roosevelt to be a Warm Springs administrator. For me, his courtesies and support were a source of strength.

Warm Springs also emphasized to me the benefits of charity. I have no doubt that my parents would have found a way to get me there once I had been admitted. But the March of Dimes picked up the whole tab—although my father gave them a generous contribution afterward so that others could receive the same benefit.

I also remember the skillful surgery of Dr. C. E. Irwin, the warmth and caring of the nurses, attendants, orderlies, and push boys who propelled us as patients in wheelchairs, and most particularly the stern medical chief, Dr. Robert Bennett. "Stern" is perhaps an understatement, although I later learned that he was a gifted physician with a huge heart, which he kept well hidden beneath a gruff and intimidating manner. Upon my arrival, I was placed under supervision of a student physical therapist to whom, for some reason, I did not see fit to provide my cooperation. Don't ask me why; I just did not want to work with her. Soon after my arrival I was in a wheelchair with arm slings, and through propelling myself by shuffling my feet I was pretty mobile. One weekend, though, I flipped over my chair trying to go through some bushes like a bold and freewheeling jungle explorer. The following Monday, my student nurse discovered my shoulder was stiff. I guess she reported me for being uncooperative.

An orderly suddenly appeared and wheeled me on a gurney to a command audience with Dr. Bennett. Dr. Bennett didn't sugarcoat the blunt message: either cooperate or get out, because you're taking someone else's place here. He put me under the supervision of a tough and talented physical therapist, Miss Lamoille C. Langworthy. From that moment on, I started cooperating. Dr. Bennett was most effective in delivering that message, and I respect him even in memory today. I count him as one of my personal heroes, right along with President Roosevelt.

On my second visit to Warm Springs in the spring of 1948, I underwent a surgical procedure called a Steindler flexorplasty. It involved taking some sinewy fascia tissue from my thigh and reattaching it between my right elbow and forearm, creating an artificial but effective bicep and restoring flexibility.

The flexorplasty surgery by Dr. Irwin was a success, and within a few months of determined practice and exercises I was able to lift my right hand to my mouth. It may not sound dramatic, but I still look in wonderment at black-and-white Warm Springs photos of medical tests showing me holding various items at different degrees of elevation, from a water glass to an empty tissue roll. Each picture provided spirit-lifting proof of my progress.

Today, I still depend on the "strong right arm" of my family and a bit of agility, plus patience and creativity, to accomplish what most folks can do with both hands. I make some reasonable and comfortable concessions, such as preferring laceless loafers to lace-up shoes. To anticipate and dispense with some questions you may deem too personal to ask but might wonder anyway: Yes, I button my own shirt, knot my own necktie, pull up my own socks, shave my own face, and blow my own nose; such daily minutiae and tasks simply sometimes take a bit more concentration and a few extra moments.

Achieving these tasks offers daily personal reminders of how far I have come in living with polio, and of course of how very blessed I have been. So many people have had it worse. But I refused then, and I refuse now, to be thought of as disabled. I am *able*—able to achieve my objectives in the most commonsense ways, which is the philosophy I carried throughout my public service as well.

I am able, but ability without action doesn't count for much. So throughout my life I have stayed active in my fight with polio. I coached my younger brothers in football, traveled solo by ocean liner to college in Scotland, and knocked around Europe as a young tourist. I escorted my boys on father-and-son trips by trains, planes, and other vehicles. I turned many law book pages as I became educated as an attorney—though I did seek and receive permission to have a typist to record my dictated answers on the Missouri Bar examination, which is taken over two days' time in Jefferson City and can inflict writer's cramp on even the stoutest young barristers-to-be. I have scuba dived in the Caribbean and helped myself into military Humvees and helicopters for tours of overseas combat zones and meetings with foreign leaders and troops on the ground and at sea. And as I have related, through the Lord's grace and the care of excellent military personnel and military doctors, I survived a military truck wreck in Iraq in 2005.

And I remain proud to have placed my right hand on the Bible seventeen times to take my oath as a member of Congress, representing the twenty-five counties of Missouri's Fourth Congressional District.

Part of my own received blessing is the Lord's gift of willingness and determination, or maybe it is stubbornness. But I couldn't have rebounded from polio on my own. Attitude is very important—this was pointed out to me a number of years ago at Lambert–St. Louis International Airport. I had time to get a shoeshine, and as I climbed onto the shine stand, I noticed a sign: "Regular Shine: $2.50. My Best: $3.50." I asked the young man the difference between the shines. He looked up, grinned, and declared: "My attitude!"

At Warm Springs, I learned how much attitude matters. Whatever the adversity, if you do not step up to seize opportunities, and do so with faith in the future, you will have regrets. And a life of regrets is not much of a life at all.

Of the many blessings that made my rebound possible, particular people moved me to pursue the post-polio phase of my life with quiet determination. There are not many contemporary household names or celebrities among them, but to me they are personal heroes who did the right thing when no one but the Lord was watching and there was no personal gain in it for them.

Chief among these were my mother and father, of course, each of whom was supportive in their own way. My rebound would not have been possible without them and so many others, including my most memorable and impactful acquaintance from Warm Springs, Miss Lamoille C. Langworthy. She was one of the Warm Springs Foundation's most experienced physical therapists, kind-natured but also a tough disciplinarian. I can still hear Miss Langworthy's words of encouragement as she helped me lift my arms in the pool—"that's good," she said, "you can do it," emphasizing the do-able. At Warm Springs, my life was centered on pleasing Miss Langworthy and earning her words of encouragement and praise. In many moments of personal reflection, that is still the case.

I believe she would be proud of me. Miss Langworthy had passed on when I was first sworn in to Congress in January 1977, but her good friend, Warm Springs's head physical therapist, Helen Vaughn, attended that special day in the U.S. Capitol.

I last visited in person with Dr. Robert Bennett during a Warm Springs stopover in 1971, when I had just been elected to the Missouri state senate. He gave me a physical exam and was his usual gruff self. Decades later, I got a look at Dr. Bennett's personally dictated notes in my medical file. He exuded pride in my accomplishments and worried that I might be working too hard as a state senator and practicing attorney and father of three growing boys. If I was indeed working too hard, it was directly because of the spirit of Warm Springs, a contagious spirit of optimism that tomorrow would be better than today. I say the spirit was contagious because so many of my fellow Warm Springs patients with whom I kept in contact went back to their homes and lived fulfilling and successful lives.

The young women I knew at Warm Springs followed a variety of paths: one became a business and civic leader; another a laboratory technician who later wrote inspirational books; one a choir director; one married a businessman, another married a college professor, and another married a railroad president, and all raised families. For one example, I cannot forget the always upbeat Ann Jones, who returned to her hometown of Cleveland, Ohio, became a leader in humanitarian causes, and married Cyrus Eaton, once America's wealthiest man.

My male pals from Warm Springs likewise had largely fulfilling lives—one became an automobile mechanic, another an insurance broker, another a physical therapist. And with that infusion of Warm Springs spirit, it's no coincidence that three patients who were there between 1947 and 1950 became members of Congress: the late Jim Scheuer of New York, the late Bo Ginn of Georgia, and yours truly of Missouri.

I once asked a doctor who was a specialist in polio treatment the reason why so many polio patients did well in later life. He told me that those who had contracted polio learned that with hard work and determination, some muscles would rehabilitate and renew, and that this knowledge transferred over into other phases of the patient's life. That was certainly the case in my life. Warm Springs, for me, meant picking up the pieces of shattered dreams.

FINISHING THIRD, AND WINNING

WHEN I RETURNED from my first visit to Warm Springs in late October 1947, I enrolled as a junior at Lexington High School, with my dreams knocked more than slightly askew by polio. My long-held goal of attending West Point was no longer within reach and I honestly wasn't sure what I wanted to do, so I didn't focus on much beyond teenaged activities. I was just grateful to be moving under my own exertions and among people who cared about me.

One interest I resumed with enthusiasm was the Boy Scouts. I had become a Tenderfoot Scout at age twelve on December 20, 1943—my birthday, and the earliest date I could join. I had completed a number of my required merit badges before I got polio, including swimming and lifesaving. Scouting was not just a boyish enthusiasm for me. Its backbone principle of self-reliance meant more to me than ever since I faced major life adjustments to continue recovering from polio.

The embodiment of a fine role model was my own scoutmaster, John Marchetti. He provided constant encouragement, even when my own belief in myself sometimes wavered. I will never forget a several-page letter he sent to me during my second stay at Warm Springs, painstakingly written in pencil. Scoutmaster Marchetti told me emphatically, *"There is no such word as 'can't.'"*

Over time, I served as a patrol leader and a junior assistant scoutmaster, and I eventually became an Eagle Scout. When I reached young adulthood in Lexington, I followed John Marchetti's example of community service by serving as his assistant scoutmaster. Through my years in elected office and legal practice, I have remained a steadfast supporter of the Boy Scouts and even received the Silver Beaver award, which honors longtime support. In 2007, I was delighted to be made honorary chieftain of Mic-O-Say, a scouting leadership organization at the Kansas City area scout camp near Osceola, Missouri. No honors have brought me more pride than those related to promoting the Scouts.

My very first Boy Scout merit badge was in aviation, and after my return from Warm Springs, I kept up my interest, stoking the fascination with flying that began years earlier when I saw the military glider in tow over Lexington and worked at the Lexington airport washing airplanes, raking the dirt hangars, picking up the grounds, and one year joining in mopping up after a river flood. I was active in a model airplane club that we dubbed the Sky Invaders. And my father was a pilot; he owned several small airplanes over the years, and I would often be found in the second seat when he flew. Though I am not a pilot, I have had the thrill—and my father would be envious—of sitting in the cockpit of the B-2 Spirit stealth bomber and other military aircraft. Their hard-working crews have my total admiration, and a little bit of my envy.

I have a most vivid recollection of becoming an Eagle Scout during the April 1948 assembly in Kansas City, hosted by the area Boy Scout Council. The sponsor was Dr. Milton Eisenhower, then president of Kansas State University and of course the younger brother of Dwight Eisenhower. My mother accompanied me to the stage to receive my Eagle medal, and I was handed a rose, which I gave to her.

As they called out my name and I shook hands with Dr. Eisenhower, he remarked, "Ike! That's what they used to call me." I never forgot that personal comment from such an esteemed man. Yet it struck me as odd, since of course his brother was well known as Ike. I related this anecdote many years later at a banquet of the Industrial College of the Armed Forces in Washington, part of the National Defense University. In the audience was Susan Eisenhower, granddaughter of the late president, and I visited with her after the speech. I asked her whether I got the anecdote right, and she said I did—all five of the Eisenhower brothers were at times called "Ike," but the nickname stuck with world familiarity to the general who became president.

The traditional senior class trip at Lexington High School was a one-day journey by school bus to Fort Leavenworth, where we toured the post, had a buffet lunch of Army chow (which almost put me off serving), and went through the museum. But to a few of us, that was just an appetizer. Jim O'Malley, Marcel Polge Jr., and I decided to make our own senior trip by bus to Jacksonville, Florida. We added side trips to Warm Springs, St. Augustine, and Little Rock—although to be honest, it wasn't until we reached Memphis that we worldly travelers realized that there was such a thing as an express bus, rather than the series of locals we'd been taking. Jim, Marcel, and I had bonded while doing a lot of singing together in Lexington, harmonizing on classics like "Sweet Adeline" and "Carolina Moon" on our front porch and serenading the neighborhood. We reprised our act for our fellow passengers on the buses and basked in the applause.

After graduating in 1949 from Lexington High School, I reentered Wentworth Military Academy as a junior college student. In this second enrollment at Wentworth, I excelled academically, which was a complete turnaround from my high school days there. Although I give all due credit to my time at Warm Springs for reorienting my thinking about my future and the amount of effort I needed to put into school to succeed, the real catalyst for the change was a five-minute conversation in my father's law office. His part of the conversation was to explain in very clear terms that I was now mature enough to stop goofing around and start really applying myself, and as I recall, my entire part of the conversation consisted of the words "yes" and "sir."

Not only did my academic work take off, but in my determination for physical achievement symbolizing my efforts to beat polio, I also became a member of the junior college track team. Although running would bring me unexpected fame, my track experience started with me standing still and at attention on the Wentworth campus. Like all Wentworth students, I was in uniform, but I was obviously no longer headed toward active military service. When we stood in formation outside "D" Hall, I stared up at an inscription above what was then an entrance (but now is a graceful archway over a large window). The inscription read: *"ACHIEVE THE HONORABLE."*

Perhaps it was the tedium of standing there, perhaps out of boredom with eyes ahead under orders, but as I stared at the inscription, I often wondered what it meant. Through formations in winter, spring, summer, and fall, I eventually figured it out: we must try to achieve something in life, all of us, regardless of physical or other challenges.

What, then, is better than setting the goal of achieving something honorable? It may be honorable military service—that was the essential Wentworth context—but for any of us it can also mean doing our best in school, being there for our family, friends, and neighbors, caring for those who are not so blessed as us. It may mean doing an honorable day's work. It means acting honorably, even when no one is watching and it may not be recorded for any history book—only in your own conscience. I was quietly determined, after my uplifting Warm Springs experience, to find ways to rebound through determination and honorable achievement.

The core values of leadership, character, vision, historical knowledge, and military strength were imbued in many young men and women at Wentworth, and I pursued them with quiet determination. Throughout my career in public life, I was content to let others have the spotlight. In Missouri, and in the finest tradition of Harry Truman, we prefer a workhorse to a show horse. And I look at the Wentworth directive in perhaps a different way, noting that "honorable" is really two words: "honor" and "able." Both words were important to me in my recovery. I meant to work harder than I had ever worked in my young life, to overcome the effects of polio. This is when I decided to go out for track.

I stood out immediately when I went loping around the oval at Wentworth. While I certainly earned my "W" athletic letter, the distinction wasn't due to my speed. I cut an unusual figure because both of my arms were taped to my sides and my fists were inserted into slits in my running shorts, securing them from flailing around while I ran.

A snapshot of me in this configuration, running on the track toward the camera, is a treasured Skelton family memento. It is published for the first time in this book. In the photo, I resemble a fleeing fugitive handcuffed at the waist—and indeed, I felt liberation in running. I drew confidence from it, thinking back to so many Warm Springs friends who could only painstakingly walk a few steps and others who could not walk at all. I ran for all of them, and for Dr. Bennett and Miss Langworthy. I ran to show polio that it could not prevail—and it did not prevail in my life.

Taping my hands to my sides worked, and I got to run the two-mile in a few meets my freshman year at junior college. In my sophomore year, I managed to finish as the top-ranking student academically and I kept running track, taped wrists and all.

I finished third that year in several more two-mile races, but I earned my letter. The last big meet of my sophomore year was in Boonville against Wentworth's archrival, Kemper Military School. In a profile a few years later when I became Lafayette County prosecuting attorney, Giles M. Fowler of the *Kansas City Star* wrote:

> Of the group of 2-milers that rounded the Kemper track that day, only three remained as the grueling race neared its finish.
>
> Last but still running—was Ike Skelton. Ike ran across the line far behind the winning two, but the grit that kept him in the race won a point for Wentworth, and won Ike wild cheers of admiration from both teams.
>
> The story later reached the ears of Dr. Norman Vincent Peale, who was so impressed that he included Ike's inspiring race in a radio program, a nationally-printed newspaper article, and finally in a book, *Faith Is the Answer.*

Today's audience may not recall what a prominent figure Dr. Peale, author of the best-seller *The Power of Positive Thinking*, was in those times. He was a renowned motivational speaker and columnist, and a multimedia star before the term really existed. To be cited in his column was like winning on *American Idol* today—it was an instant ticket to national fame.

I credit the flattering attention from Dr. Peale to my mother's relentless cultivation of publicity—I don't know this for certain, but I always suspected that she tipped him when the original newspaper account of the Wentworth-Kemper meet appeared in a Boonville newspaper. I later had the pleasure of meeting Dr. Peale. We became friends, and he publicly endorsed me when I ran for Congress—a heck of a favor to a young public servant from a nationally respected and popular celebrity.

But because I wanted to be elected on my own merits, not from sympathy votes, I have rarely spoken publicly about my polio and the rebound from it.

I figured that family and friends already knew the story, and others could figure it out, if they cared. Or they could read the accounts of Giles M. Fowler or Dr. Norman Vincent Peale. What I did not want was anyone's pity. What is important to me is keeping the positive mental attitude Dr. Peale famously espoused, and which President Franklin D. Roosevelt so admirably embodied.

I am sometimes asked if I thought Franklin Roosevelt did the right thing in keeping his polio private. I certainly understand why he did. It didn't affect his ability to be president any more than mine affected my ability to represent the Fourth District. And as long as my left hand was tucked in my pocket, most people wouldn't know I had had polio. In President Roosevelt's case, it was rather more obvious—but no more relevant.

I am finally relating my own polio experience in some detail in this memoir because I have come to realize that by sharing their own stories, public figures can both encourage others and spread the understanding that anyone can achieve the honorable through hard work and quiet determination.

DAD

THE LESSON OF quiet determination also came from my greatest hero, my father. He was sturdy in every way: respected as a man, as a lawyer, and as a public servant. Isaac Newton Skelton III could juggle many tasks, and he did them all so well because he brought considerable intellect to bear upon them. But unlike many, he didn't just rely on talent; no matter how familiar a task or how fully he had mastered it, he always added focus and effort—he worked at it.

Certainly, my inclination toward military affairs came from him. I'm convinced that his service in the Navy aboard the USS *Missouri* was the defining moment in his life and formed the man he became. He was very pro-military and in particular pro-Navy.

Dad would go into a room full of people and, without anybody being envious, take over the room. He was very warm, very bright. He liked people. People liked him. He was the hardest worker I've ever known. He would know a case better than any lawyer who walked into a courtroom, which helped him a lot.

One enduring lesson my father taught me was to be able to move on many fronts at the same time. In the case of his legal practice, he was so disciplined, and he didn't just work on one case, milk it for all it was worth, and then move on to the next case. He moved multiple cases forward at the same time, sometimes through very complex law and research and courtroom argument. It was possible only through diligent preparation, and because of my father's example, I learned to move on multiple fronts and did very well in my own law practice.

My love of the law was cultivated by watching its exercise up close. For five summers, I worked for my dad in his Lexington law office, initially being paid seven dollars a week for taking papers to the courthouse for him and doing chores.

The case I mentioned earlier, involving my poor soda pop etiquette, was a showcase for my father's fine ability to think on his feet in the courtroom. It was 1943 and a group of Jehovah's Witnesses, who were famously pacifists in this time of World War II, were passing out their church literature in Odessa. The city fathers bodily threw them out of town, injuring some of them, an act that was as wrong then as it would be today if we prize freedom of speech, religion, and assembly—but such was the depth of pro-American patriotism. So some of the Jehovah's Witnesses sued the mayor, the city marshal, and other town leaders, along with the city of Odessa. My father was the Odessa city attorney, and he set to work defending the city, intensely studying the religion and practices of the Jehovah's Witnesses.

I remember he cross-examined each witness and got into the record that their faith precluded them from swearing an oath on the Bible to be a truthful witness, which no doubt offended many jurors. And my father, aware that some of the jurors were veterans and that all of the jurors were deeply patriotic, compelled the witnesses to acknowledge that they did not as a practice salute the American flag next to the courtroom bench.

Juries are the conscience of a community, and in that time, in that context, the jury was not of a mind to side with conscientious objectors. My father's defense was successful, and as a patriotic veteran himself, he never expressed any regrets about his arguments, though of course the jury's verdict would be a questionable one today. But it was my father who taught me that juries are the community conscience, and the verdict reflected the mind-set behind that conscience in that time of world war.

My father was the example of someone who fully used his talents and poured all he had into the job at hand. But he only had a partially successful political career. In 1926 he was elected prosecutor of Lafayette County and was reelected in 1928. In 1932 he ran for Missouri attorney general, and he carried a large number of counties but still lost in the Democratic primary. In 1946 my father ran for Congress and finished second in the primary. Still, he was the greatest public speaker I ever heard—of course as his fourteen-year-old campaign manager, I was then and remain today rather biased.

I'll never forget when he got up on the stump in Centralia during that 1946 campaign. He was running as the only veteran in the race, and his sheer patriotism simply held that audience. It just didn't hold enough of them to prevail at the ballot box.

The primary winner was Will Nelson, who lost to the Republican incumbent, Max Schwabe of Columbia. Another losing Democratic primary candidate in that race was Bill Wright from Salisbury, who served as a state legislator, and whose son, Marvin "Bunky" Wright, went on to become a fine attorney and served until his retirement as general counsel for the University of Missouri. As for Max Schwabe, he was unseated the next election outing. But by then, my dad was focused on the law.

After his 1946 loss, my dad poured everything he had into being the best attorney he could be, and he was a big success, receiving cases from all over the state. He became a real master of the courtroom and was chosen to become a fellow of the American College of Trial Lawyers, the most prestigious such professional association in America.

My father taught me to take advantage of opportunities—not just in the courtroom, but in life. He was an example of the rule that the way a person thinks makes all the difference in the world—that talent is the ability to work hard and use all of your resources and watch for opportunities and seize them.

For instance, my father told me when I was serving as prosecuting attorney that if a criminal defendant ever takes a change of venue to another county, never tell the jury it is a change of venue—that is reversible error for a prosecutor to commit. Years later, in private practice, I was defending a man accused of stealing and burglary in Lafayette County who took a change of venue to neighboring Johnson County, where James G. Lauderdale, the prosecutor, told the jury the defendant was there on a change of venue at his request. I immediately objected to Judge William Kimberlin and asked for a mistrial. I was overruled. I asked that the jury disregard the prosecutor's remark. I was overruled. I thought, "I sure hope my dad's right," and I just objected generally. The jury, after a great deal of deliberation, returned a verdict of guilty and the man was sentenced to five years in prison.

I went through the law books and found three cases right on point proving my father was right. I made that argument, the judge granted a new trial, and I withdrew from the case. Another attorney handled the defense in a second trial. My former client was still found guilty, but he got a sentence of just three years in the second trial, so I saved that guy two years behind bars by listening to my father.

My Aunt Irene Skelton Baldwin told me once that her brother Ike was very determined and whenever he wanted something, he got it. He came by that determination in part from facing youthful challenges of his own.

I had mentioned that my father's own father figure was his grandfather, Washington Mason Skelton, after his actual father was struck and killed by a train while walking along a railroad track on Election Day in 1908. As the oldest of three children, my father had to go to work at a young age. He worked as a shoeshine boy and a store clerk. He later worked his way through the University of Missouri as a salesman at a ladies ready-to-wear shop in Columbia. He was Phi Beta Kappa his junior year. In law school he was a member of Order of the Coif, the honorary society for the top law students, and he was a member of QEBH, the top honorary leadership society at the university.

He also served as president of the all-senior student body at the University of Missouri. One of his proudest moments was presiding at the dedication of the tower of Memorial Union, which was constructed in remembrance of the university boys who lost their lives in World War I. Memorial Union, with its soaring clock tower, is now an iconic landmark at my alma mater, and I think of my father every time I visit the Union for a speech or a lecture.

At the time of the Memorial Union dedication, my father was already a military veteran, not an unusual situation in that period when young men were called upon to put on hold their lives on the home front in the service of a greater national cause. As I mentioned, my dad actually misrepresented his age when he joined the U.S. Navy—he was just seventeen, and his mother would not give her signature allowing him to enlist. So he told them he was eighteen and entered basic training at the Great Lakes Naval Station at Chicago, which led to him serving on the USS *Missouri* in 1918 and 1919. That ship had earlier been part of the "Great White Fleet" which President Theodore Roosevelt sent around the world from 1907 to 1909 as a display of U.S. sea power.

After his Navy service, my father came back home and finished high school. He and my Aunt Irene were debate partners, and she told me that after his brilliant remarks, he would say, "Now my old-maid sister will address any questions." He was a great tease, and she and the audiences loved him and responded to him.

Indeed, in the eyes of some, I could never measure up to my father. There was one woman from Lafayette County who had an unrequited crush on him. One day after I joined the practice and my father was out of the office, she appeared and agreed to meet with me in my father's absence. I greeted her warmly. She looked me up and down, and said with obvious disappointment, "Well, you're certainly not as good-looking as your father." That was not exactly a confidence builder.

He was a very difficult act to follow, but follow him I did, becoming Phi Beta Kappa, Sigma Chi, and eventually being elected as Lafayette County prosecutor. Dad didn't live to see me serve in the Congress he once aspired to join, but I know he would have been proud of me.

On November 11, 1941—the anniversary of the 1918 Armistice ending the War to End All Wars—my father took me out of the fifth grade at Central Elementary School in Lexington and we drove to Odessa. He was the keynote speaker at a high school assembly in honor of Armistice Day. The program was very dramatic, with drums simulating artillery fire.

As a skilled trial attorney, my father was a gifted and impressive speaker, and he knew "In Flanders Fields" by heart. That day he told the assembly, "There are those in this audience who may very well have to fight again for America's freedoms."

Then, as one who had years earlier returned from warfare, he recited that moving tribute to faith and the fallen.

> In Flanders Fields the poppies blow
> Between the crosses row on row,
> That mark our place; and in the sky
> The larks, still bravely singing, fly
> Scarce heard amid the guns below.

We are the Dead. Short days ago
We lived, felt dawn, saw sunset glow,
Loved and were loved, and now we lie
In Flanders fields.

Take up our quarrel with the foe:
To you from failing hands we throw
The torch; be yours to hold it high.
If ye break faith with us who die
We shall not sleep, though poppies grow
In Flanders fields.

Less than one month later, on December 7, 1941, came the Japanese attack on Pearl Harbor. And from the Odessa High School graduating class of the following spring, there were two young men who were indeed killed in Europe during World War II.

Thirty years after my father's speech in Odessa, I had my own experience reciting "In Flanders Fields" after a luncheon at the National Guard armory in Boonville, Missouri, with Susie and my young boys along for the event. I couldn't match my father's delivery, though there was no less feeling underlying the oration.

Still, my eight-year-old son Ike wandered out to go to the bathroom, and his two bored little brothers followed him during my big moment. They never returned to their seats. I was a bit disturbed and let them know later how much the poem meant, or should mean, to them.

When my annoyance passed, it turned into a special learning moment between generations. My sons, two of whom now serve in uniform, have by this time heard me recite the poem on numerous occasions. For twenty-four straight years I made "In Flanders Fields" a centerpiece of my remarks at the annual Veterans Day breakfast at Lincoln University in Jefferson City, and I hope the poem's powerful significance will be appreciated by new generations.

My father is a central figure in one personal memory of World War II. A family friend, Ralph Soule, lived in an apartment of my dad's. We called him Uncle Pinkie because of his red hair. On Sunday, December 7, 1941, we went to my dad's farm at Wellington, where Uncle Pinkie and I had discussed going into the rabbit-raising business together.

On the drive home, with me sitting in the front seat between my dad and Uncle Pinkie, we heard the urgent radio news bulletin about the Japanese attack on Pearl Harbor. Uncle Pinkie, who was in his late twenties, turned to my dad and said, "Ike, you know what that means—I join tomorrow."

Indeed, Uncle Pinkie went to Kansas City to join the Navy, as my father had done in World War I, but they told him his eyesight was not good enough and he was rejected. Uncle Pinkie followed my father's example of staying focused on his prime goal; a few days later he went back to Kansas City, and this time he was able to enlist in the Army. He later served as a company commander in New Guinea.

Such was the patriotism of my father, my hero, that he also tried to rejoin the Navy during World War II, but he was not allowed to serve because he had undergone an ulcer operation several years before. He even wrote to his old friend, Senator Harry Truman, pleading to serve again in uniform, but it didn't do any good.

My father was very Confederate-oriented and most proud of Lexington's place in the Civil War. One day not long before he died, Dad and I were driving past the Lexington battlefield. He recalled that in 1932, the remains of five Union soldiers were uncovered there when an old trench fell in. The five were reburied on November 11, 1932—on Armistice Day, which we now call Veterans Day—and my father was asked to serve as the guest speaker. As we drove past, he noted the Union soldiers' grave marker at the battlefield and told me, "I never enjoyed anything more than burying those five Yankee soldiers!"

My father practiced law until his death in 1965. At the time, he also served on the University of Missouri's governing body, the Board of Curators, which was a great source of family pride as we love the oldest public university west of the Mississippi River; it is a leader in higher education and a cultural center for our state.

When my father died, the entire Board of Curators came to Lexington for his funeral, and they stopped to visit with me privately and pay respects. The curators also came with a surprising and generous offer, made more out of their tremendous regard for my father than for my own comparatively limited résumé. The curators said they would unanimously recommend to Governor Warren Hearnes that he appoint me to fill my father's unexpired term on the board.

It turned out that Governor Hearnes had another idea. I had supported his gubernatorial primary opponent, Hilary Bush. So despite the curators' entreaty, the replacement appointment went to William Tucker of Warrensburg, publisher of the *Star-Journal*. Mr. Tucker died in 1966, and his wife, Avis Green Tucker of Warrensburg, was appointed to succeed him on the Board of Curators. Avis, a good friend, eventually became the first woman to serve as president of the board. She served with distinction and went on to serve by appointment to many important state boards and commissions, so highly regarded was her honesty and leadership ability.

COLLEGE YEARS

AFTER MY TWO years of junior college at Wentworth Military Academy, I transferred to my father's alma mater, the University of Missouri in Columbia. Then, as now, it is a very special place of learning and tradition, producing national and international leaders.

Arriving as a junior in the fall of 1951, I pledged Sigma Chi, just like my father. My goal was to be Phi Beta Kappa, and I studied hard and achieved that goal in my senior year. My father teased me that it only took him three years to make Phi Beta Kappa and it took me four. He was actually one of what they referred to as the "junior five," the five students from the entire student body who were so gifted they made Phi Beta Kappa their junior year. I loved his teasing, as it also motivated me.

Another of my life's heroes—a true mentor—awaited me at the University of Missouri. He was Dr. Lewis Atherton, professor of history, a native of Carrollton, Missouri, who in his early career coincidentally taught at my hometown alma mater, Wentworth Military Academy. By the time I arrived on the Columbia campus, Dr. Atherton was nationally known as a historian of the American frontier, and he was a very popular professor because his lectures were so interesting.

He was of average height and build, wore glasses, was balding—there was nothing really distinctive about Dr. Atherton's appearance. He was pleasant but never flamboyant or even overly warm. But he taught our nation's history with such deep and vivid scholarly knowledge that he brought you along on every adventure.

I spent five hours each week on his course, the History of the South, and he knew the subject so well that his old notes were rather dog-eared when he turned to them. The final exam in that course called for essays on a couple of questions, the most memorable of which was, "What is the South?" I wrote, "The South is a state of mind." That declaration and my elaboration helped me make a "B" in the course, which for the demanding Dr. Atherton was quite good.

Another class I loved was an English poetry class taught by Dr. John G. Neihardt, who had written epic poems on the subject of our American West. The class was in fact named for his epics, entitled *A Cycle of the West*. Dr. Neihardt was a dramatic figure, scarcely five feet tall but with long gray hair when long hair wasn't fashionable. He had lived with a Sioux medicine man during the 1930s, which inspired him to write the classic *Black Elk Speaks*, a book that is still in print and still on college reading lists.

I was so lucky to have these teachers who recognized and cultivated my boyhood love of history. I also had an interesting seatmate in Dr. Atherton's class. We were seated alphabetically, and next to me was someone with the last name of Scott, nicknamed "Scotty."

"Scotty" was a veteran, a bit older but a very pleasant guy. He was interested in acting and performed some of the male leads at the playhouse at Stephens College, the ladies' academy across town. Years later I went to the movies to see *Anatomy of a Murder*, and there on the big screen was my friend Scotty—better known today as Academy Award–winning actor George C. Scott. This was one of several memorable college brushes with celebrity, or in "Scotty's" case, a celebrity-to-be.

The early 1950s were a very different era, and segregation was a fact of life in Lexington. Schools were segregated and most of the black adults worked in white people's homes. We always had help. Katie Jackson helped us when I was quite young. Then in the summer of 1948 her daughter-in-law, Margariet Jackson, started working for us, first for my mother and then for Susie and me after we got married. She continued with us through my first year of Congress, when she retired and went home and became a leader in her church, the Second Baptist Church in Lexington. She and a few other selected senior ladies in that church were all designated as "Mothers," so she was known as Mother Jackson. They normally wore white dresses to church.

It's interesting, though, that despite the segregation, I always felt welcome in any home in my hometown. But in the fall of 1950, I think I was the one that broke the race barrier in town. I was going to Wentworth at the time and oversaw a sixth- and seventh-grade football team that practiced in my front yard. We played other teams around the county.

A teacher from the Douglass School, the school for black kids, was walking by one day and saw us. He stopped and visited with me and said, "Why don't your boys play my boys?" I said, "Good deal," and we did.

We played on the Douglass School football field. It was a hell of a game, tied six to six. One of their players, I forget which one, was on the way to a touchdown. My brother John nailed him, and that was the last play of the game. Everybody got up except my brother; he was down for the count. But it was no serious injury. I'm convinced that this game was the first color barrier that was broken in Lexington.

During this time, I started seeing the world beyond Missouri. After working for my father in the summer of 1951, I took a long trip that wound from

Massachusetts to New York, where I was reunited with Warm Springs friends. I went down the coast to Jacksonville, Florida, to visit my maternal grandmother, the widow of the esteemed local minister known as "Brother Boone." Then it was on to New Orleans and Little Rock, Arkansas, for fun and friends. I kept up my travels in 1952, touring Miami and Nassau, Bahamas, a place to which I would return often with my wife.

Prior to my graduation from the University of Missouri in arts and science in 1953, I learned of an opportunity to travel overseas to Scotland and attend the University of Edinburgh for a summer course in history. My father had promised me that if I made Phi Beta Kappa he would pay my way to Scotland, and he kept his word. My world continued to expand as I embarked on a ship from Montreal, landing in the Old World at Southampton, England.

On the ship, I met and fell into youthful infatuation with a beautiful dancer from the London Festival Ballet whose troupe was returning from North America. I made friends with several of the company, and they made me an honorary member of the ballet. I felt very sophisticated and even wore an ascot during my travels in Europe—a practical accessory, I learned, because it kept your shirt collar from getting dirty between launderings.

I made lifelong friends during my time at the University of Edinburgh, including Doug Spear from Iowa, who later became a professor in Eugene, Oregon, and who sadly passed away in 2009. Doug didn't know it at the time, but I helped him launch what became a wonderful marriage. He and another student named Mary Ann were very fond of one another but also very shy. After Doug and I toured the Continent and he returned to Iowa, I met up with Mary Ann in Paris and we began plotting how she could encourage his continued interest.

Our plan centered on her inviting him to visit her in Nebraska, and it worked—the following summer I was in Nebraska myself for their wedding. When I stepped off the plane, Mary Ann ran up to me and whispered, "Did you ever say anything to Doug?" It was a reference to our Paris conspiracy, and I told her no, and that I never would. But I will say it was a conspiracy with a happy outcome for two such lovely people.

Other U.S. students at Edinburgh who became great friends were Art Kline and Horace Speed, who joined me in visiting the quaint pubs there in the interest of good neighborly relations. In one pub we beheld a Scottish soldier standing at the bar and having a drink, wearing his kilt and a military hat with a ribbon dangling down the back.

Appreciative of all things military and noting he was by himself, I went over, introduced myself, and asked him to join our table. He was Regimental Sergeant Major Ernest Whiteoak, and we became fast friends until the day he died. Susie and I visited Ernie and his lovely wife, Molly, at their home in Scotland, and they visited us in our home. I still stay in touch with Molly, since she and Ernie took quite a shine to our son Page, who was ten years old when they first visited us.

When Page turned eleven, he went over to visit the Whiteoaks, who took him on a tour of Scotland and England. Page still remembers that trip fondly, and I relate so well to his having the eye-opening experience as a young man of starting to see the big world beyond home.

One indelible memory of my time in Scotland was going downtown to a movie in Edinburgh. They also had a live stage presentation for entertainment after the movie. The entertainer was a husky American singer, Burl Ives, who of course went on to international fame as a beloved balladeer and actor. But in 1953 Americans were not universally popular in Scotland and Great Britain because some soldiers during the war came across as overbearing and overly amorous. The British described the Americans as "overpaid, oversexed and Over Here."

There were actually a good number of boos when Burl Ives was introduced as an American visitor and took the stage. But soon his charming way with old folk songs won over the audience, and there was such applause that he performed encore after encore. They wouldn't let him go.

That was an important lesson for me. As an ambassador in another land, whether formally designated or as an informal traveler, what's important is not so much what went before, over which you had no control or involvement, but how you conduct yourself in the present. And indeed, that lesson applies well to all of life.

When I came back to Missouri for law school, I was obsessed with academics. I was fortunate to make Law Review at the end of my first year, and in my senior year, I won the University of Missouri's Guy Thompson Award for best Law Review article, on demonstrative evidence. I served on the law school's student board of governors for all three years, and in the second semester of my senior year, I served as the board president, which came with the honor of presiding at the Law Day dinner where we mingled with esteemed graduates and legal educators.

I studied hard, but life wasn't all work. I volunteered to go across town to Stephens College, the all-women's school, to assist with Sunday services. That helped me meet some lovely girls. As a senior in my undergraduate days, I gained a serious affection for a nineteen-year-old Stephens girl and gave her my fraternity pin, which meant we were serious.

There were mutual pledges of being true during the summer, and we awaited a joyous reunion that fall when I returned from Scotland. I returned to find that my girl, who was from Alabama, had developed a good friendship with a University of Alabama student named Walter during the summer. We continued dating sometimes, but I took back my fraternity pin.

In October she asked whether I would do her a big favor, and I said of course. Then I heard the request: Walter was coming up from Alabama for the weekend, and although we had resumed dating, she wanted me to ask her roommate out while Walter visited. I agreed. But later, the more I thought about what she was asking, the more irked I got. So I stopped by a florist shop in downtown Columbia and sent the young lady a dozen roses to her dorm room, along with a card that read, "Looking forward to this weekend." I didn't sign the card.

When Walter showed up on Friday, she came bounding down the stairs, draped her arms around him, and cried, "Oh Walter, Walter, the roses are beautiful!"

Walter replied rather coolly: "What roses?"

I stayed true to my word and took out her roommate that Saturday night. I got to meet Walter, who was none too happy, and neither was my former girlfriend. Walter went back to Alabama and never returned. She was upset with me, of course, but I noted that there was no signature on the roses I sent to her. Sometimes making assumptions is dangerous.

History had a way of reaching out and touching me even when I didn't expect it. My first year in law school, I stayed in the attic of a home owned by Mrs. Florence Bill on Bingham Road in Columbia. Her late husband had been an architecture professor at the University of Missouri. It was a ritual with me about every Sunday to have biscuits and tea with Mrs. Bill. She was seventy-five years old and just bright as a tack. We would talk about yesteryear at the drop of a hat.

I was about to walk out the door one Sunday morning past a beautiful Chinese tapestry by the front door when I asked, "Mrs. Bill, tell me about this tapestry." She said, "My fiancé gave it to me. He was a Marine and was killed in the Boxer Rebellion." I figured out she was about twenty-three years old during the Boxer Rebellion. I never expected to be visited by an artifact of gunboat diplomacy at law school.

I got involved with student government and served as chairman of the MUST party—the Missouri University Student Ticket party. Nothing seems so intense at the time as student government politics.

Our party initially thought we lost all four of our races. But we later learned there were irregularities in ballot counting for two of the races. It was my first personal exposure to suspicions about the lengths others would go to win elections. I later had adult lessons in such rotten political games played by others.

I moved back into the Sigma Chi house for my senior year of law school. My roommate, Tom Fenner, who was very active in student activities, was a member of the prestigious QEBH honor society at the University of Missouri. Thanks to Tom, and based on my law school activities and other student interests, I was recommended to become a member of QEBH. At the time, my father and I were the first father-and-son QEBH members—he had joined in 1926.

One honor my father received that I did not was Order of the Coif, the highest law school honor, the very top. But more than four decades later, the law school named me an honorary member of Order of the Coif, and what meant the most to me was joining my father at last in this association.

There was one more path of my father's that I was intent on following—serving as a prosecutor. I filed for Lafayette County prosecutor in March 1956, precisely three decades after he first held the job.

I graduated from law school that June and took the bar examination, learning on August 4 that I had passed. Passing the bar exam was no small concern, since I was already campaigning door to door to be prosecutor.

THE LAW, DEWEY, AND GENE

WHEN I CAMPAIGNED for Lafayette County prosecuting attorney in 1956, I was the youngest person ever to try for the office. I was fortunate to be "Ike's boy"; my father was very popular, and I was welcome in every home in town. Even the African-Americans in town, who were pretty solidly Republican in gratitude for what President Lincoln had done, went for me in the election.

A great Missourian made a big impact on my political future by befriending me at a fancy reception in Washington, D.C., for President Truman's January 1949 inauguration. Thomas Hennings Jr. was a lawyer from St. Louis, and he told me he was going to be a U.S. senator. And indeed, Missourians elected him their senator, and he remained my friend.

One day as I was campaigning door-to-door in Lexington and hiking up a big hill in town, up rolled a big black car, and when the window came down, I was greeted by none other than Senator Hennings. The senator invited me into his car and asked how things were going. I told him, "They're using my age against me." In fact, I was fresh out of law school and had just passed the Missouri Bar examination. The wise senator just laughed and gave me some wonderful, inspiring advice.

"How old are you?" he asked. I replied that I was twenty-four.

He turned to look at me and said, "Ike, just remember William Pitt was elected prime minister of England at twenty-four. Now go out and *win*." That was such a psychological boost for me; it let me turn my youth into an asset. I never forgot Senator Hennings's encouragement.

In November 1956, I defeated the Republican nominee for prosecutor, Forrest Roberts, a lawyer who also ran a drugstore. I was of course pleased to win my first political race, and I was doubly pleased to have improved on a record set by my father. Dad was twenty-six years old when he took his oath as Lafayette County prosecuting attorney, the youngest person ever to hold the job. That is, until I took my oath in January 1957, at age twenty-five, for that same office, in that same Lafayette County Courthouse, which to this day is still the oldest continuously operating courthouse west of the Mississippi. We kidded one another about that, but my father was proud of me, and he continued to share advice from his own vast legal experience.

I needed all of the advice I could get. Fortunately, I had another outstanding adviser in the practicalities of law, and he never went to law school.

Dewey Parrott's professional background was running a barbershop in the small town of Odessa, but he was hired as a Lafayette County sheriff's deputy in 1932. Back then, Missouri sheriffs were limited to serving one four-year term, so in 1936 Dewey ran for and won the sheriff's job.

He was considered a good lawman and a fair person, and he was popular. He was able to speak softly and gently coax the information he needed to build a case. I never knew Dewey to have to fire his pistol in the line of duty. But while he was serving as deputy, it accidentally misfired and struck Dewey in the leg, causing a serious wound. Part of his leg had to be amputated. From then on, Dewey had a wooden leg.

After the 1940 election, with Missouri's mandatory term limits for sheriffs, Dewey became a farmer. He remained popular and respected, and when I ran for prosecutor, Dewey was on the Democratic ticket with me, running for sheriff once again. Dewey was fifty-eight during the 1956 election. Since he and his wife, Mildred, had only a daughter, he considered me like his son during the four years we served together as courthouse officials. We both won by a margin of about fifteen hundred votes in the general election, although our strengths were in different parts of the county. I often teased Dewey about my getting three more votes overall than he received.

My fond nickname for Mildred was Polly—yes, Polly Parrott. I was a bachelor and was welcomed to share her great cooking in their living quarters at the county jail. She also kept the books for the sheriff's office and prepared meals for the prisoners, who ate pretty well; usually they had whatever the Parrotts were having.

In that sense the sheriff's office had a bit of the relaxed atmosphere of the easygoing Mayberry jail on the *Andy Griffith Show*. And in the best sense of that analogy, Dewey Parrott had many of the admirable qualities of the fictional Mayberry sheriff, Andy Taylor. Dewey was not a man with a great deal of formal education, but I considered him brilliant in terms of common sense and country wisdom.

I saw an example of his wisdom when I met and started dating my future wife, Susie, while I was prosecuting attorney. The Parrotts were delighted for me, and they adored Susie. When we decided to get married, Dewey gave me two pieces of advice, both of which sound simple but are nothing short of profound. Number One: Don't get mad at each other at the same time. And Number Two: If one of you offends the other, let that offense go right on down the river and never bring it back up again.

Dewey's primary point was that if you are working on a loving marriage with sincerity and commitment, it means being unselfish and sensitive to your spouse. As strong Baptists, Dewey and Polly were great role models in this regard. But that wasn't his only good advice. From time to time we got a bad check case, and Dewey would admonish that a man needed to be extra careful with two things—where he put his pencil, and where he put his . . . well, something more private.

Indeed, Dewey was a fountain of the type of wisdom you don't obtain in a college classroom. Although Dewey didn't attend law school, he knew a great deal of law from practical experience. He had a superb mind, and he absorbed and retained so much about areas of the law such as criminal evidence. Dewey never seemed to forget details and notable aspects of past cases.

When I was sometimes baffled about where to go with a case, Dewey would guide me. He would lean back in his chair, gesture to the tall bookshelf, and drawl, "Ike, if you go and look in them there law books, it will tell you . . ."—and sure enough, I would do the research in the section of law he suggested and we would build a successful case.

It's also important to note that many cases never got to trial because of Dewey's easygoing but highly effective way of talking to those who were under investigation or accused. He was a great communicator and listener and didn't raise his voice or threaten or intimidate in any way—he just visited with them, and eventually he would catch small contradictions in their stories.

He would take out his chewing tobacco and think about what they had told him, and then he would point out the inconsistencies. They would finally relent and say, "Well, Mr. Dewey, you're right, I did it," and there would follow a guilty plea and the sentencing. Dewey was just that good at reasoning with people and listening closely, and I owed a great deal of my success as prosecutor to Dewey's success in dealing with the accused and getting confessions.

Don't get me wrong—Dewey Parrott was a brave man, and he was an excellent shot, the leg mishap notwithstanding. We would ride across to the other side of the Missouri River to have target practice along with his deputy, Charlie Burns. Once we were taking turns shooting at a couple of dozen tin cans about fifty feet away. The first one I shot at went flying, and Dewey exclaimed, "That's real good, Ike!" I replied, "Yeah, but that was the wrong tin can."

Another time we learned of some serious gambling happening in Lexington, and Dewey and I planned a raid on a house down on Tenth Street. When we burst in there was a big card game going on, with some familiar faces holding the cards. One of the fellows looked up at Dewey and said, "Aww, Mr. Dewey—just when I got a winning hand."

When I took the oath of office as prosecutor, my first case was already waiting for me. Right after my election, I traveled to Florida and Nassau to visit friends. When I returned, I stayed overnight at the Kansas City home of my fraternity brother Ed Setzler, and it was there that I sat down to read the morning newspaper. It reported that the janitor at the Lafayette County courthouse, a man named Delbert Porter, had been arrested for stealing twenty-six thousand dollars from the county collector's office.

The theft was reported to have happened on Christmas Eve, and charges were filed by the man I was succeeding as prosecutor, Warren Sherman Jr. The deputy collector was reported to have left a locked leather bag containing cash and checks on the office counter when he locked the office and went out for several hours. The bag was gone when he returned.

The sheriff, Lambert Schlueter, knew that as janitor, Delbert Porter had one of the few keys to the office. Delbert denied knowing anything about the missing money, so the sheriff sent Delbert over to help look for it in the courthouse.

Sure enough, the leather bag with the money mysteriously "reappeared" in the collector's office. The charge was thus filed and pending when I took office on January 1, 1957. I investigated thoroughly and put together the case, which was indeed a circumstantial case—no one had seen Delbert take the money, and he had not spent any of it.

I told the jury that while this was my first case and of course I wanted to win it, I primarily wanted justice to prevail. The defense attorney was the great William Aull III from Lexington, who would prove to be a regular opponent over the years. He was an honorable man who had commanded a company of Nisei soldiers in the Second World War. Afterward, he became an outstanding lawyer; not as good as my father, of course, but a close second, and it made a headline when he told the jury my case was as "full of holes as Swiss cheese." But the jury convicted Delbert, and he was sentenced to six months in jail—for a crime that under law could have been punished with as many as ten years in prison.

Delbert was a nice fellow, and of course I had known him for quite some time. His lawyer asked the judge for a new trial or dismissal, saying the evidence was insufficient. The judge agreed and dismissed the case, setting Delbert free.

So I had won my first felony prosecution, only to have the judge set aside the conviction. Whenever I saw Delbert around town, he was always friendly and never seemed to hold a grudge. In fact, he supported me when I ran for the Missouri state senate in 1970. I learned to speak and deal with everyone, even criminal defendants, with courtesy and respect, while making clear I had a job to do. It was an enduring lesson from Dewey Parrott.

About this time, I joined the Lions Club, and guess who sat across from me at the first meeting? My old boss, the airport manager, Mr. Van Camp, who was lovely to me. I guess he saw that I had learned to work some after all.

Even with Dewey's help and gentle persuasion, I insisted on being a tough prosecutor, and early in my career I proved it. Two men who had prior felony convictions were caught burglarizing a gas station in Odessa. In Lafayette County, the tradition was that if the prosecution and the defense had a discussion and worked out a plea, the prosecutor might recommend a sentence that was not the maximum, subject to approval of the judge, which was often forthcoming. But I charged these two with the separate counts of burglary and stealing—burglary carrying a maximum ten-year sentence and stealing carrying a maximum five-year sentence. I wanted to get each defendant sentenced to ten years.

A good friend of mine, a deputy court clerk named Joyce Neville, came into the prosecutor's office, closed the door behind her, and asked me whether I knew what they were saying about me in the courthouse. I told her I had no idea.

"They're saying, 'Ike is crazy, seeking those ten-year sentences for that filling station break-in.'" That just made me more determined to see that these two repeat offenders were punished. I went to trial and the first one was convicted—the jury sentenced him to fifteen years. That led to the second defendant entering a guilty plea, and he was sentenced to ten years. The judge commuted five years from the first convict's sentence, so they both wound up with ten years in the penitentiary, as I wanted. Nobody called me crazy as a prosecutor after that.

One case of mine that drew national attention was a robbery and kidnapping by an escaped Ohio convict who was picked up hitchhiking on Highway 40 by a young Air Force airman and his pregnant wife. The convict pulled a gun on the couple and stuffed them into the trunk of the car, stopping occasionally to intimidate them and pistol-whip the husband bloody. The convict drove the car into Kansas City, with the couple still captive in the trunk, and by happenstance a driver's license examiner administering a driving test saw the husband's bloody hand reaching from the trunk, which he had pried partially open.

The examiner alerted a motorcycle police officer, who stopped the car and rescued the couple. It was later learned the abduction had happened in Lafayette County, so I was responsible for filing charges, which I promptly did. But our headaches with this convict were just starting—he turned out to be an escape artist. He made it through one door on his way out of the county jail in Lexington, so I got a court order to transfer him to Jackson County, where he again tried to flee but was caught before leaving the jail. I got another court order to put the slippery fellow into the maximum-security state penitentiary in Jefferson City pending trial. On the morning of the scheduled trial, the convict pled guilty and was sentenced to twenty-two years behind bars. After serving his Missouri sentence, he was to be extradited to Ohio to finish his previous sentence there. By my calculations, he had no chance of release before he was at least seventy-six years old. An account of the bizarre series of events culminating in the arrest was published in *Reader's Digest*.

Back in Lexington, Dewey's deputy, Charlie Burns, got a job as a truck weight inspector for the Missouri State Highway Patrol, creating a vacancy in the sheriff's office. I recommended that Dewey hire an Army veteran who was working at the Ford assembly plant near Kansas City, a Dover resident named Gene Darnell. Gene was a perfect fit and Dewey hired him, launching Gene's career of almost four decades in law enforcement.

I served two terms as prosecutor, from 1957 to 1961, and then I resumed private law practice in my dad's office, where he had a strong and thriving partnership with a wonderful attorney, Newton Bradley.

Meanwhile, the law limiting sheriffs' terms had been changed to allow them to run for unlimited terms, so Dewey Parrott, ever popular, stayed in office until he decided not to seek reelection in 1964. Dewey's retirement meant an opportunity for Gene Darnell, who filed for sheriff. Gene had gained an excellent reputation, as had Dewey, for fair and professional law enforcement. He was not a physically large man, but people didn't test Gene because he meant business. Still he was very popular, perhaps as much so as our dear friend Dewey.

Gene was so popular that he kept getting reelected as Lafayette County sheriff, eventually serving a total of thirty-two years in the office, including his prior tenure as deputy. Few Missouri sheriffs have served comparable tenures, and Gene was known and respected statewide in law enforcement for his time in office and for founding and leading the region's Major Case Squad for the most serious criminal investigations across jurisdictions.

Gene's widow is a wonderful lady named Leona, and as with Dewey Parrott's wife, Polly, she was Gene's rock and his partner. They would tease one another with great love. Leona was a waitress at the Victory Café, and she would change her hair color from time to time. We were sitting with a bunch of fellows around a table at the café one day just after Leona had changed her hair color to a really light platinum blonde.

Gene quipped, "You know, I sat up in bed this morning and there was this blonde woman lying next to me, and I said, 'You better get up honey, because my wife will be coming home soon.'" Leona didn't exactly appreciate that joke, but they always shared laughter, eventually.

SUSIE

ALTHOUGH I'D ONLY won one election so far, politics were becoming a bigger part of my life. I was very nearly nominated for Congress in 1959, while serving as Lafayette County prosecutor. I was all of twenty-eight years old when the incumbent congressman, George Christopher from Butler, Missouri, died in office. The congressional district committee, composed of county Democratic leaders, was convened to select a nominee for a special election to fill the suddenly vacant post.

A "rural" candidate was proposed from Nevada, Missouri, and a "city" candidate proposed from more populous Jackson County, which includes Kansas City and Independence. The committee vote was tied between those two.

The Jackson County people went to my Lafayette County Democratic chairman, who would have been expected to be my strong ally, and proposed breaking the deadlock by nominating me as the compromise candidate. That would have combined the "city" votes with the "rural" vote of my county chairman—and likely others. But unknown to me, while smiling to my face and expressing support, my county party chairman refused to agree to the deal. The nomination eventually went to William J. "Bill" Randall, who won the special election.

In 1960, I was helping my pal Cleo Crouch campaign for U.S. Senator Stuart Symington, a great Missourian we were supporting for the Democratic presidential nomination against contenders John F. Kennedy and Lyndon B. Johnson. We felt like political veterans when we were assigned to travel to Colorado to organize area Democrats for Symington, and we wound up with tickets to the Democratic National Convention in Los Angeles.

One morning during the convention, Cleo and I were standing in the Beverly Hilton Hotel when a young lady in a yellow linen dress came up to us, followed by her brother. She asked me, "Hello Ike, do you remember me? I'm Sue Anding."

I said, "Who?" She said, "Sue Anding!" and I said, "Oh yes." I did remember having met her mother, a graduate of the Missouri law school, at University of Missouri Law Day.

As Susie later told it, usually with a knowing smile, we had actually met at that same Law Day event, but I was so busy buttering up her mom that I didn't pay much attention to her. And to make me blush a bit in the retelling, Susie would recall the times at the University of Missouri when she worked at her Delta Delta Delta sorority front desk during "date call" and went upstairs to alert other lucky young ladies that the dashing and elegant—that is, full of himself—Mister Skelton had arrived.

After she and her brother walked away, Cleo Crouch turned to me and said, "Ike, that's the girl you should marry." It was more command than suggestion. We may not have picked the winning primary candidate in the Kennedy year of 1960, but with his matrimonial declaration, Cleo was absolutely correct.

Susie and I began dating, and we fell in love. On Christmas Eve 1960, I was in Susie's hometown of Pacific, Missouri, to pop the question and present her with a ring after her mother had gone up to bed. The big moment was upon me—and the phone rang. It was my dad, calling from Lexington, wondering whether Susie had accepted my ring (he adored Susie until the day he died). I told him, "No Dad, not yet—call back later."

We confirmed for him in a later call that indeed Susie had accepted my proposal, right there by her mother's Christmas tree. There may have been some mistletoe hanging around, too.

Cleo Crouch came to our wedding precisely one year after the Los Angeles convention, and I was delighted his advice proved so resoundingly correct when he declared I should marry Susie.

Susie had been born in St. Louis on August 19, 1936, and she was raised in Pacific, southwest of St. Louis. Susie's father, who held engineering and law degrees, died of a heart attack when she was very young. Her widowed mother, Virginia Booth Anding, was an attorney and businesswoman. Like me, Susie was a graduate of the University of Missouri in Columbia, earning her bachelor's degree in education. Her leadership skills were on display in college, as she was elected president of the Panhellenic Association.

Susie put others first. She made my goals her goals, without complaint, sometimes when a complaint or two would have been understandable and justified.

Our first home after our July 1961 wedding was a very small bungalow at 1721 Bloom Street in Lexington. But in 1964, my father bought a big rambling house for us. It was built in 1850 on two acres of land and had a commanding view of the Missouri River from a soaring bluff. My father said to Susie and me, "I bought you a house. It's yours. And all you have to do is pay for it." It was a beautiful home that Susie and I fixed up over a period of years. We moved in and worked on different rooms from time to time. We didn't have them all complete by the time I got to Congress, but Susie did a magnificent job in fixing up what we had. It had a usable stable and an old cookhouse in the back. At night in the summertime when the barges went by, they'd flash their lights up at us. And we did pay for it, eventually.

My father was devoted to Susie and our oldest son (Dad passed away in 1965, before the birth of our other two sons), and he usually joined us at our home for at least one meal a day, often arriving for breakfast. He was always a welcome visitor, but one day he landed in Susie's doghouse.

Susie and I had traveled to Columbia for a University of Missouri football game. My father got the idea that a tall row of lilacs lining our driveway might provide concealing cover for a prowler, and that wouldn't do, since Susie was often at home alone. So with the best intentions, my father had the lilacs cut down, figuring we would be pleased upon our return that night. But Susie, who loved gardening and had been cultivating the lilacs, was livid—and she stayed angry for some time, which was excruciating to my very apologetic father. They eventually reconciled, of course, and Susie was once again like his daughter, and he provided a protective paternal presence she didn't have while growing up.

Meanwhile, I was enjoying private practice with my father and his partner, Newton Bradley. Dad was a strong Democrat and "Brad" was a staunch Republican, but politics never entered into the equation when they were doing their jobs as attorneys. Later we were joined by another fine attorney, Bud Schelp, and two bright young attorneys, Gary Bradley, Newton's son, and Robert Langdon. I worked closely with Bob Langdon, who helped me prepare numerous jury cases, and he went on to national distinction as a highly successful trial attorney, specializing in product liability cases. Bud Schelp went through Navy ROTC and the University of Missouri about when I did, although I didn't know him back then. He went into the Navy for a number of years and flew P2V sub hunters. Then he came back and applied to law school. His undergraduate grades were not quite up to snuff, but he said to the dean, "You let me into law school. It will take an act of Congress to get me out." The Cuban Missile Crisis came along during his senior year, and he got recalled. So it wasn't quite an act of Congress, but close.

Just as my father had defended the City of Odessa in the Jehovah's Witnesses case, another memorable case involving a defense of Odessa put my own legal skills to the test. In 1960, Leonard Alkire was the Odessa city marshal and my father was the city attorney. The city council passed an ordinance declaring that no one past the age of seventy could be elected or serve as city marshal. Mr. Alkire had been marshal for many years, but when he went in to file for reelection, his papers were rejected pursuant to the ordinance because he was older than seventy. Mr. Alkire sued, and my father asked me to handle the city's defense in a non-jury trial before an out-of-town judge.

I made the argument that the ordinance was within the rights of the city council to enact because they could establish standards for law enforcement, including the reasoning that the physical demands of such an active job might be too much for a man older than seventy. I won the case, and when I got back to the law office, my father inquired about how it had gone in court. I told him of the victory. "What? You were supposed to lose!" my dad exclaimed. His surprise quickly turned into pride in my unexpected triumph, which made me very proud indeed.

That wasn't the end of Mr. Alkire's story. He ran as a write-in candidate and was elected. But the city clerk refused to certify his election because of the age ordinance, so Mr. Alkire sued the city again. This time my father handled the city's defense, employing the same arguments that helped me win the first round. Mr. Alkire lost his second lawsuit too, but he received a great deal of publicity, which seemed to please him, since he was a colorful character. For me, the thrill was paving the way with winning legal arguments and, in a rare situation, having my father follow my footsteps for a change.

Of course, as the years have gone by, my own attitude has become that some people make their greatest contributions when they are past seventy and can employ their accumulated wisdom.

MR. TRUMAN

IN THE SPRING of 1962 I was working a part-time job as a special assistant under Tom Eagleton, Missouri's attorney general, in which I got to brief and argue three cases a year before the Missouri Supreme Court. I had an office in the Supreme Court Building in Jefferson City, and Susie sometimes accompanied me down from Lexington, where I still worked with my father in private law practice.

I was in the back office visiting with George Draper, an assistant attorney general in charge of the criminal division, when a secretary came in and said a Mr. Burrus was on the phone. I thought it might be a Wentworth classmate named Burrus, but it turned out the man on the phone was his father, Mr. Rufus B. Burrus, an influential lawyer from Independence and a confidant of former President Harry Truman.

Mr. Burrus told me in that call, "This is the last day of filing for the 1962 primaries and President Truman wants you to file for Congress against the Democratic incumbent, Bill Randall."

Well, I thanked Mr. Burrus but told him I had been married just a short while and wanted to get my law practice going, and that was the end of the conversation. But pretty soon another secretary came running into George Draper's office, crying out that Harry Truman was on the phone!

Indeed he was. In that familiar confident voice, President Truman was urging me to file against Bill Randall, who was no favorite of the Man from Independence. I told him the same thing I had told Mr. Burrus—I thanked him for his interest, but I didn't think this was the time for me to run for Congress. I wrote the former president a follow-up note on April 27, 1962:

Dear President Truman,

May I take this opportunity to express my appreciation to you for your encouragement and kindness when you called me in Jefferson City the other day. It was a most difficult decision to make, especially after we talked on the phone, but I sincerely felt that it would be best not to run at this time. Earlier this year, I had considered the race for Congress, but I could not see my way clear to enter it. I felt that present circumstances compelled me from filing, and to continue in the practice of law for the time being.

Mr. President, let me again thank you for your interest and encouragement. I hope to someday merit your kind thoughts. At some convenient time, Susie and I would like to come by Independence and have a visit with you.

Most sincerely,
Ike Skelton, Jr.

On May 16, Mr. Truman replied:

Dear Ike,

I appreciated your letter of April 27, and I am as sorry as I can be that I have been so long in acknowledging it.

I understand the situation and all I am interested in is to see that we have a Democratic Congressman in Washington who will have an interest in the welfare of this district. I hope we will get him before we get through.

Sincerely yours,
Harry S. Truman

The Man from Independence and I remained friends until his death in 1972—a decade after Mr. Truman first urged me to run for the congressional seat I eventually assumed from Bill Randall in 1977.

And as Mr. Truman wished, I have tried to be what he wanted—"a Democratic Congressman in Washington who will have an interest in the welfare of this district." I am particularly honored that, as far as I can determine, I was the only member of Congress in 2011 who was personally urged by Harry Truman to run for the House—even though I initially turned him down.

The Skelton family's relationship with the Truman family dated back to September 17, 1928, when Mr. Truman's daughter, Margaret, would have been a four-year-old and I wasn't even a twinkle in my dad's eye, since he didn't get married until that December. On that day, a monument was dedicated in Lexington to the pioneer mothers of America's westward movement. The keynote speaker at the dedication of the Madonna of the Trails was the county court judge from neighboring Jackson County, Harry Truman. Representing the American Legion at the same event was my father, who like Judge Truman was a World War I veteran. They shook hands and hit it off instantly.

My father and Harry Truman remained friends. In 1940, Truman, then a U.S. senator, was in a tough primary renomination fight against Governor Lloyd Crow Stark and Maurice Milligan, U.S. attorney for the Western District of

Missouri. At the time, Mr. Truman's mentor (or "patron," to those less charitably minded) was the Kansas City political boss Tom Pendergast, who had been tainted with corruption. The criminal conviction of Tom Pendergast for income tax evasion hung around Mr. Truman's neck politically, but my father stuck with him in 1940 and their friendship continued.

In 1948, when Mr. Truman was running for the presidency in his own right, the Gallup Poll showed he was not going to win. I asked my father right before the election whether Harry Truman could be reelected, and my father told me, "Don't count Harry Truman out."

I stayed up all night listening to the radio commentator H. V. Kaltenborn, who was very much for Dewey, saying in his high shrill voice that Truman would be defeated. But as we all know, Truman won the election.

My dad took me to Truman's inauguration in January 1949. We rode up with all the Democratic political leaders on a train designated the "Forrest Smith Special," because Mr. Smith was the newly elected governor. The Washington festivities were great fun and very impressive to me. I must say, though, that I was less interested in the politics than in gawking at the blonde bombshell actress Joan Blondell sitting just one table away at the Electors dinner. It was at this dinner that President Truman famously mimicked the pompous radio commentator Mr. Kaltenborn, who had insisted on the air that Truman could not possibly prevail, even though the actual numbers were showing otherwise.

I'm not sure historians fully understand some of the remarkable traits of Harry Truman. A couple of those traits stand out in my mind. First, he did not suffer fools or people he felt were disloyal; he did not like my predecessor, Congressman Randall, and I saw Mr. Truman on occasion look right through him and ignore him.

Mr. Truman's second remarkable trait was that he was so very thoughtful of other people. I was a recipient of that kindness. He wrote me that letter of encouragement when I was in the hospital with polio, and there was a notable event in September 1952 that I cannot forget, when young Rufus Burrus and I were students at the University of Missouri.

We learned that President Truman would be giving one of his famous speeches from the rear platform of a train in Jefferson City on behalf of Democratic presidential nominee Adlai Stevenson. So Rufe and I went over to the train station, and we went to the front of the last car of the train. Rufe told the Secret Service agent he was Rufus Burrus II of Independence and that I was Ike Skelton Jr., and that we would like to see the president. We were eventually allowed to board the train, and Mr. Truman called Rufe by his known name of "Sonny." After visiting briefly with Mr. Truman, we stepped off the train, worked our way to the rear, and were standing maybe eight feet from the platform.

There right beside me was a man who had no legs. The fellow wheeled himself around on a little cart made of 2-by-4s and roller skates. President Truman came out onto the platform, with the crowd cheering, and he looked down and saw this man and just stopped. Then he climbed down and went over to shake hands with the man, thanking him profusely for coming to hear him speak.

While Mr. Truman was talking with the gentleman with no legs, a news photographer came up. But Mr. Truman waved the photographer away, thinking the man might be embarrassed by all the attention. Only after he thanked the man again for coming did Mr. Truman get up and deliver his political address for Adlai Stevenson. It was an example of his great kindness.

Kindness in its many forms can be a great balm. My private law practice was varied, sometimes including defending those accused of serious crimes. One such defense led to one of the most profound acts of forgiveness I have ever witnessed.

Skelton's Confederate
great-grandfather
Washington Mason
Skelton, circa 1850.
Skelton's Family Collection

Skelton's grandfather
Isaac Newton Skelton II,
circa 1900. Skelton's Family
Collection

Skelton's father, Isaac Newton Skelton III, fireman second class, aboard the USS *Missouri*, 1918. Skelton's Family Collection

Skelton's father, prosecuting attorney of Lafayette County, 1927.
Skelton's Family Collection

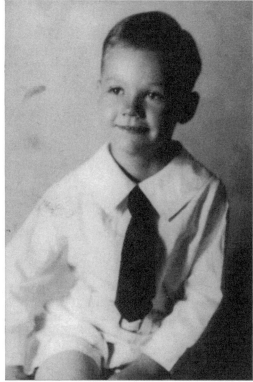

The author, age six.
Skelton's Family Collection

Rev. J. T. Boone, author's grandfather, 1941. Skelton's Family Collection

Scoutmaster John Marchetti, Troop 418, Lexington, Missouri. Courtesy of Roy Gene Marchetti

The author as a high school sopho-more at Wentworth Military Acad-emy, 1946. Skelton's Family Collection

Georgia Hall, Warm Springs, Georgia. Skelton's Family Collection

Dedication of the Little White House, Warm Springs, Georgia, June 1947. Author peering from behind roommate Peter Hanson. Skelton's Family Collection

The author with fellow Warm Springs patient Lynn Long-bottom, 1947. Courtesy of Lynn Longbottom Rice

The author and father in front of father's Luscombe, 1950. Skelton's Family Collection

Author's mother, Carolyn Boone Skelton, 1951. Skelton's Family Collection

The author running track, Wentworth Junior College, 1951.
Skelton's Family Collection

The author on Wentworth Junior College graduation day, 1951.
Skelton's Family Collection

The author and father, law school graduation, University of Missouri, 1956. Skelton's Family Collection

The author's father, Isaac Newton Skelton III, 1963. Skelton's Family Collection

The author and Susie Skelton with former president Harry Truman, 1963.
Skelton's Family Collection

The author, Senator Tom Eagleton, and Congressman Jerry Litton, 1974. Skelton's
Family Collection

The author and Susie Skelton with sons Jim and Page and friend Nick Iman, 1975.
Skelton's Family Collection

The author and Dr. Norman Vincent Peale, 1975. Skelton's Family Collection

The author with State Senator William Cason addressing group of constituents, 1975. Skelton's Family Collection

The author with Emory Melton and Norman Merrell, state senators, 1975. Skelton's Family Collection

State senator Ike Skelton and presidential candidate Jimmy Carter, 1976.
Skelton's Family Collection

Skelton with U.S. senators Edmund Muskie and Stuart Symington,
1976. Skelton's Family Collection

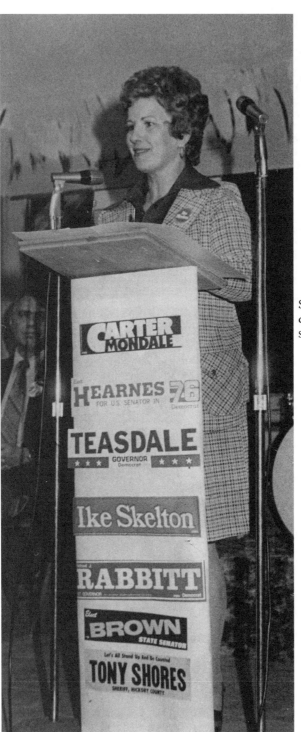

Susie Skelton on the
campaign trail, 1976.
Skelton's Family Collection

MEMORABLE COURTROOM MOMENTS

IN NOVEMBER 1967, Ronnie Melton, a Virginia resident and recent graduate of William and Mary then attending graduate school at the University of Georgia, drove along Interstate 70 in Missouri. He went into a grocery store in the small town of Emma, ripped the telephone from the wall, and robbed the store of a good deal of money. He sped away and then stopped in Lexington, checking into a motel run by an elderly couple. After dark he went into the motel office and shot dead the wife, who was on duty at the desk. Her husband arrived just in time to see Melton driving away in his car with Virginia plates. The Missouri State Highway Patrol was alerted, and they found and arrested Melton.

It was a shocking crime in a peaceful small Missouri town. Melton denied everything, but officers found the gun under his car seat and the ballistics investigation matched it with the weapon used to kill the woman. The case looked obvious to me, but there were questions about Melton's sanity. His family hired me to defend him, and in the spring of 1968, we had at least two full days of witness testimony and evidence about Melton's mental state. The non-jury trial was held before a visiting judge. The judge found that Melton was not guilty by reason of mental disease or defect, which spared him the prospect of the death penalty, but it also meant he would be locked up for life or until pronounced cured, a possibility which seemed highly unlikely.

After Melton had been sentenced and removed from the courtroom to be taken to the state's prison for mental patients in Fulton, I stood talking with a deputy sheriff. The husband and daughter of the slain woman walked up to us and asked me whether they could speak with Melton's parents, who were on the other side of the courtroom. I thought, "Oh, my Lord, what is this?" But I went over and brought Melton's parents back with me.

The victim's family had been in the courtroom and heard all of the expert witnesses on mental illness and the other testimony. To my amazement, the daughter of the slain woman expressed very sincere sympathy to Melton's parents for the obvious sickness of their son. I have seen nothing in the practice of law, and few events in life, comparable to this generous gesture.

A postscript to the case: In 1973, while incarcerated at the state hospital and working on its inmate newspaper, Ronnie Melton escaped and seemingly disappeared. He is presumed to be either dead or out there, somewhere.

Not every case for a country law firm gains you national distinction, a big payday, or even a memorable anecdote. Sometimes there's a great deal of aggravation—even in trying to collect your fee. After all, lawyers have families to feed, just like everyone else. At times you just have to laugh and learn.

One such case involved a woman I represented in a divorce lawsuit. She had the memorable name of Zephyr Rabius. She went to the hospital for back surgery, and while she was recuperating, her husband was untrue to her with her best friend. Zephyr became aware of this infidelity and hired me to represent her. So I hired a private detective to gather relevant facts, which he accomplished in part by feeding lunch meat to the other woman's guard dog to distract the canine while he peered through the window at the activities within.

Zephyr got her divorce, including a handsome alimony award, but she remained angry about the whole matter and wanted to do more in court. I advised her that she could file a lawsuit against her best friend alleging alienation of her husband's affections. Zephyr wanted to do it, and we agreed on a fee for my firm of one thousand dollars to file the petition.

We tried the case, including the evidence produced by the private detective. It was all going well until the defense put on the witness stand a bartender who testified that during the period when her husband's affections were in the process of being alienated, he, the bartender, had intimate relations with Zephyr.

Zephyr spoke up in court, shouting, "That's a lie!" The bartender looked at her from the witness stand and declared, "Zephyr, you know that it's true—right there on your sofa in your front room!"

I gave an outstanding closing argument to the jury about the sanctity of marriage, but I knew the bartender's testimony was a major setback. Still, when the jury went out, Zephyr turned to me and said, "I don't care what the jury does; you've done a marvelous job, Ike."

A little over an hour later, the jury returned a verdict against Zephyr Rabius for her claim of alienation of affection against her former best friend. And despite her courtroom words of praise for my work, thereafter on late Wednesday nights or early Thursday mornings, she would call Susie while I was serving in the Missouri senate down in Jefferson City.

With slurred words, Zephyr would complain bitterly to my sleepy wife about what a terrible lawyer I was. She kept this up for several weeks running, and finally Susie said between irritated yawns, "Zephyr, I don't mind you calling and waking me at 2 A.M. every Thursday morning, but the least you can do is come and pay your legal bill."

The following Saturday morning Zephyr showed up at my law office with a thousand-dollar check. She never rang the house again, at any hour.

BACK INTO POLITICS

PEOPLE CALL ME a politician. I've never thought of myself that way, and it may surprise you to learn that many members of Congress (and people who get elected at all levels of government) don't consider themselves politicians. We are public servants; our goal is to make government work for our fellow citizens. Engaging in politics—campaigns, elections, and all that—is something we have to do to get elected to those public service positions, but it is not what we look forward to, nor is it how we define our careers. Many Americans serve the public—as firefighters, in the military, in government at all levels—without having to engage in politics, but to some of us who are called to offices that require election, politicking is a necessary part of getting the job.

Others, of course, relish the rough-and-tumble of politics and may consider actually doing the job to be anticlimactic. As I mention elsewhere in this book, I believe that an attitude of constant competition does not serve the American people well.

Fortunately, that competition often gives way to a more human spirit. I have been blessed with many good friendships across the spectrum of politics and public service. One of my greatest friendships was with a man I met in the late 1950s, when I was the Lafayette County prosecutor and Tom Eagleton was circuit attorney for the city of St. Louis. When Tom decided to run for state attorney general in 1960 and asked me to campaign for him, I agreed, and he did win the election.

Tom Hennings, who had given me such good advice during my campaign for prosecutor, served as Missouri's U.S. senator until 1960, when he died in office. He was succeeded by Edward Long, until my old friend Tom Eagleton decided to challenge Senator Long in the 1968 Democratic primary.

Senator Long called me one day at my law office in Lexington and asked who Tom Eagleton had supporting him locally. I told him truthfully, "Tom has *me*." I worked hard for Tom Eagleton in Lafayette County, and he carried the county in his unseating of Senator Long.

About the time Tom Eagleton set his sights on the U.S. Senate, I began rethinking my decision some years earlier to turn down President Truman's request that I run for Congress. But I was a horse without a horse race. Democrat Bill Randall was still the incumbent congressman, and a poll I commissioned indicated that I couldn't defeat the veteran lawmaker. However, the poll showed there was good potential for political victory in a Missouri state senate district that partly overlapped the congressional district. So I decided to run for the state senate seat and filed for the race in 1970.

This time I tried to work the supposed age issue to my advantage. I took out a newspaper ad stressing the advantages of having a youthful and energetic thirty-eight-year-old lawmaker—rather than a sixty-five-year-old Republican incumbent. This tactic, which it embarrasses me to acknowledge in retrospect, very nearly backfired. An editorial in the *Sedalia Democrat* blasted me with intense heat, declaring the issues were too important to devolve into a petty argument about the candidates' respective ages. In fact, the editorial raised questions about my own maturity.

I did win that hard-fought election, although barely—by 348 votes out of about 42,000 cast. That victory taught me a lesson—focus on the issues, and stand on your own principles, not your birth certificate. Of course, as I have gained a bit more gray hair, I like the notion of wise seniority in public office, especially in the Congress, where seniority really counts. Unfortunately for me, later in life the Republicans scored points the same way, with advertisements saying that while I had served Missouri well for many years, it was probably time for me to come home.

In the Missouri senate, I took on some major issues—and some that may not sound so big, but had lasting effects. Easily the most ambitious (but probably not too surprising for a young prosecutor to take on) was a comprehensive rewrite of Missouri's criminal code. Over time, as laws are amended and new ones passed, inconsistencies can turn up. In the criminal code, these inconsistencies can complicate not only the definitions of certain crimes but also the penalties they carry, leading to harsher penalties for lesser offenses and vice versa. And some laws just become antiquated. The Missouri criminal code hadn't been rewritten since the nineteenth century, so there was a lot of room for obsolescence! Therefore, with Senator Paul Bradshaw, I proposed and led a top-to-bottom revision of the code. I say "revision," but it was so comprehensive that it was really a replacement. It changed so much of the code that members needed to study it in depth, so it didn't get the votes to pass while I served in the state senate, but it did become law shortly after I left.

Another initiative I'm proud of to this day was changing the voting age to eighteen. On the face of it, the logic was simple. The Vietnam War was in full swing during my senate term, and the United States still had the draft. Eighteen-year-old Missourians were being called every day to put their lives on the line for their country. It only made sense to me that they should be able to receive the benefits of the democracy they were being asked to defend and to have a voice in where and how America used its forces.

A third successful effort may not sound as serious, but it was unfortunately necessary. I saw reports of cases in which horrible people had, for whatever reason, put dangerous items like razor blades or needles into children's Halloween treats. You might think that would be against the law, but at the time, it was covered only by general prohibitions against endangering another human being. I drafted language specifically making adulteration of such treats a felony and the legislature passed it. As the parent of three sons then of prime trick-or-treating age, I knew the peace of mind this law helped give to parents. Governor Warren Hearnes called it the best bill he signed.

I was reelected to the Missouri senate in 1974. Midway through my second term, Congressman Randall sent signals that he planned to retire, so I laid plans to run. So did two of my state senate colleagues, Don Manford and Jack Gant, both fine gentlemen who later became judges in the Missouri state courts. There were six other Democratic primary candidates on the day filing closed, for a total field of nine in my party contest. But I turned the race into a battle pitting the district's fifteen rural counties against the cities—Jack was from Independence, and Don from Kansas City—and I managed to emerge as the primary winner, finishing more than ten thousand votes ahead of the second-place finisher, who hailed from Jackson County, the most populous county in the district. One reason for my primary win was a key endorsement from a prominent Jackson County resident: Mrs. Bess Truman, widow of the late president who had first encouraged me to run for the congressional seat fourteen years earlier.

Another reason I did well was that 1976 was America's bicentennial year. I was vice chairman of the Missouri Bicentennial Commission, which allowed me to travel throughout the district and the state, meeting people, making speeches, and handing out bicentennial flags. So when the time came to run for Congress, I had friends in a lot of Missouri's small towns.

As the returns came in on primary night, what should have been a celebration turned quite dark. Senator Stuart Symington, a great friend of national defense, had retired, and former Governor Warren Hearnes, Symington's son Jim, and two-term Congressman Jerry Litton were involved in a vigorous Democratic primary fight for the seat. Jerry Litton and his family boarded an airplane in Chillicothe, bound to an election-night party in Kansas City. In the middle of the returns, I learned that the plane had crashed on takeoff, killing all aboard. Jerry Litton never knew that he had won the primary.

Naturally, Jerry and I had crossed paths throughout the primary season. He made a real art of being late. At one dinner, I was the master of ceremonies with a dais full of Democratic hopefuls and officeholders. As usual, Jerry's seat remained empty as the program went on. Then his staff started going from table to table, passing the word: "Jerry Litton is here! Jerry Litton is here!" People started craning their necks, and about a minute later, just as choreographed,

Jerry walked in the door. His arrival drew a huge ovation—far greater than was given to those of us who were there on time.

My Republican opponent was the mayor of Independence, Richard King, and we ran a spirited race. On the night before the election, we had our only televised debate, on cable TV in Warrensburg, after which Mayor King rather dramatically flew off in a helicopter to get to a huge Republican rally on the Independence Square, right in front of a statue of President Truman.

The keynote speaker at the GOP rally was the 1976 vice presidential nominee, Kansas Senator Robert Dole. Senator Dole got revved up and was getting big cheers as he rattled off the names of his party's candidates. His recitation relied partly on the sea of waving campaign signs and shouts from the audience. So several of my supporters worked their way into the crowd near the podium, carrying "Ike Skelton" placards. Here's a transcript from a radio station's tape of the rally:

> DOLE: . . . And so tomorrow, when you're voting for Bill Phelps and Kit Bond and Dick King, Joanne Collins and Jack Danforth . . .
>
> AUDIENCE MEMBER: And Tom Coleman!
>
> DOLE: . . . and Tom too, and Ike Skelton . . .
>
> *(Audience boos and jeers)*
>
> DOLE: . . . No? No? I didn't think he was very popular. I just thought we'd give it a try, but there's nobody here for him, so we'll move on to someone else . . .

What a moment. Bob Dole, a true American hero in World War II, later became a good friend of mine in mutual efforts to build national security and honor the men and women who serve in the military. He usually teases me about how his 1976 endorsement carried me into Congress. Indeed, I was elected with about 56 percent of the vote in my first general election for Congress, carrying Jackson County, which includes Independence, by more than twenty-two hundred votes.

I didn't have a helicopter, but my campaign did have a distinctive feature for a short while. One day, the phone rang at 7 A.M., and I heard a question I did not expect:

"What are you going to do with the mule?"

"What mule?"

Well, it turned out that the previous night, my friend Nick Iman had paid eighty dollars for a mule, thinking it could somehow be used in the campaign. I convinced my brother John to house the mule at his farm, but it turned out to be ornery and rambunctious, good neither for campaigning nor farm life. John wound up selling it—for forty dollars.

After the 1976 Christmas holidays, Susie, the boys, and I boarded a train for Washington from the old Warrensburg depot and we traveled in the railroading style of Harry Truman to attend my swearing-in ceremony on Capitol Hill. The event was organized by my old Warrensburg friend Bob Welling. He gathered our neighbors and supporters from across the district to give us a fine send-off, for which I will always be grateful.

When I went to be sworn in as a member of Congress, many aspects of my life came together. Susie and my boys were there, of course; in fact, my entire family was there, including both brothers. A few folks from Missouri came out. But my Warm Springs experience was represented as well. Helen Vaughn, who was the head physical therapist at Warm Springs, had moved to nearby Maryland, and she attended the swearing-in. Although her roommate, my Warm Springs physical therapist Lamoille Langworthy, had passed away, Helen's presence was quite a highlight for me. As I looked around with my hand on the Bible at all these loving people, I felt as though I'd just won the gold cup.

But then it was time to actually start doing the job my friends back home had elected me to do. I asked for and was given a seat on the Agriculture Committee. Agriculture meant a great deal to my rural district, but to be honest, the weather and the markets control agriculture more than Congress does. We could do some good when international trade issues loomed, such as in 1980, when President Carter responded to the Soviet invasion of Afghanistan by declaring an embargo on some grain exports to Moscow. That hurt a lot of farm families in my district, although—as I said publicly at the time—I never heard an unpatriotic comment from any of them. I introduced a bill to establish a revolving agriculture credit fund to help carry farmers through the embargo, and overall, we in Congress were able to patch together safety nets to keep farming viable.

About the same time, another big agricultural challenge was trying to sell beef to Japan. I remember very well when a group of Japanese parliamentarians came to visit, hosted by my friend and classmate Andy Ireland of Florida, who was then a Boll Weevil Democrat. Andy turned them over to me for lunch. I bought them lunch in the members' dining room, and around the table they spoke English as well as you and me. Then we went into a formal discussion about trade, and the very same parliamentarians read and said everything in Japanese through an interpreter, which slowed the whole process down. At the end of the day we had made no progress on selling more beef to Japan. In years since that has changed some, but it gives you an idea of what we were facing then.

Harry Truman said when he first came to the Senate, he wondered how in the world he got there, and then after six months, he wondered how in the world the others got there. But as I came to know my fellow House members, I could see that for better or worse, it's really a cross-section of America. The diversity of backgrounds, abilities, and prejudices runs the gamut.

I was part of a very large class of new congressmen; the class of 1976 was heavily Democratic, as we were the first class elected following the Watergate scandal. It was a very interesting group, including Dan Quayle and Al Gore, both of whom became vice presidents; Leon Panetta, who became secretary of defense; eventual majority leader Dick Gephardt; and some like Norm Dicks who are still in Congress. Andy Ireland was a very close friend. I'd been down to his district, and he'd been to mine. One day Andy told me that something unusual had happened over the preceding weekend. He was giving a graduation speech at a high school, and a young man, I guess the valedictorian, gave a talk about a young boy running track who had had polio, a story he found in a book by Dr. Norman Vincent Peale, and Andy got up and said, "That's my best friend."

I should note that I wasn't the most newly elected Skelton by then. After I was elected to Congress, Susie was elected president of the ninety-fifth Congress Group, which represented spouses of the members. During the one hundredth Congress, Susie became only the second Missourian to serve as president of the Congressional Club, an organization for the congressional, Supreme Court, and cabinet spouses.

Thanks to my love of history, I found kin in Congress as well. The Boone family was rather prolific, as Daniel had numerous brothers, including the one from whom I am descended, Samuel, the father of Squire Boone. It turns out that the Boone family tree has branches that descend to at least four other recent members of the U.S. House of Representatives that I knew: Dan Boren of Oklahoma, who served with me on the Armed Services Committee; Louise Slaughter of New York; Alan Mollohan of West Virginia; and Brian Bilbray of California. My colleagues and I discovered these Boone connections through congenial conversation, and we were quite proud to be the House's informal "Boone Caucus."

In that 1976 election, Missourians also sent to Congress a new senator. The state attorney general, the Reverend John Danforth, had succeeded Stuart Symington. Danforth was a moderate Republican, and we saw eye to eye on a lot of things. I can't say we were close, but he was a friend and a very able, sensible guy.

His grandfather, William Danforth, was the founder of Ralston Purina and had written a self-help book for young boys entitled *I Dare You*, very simple but very good. For many, many years, it was given to 4-H members across the state. My grandfather gave me a copy when I was nine years old, and I got copies for my boys as they were growing up. Jack used that phrase, "I dare you," as his slogan when he ran for attorney general, and people in rural Missouri, who knew about the 4-H program, knew where the phrase came from. And it worked.

Jack Danforth and my mentor Tom Eagleton, Missouri's other senator, became very close friends. Tom was a dyed-in-the-wool liberal, and though Jack Danforth was a centrist Republican, he was still a Republican. But they had a very close relationship. That was possible back then, when Congress ran on goodwill; there was a sense of purpose, of getting the job done, that superseded party differences.

Similarly, Charlie Whitley of North Carolina, Wes Watkins of Oklahoma, and Bob Whitaker of Kansas became my very good friends. The four of us—and later Jim Lightfoot of Iowa—would meet at 7:30 on Wednesday mornings for Bible study. It was two Democrats and two Republicans, although Wes later became a Republican after he left Congress. But at the time, nobody gave that part a thought. Charlie Whitley had taught Sunday school, at that time, for more than twenty-seven years and had never missed a class. In fact, he taught Sunday school when he came out to my district one time, so that he could keep his string going. Charlie was our biblical expert.

Thursday mornings were the weekly prayer breakfast, which I attended most of the time; I was even chairman of it one year. One of the members there was my first friend in Congress, Bob Stump of Arizona. Bob served coffee to everybody that came in. He was a Democrat then, but even after he left the Democratic Party, our friendship remained strong.

Reverend James Ford, the chaplain of the House, came to the prayer breakfast quite often and became a very good friend. He gave a prayer at my son Page's Eagle Scout Court of Honor, and years later he came down to North Carolina and married Page and Caroline.

My chief mentor in Congress was Dick Bolling from Kansas City, Missouri, whose district was right next to mine. In many respects Dick was bigger than life. He was a hawkish liberal, very much pro-union, did not suffer fools—he was a great guy. Moreover, he was a master of legislation, one of the few true legislators that understood the process from A to Z, which was why he later became chairman of the Rules Committee. Dick was a great mentor despite the fact that on many issues I voted contrary to his position.

One of those occasions arose in March of 1977, when we were getting ready for a big vote on what was called common situs picketing, the question of whether unions could shut down an entire construction project if they had an issue with just one subcontractor. Dick came to me and said this was a litmus test for unions. I felt that it would needlessly stall projects and hurt the economy, so I voted "no" on the bill when the position of most Democrats was to vote "yes." Needless to say, that infuriated the unions, including some that had supported me. One of my aides at the time, aware of the strong labor support I had just enjoyed in the election, predicted my political demise as the result of my "no" vote. But there was another effect—it declared my independence, which turned out to be the best thing that I could have done early in my career. Yes, some labor leaders were upset, but the residents of my district understood that I was voting for their larger interests. They kept favoring me with their votes, and I never had a serious Democratic primary challenge after the crowded 1976 contest.

By the way, the union position on common situs lost by about fifteen votes, which surprised everybody with the heavy Democratic majority that we had. Speaker Tip O'Neill and all the Democratic leaders were shocked by the loss.

I've been asked from time to time what the toughest votes were I had in Congress. But on most votes, like the common situs bill, if my vote was not in line with the party, it was in line with my district. I suppose some would see the divide between party and constituency as a problem, but for me it was an opportunity to bring Missouri values to bear when helping to shape my party's positions. And if the party took a position I thought wasn't right for Missouri or America, I would vote against it.

One of the biggest questions facing any congressman is whether you are there simply to represent the will of your district, or to take a broader view and try to do the right thing even if it's not popular. I felt that the people at home sent me to use good judgment in reflecting what's good for them and the country even though it might momentarily be unpopular. There are some things on which you're always in tune with the people at home, but on a lot of issues Congress handles, there is no precedent. So you have to use your good judgment to do what you think is right in the long run, even if it may be unpopular at the moment. It's not easy to take the long view when you have to stand for election every two years, but it can be done if you're very careful in identifying which votes are really the tough ones and worth bucking the trend. I believed I was not hired to be a rubber stamp, and that philosophy worked well for thirty-four years.

From time to time, I was approached to switch parties. Sometimes it was just joking, sometimes more serious. But I had good Democratic support because many of the Democrats were of a conservative moderate type, with some exceptions. And I'd always had interesting conversations with the exceptions!

Even some of my votes that resonated well back home weren't popular with everyone. The most dramatic example I can recall came after I supported aid to the Contras in Nicaragua, most definitely not a mainstream Democratic position. I attended church in Wellington, Missouri, one Sunday, and it turned out the pastor had let people know I'd be there. On emerging, I found about a hundred protesters from St. Paul's Seminary in nearby Kansas City picketing me as a "murderer." That got a lot of attention in the area, but it turned out the protesters weren't representative of the community—in fact, their protests helped me carry Wellington handily in the next election.

Just as I feel I have the spirit of Missouri running through my veins, Tip O'Neill, the Democratic Speaker of the House, was Boston through and through. He had a reputation as a great arm-twister, although I have to say he pretty much left me alone in that regard. Tip was just a warm individual, and he and Susie became good friends.

Tip was not seriously challenged for Speaker during my time, but I did get involved very early in a dramatic race for the majority leadership. Phil Burton from California was running, and Phil was a pretty controversial fellow. Dick Bolling didn't like him at all and entered the race against him. Jim Wright from Texas ran, as did a fellow by the name of John McFall who was then the majority whip. It boiled down to an elimination vote, and as I recall, the final two standing were Phil Burton and Jim Wright. Jim won by one vote, and many people, including me, would remind him regularly, "It was my vote that elected you majority leader." Jim ran into trouble later, but I had regard for him because he had received the Distinguished Flying Cross while flying in B-24s in the Army Air Corps.

I was privileged in August of 1978 to be one of eight members who traveled to Hanoi, Vietnam, to bring back the remains of fourteen American servicemen in a mission led by the late, great Congressman G. V. "Sonny" Montgomery of Mississippi, about whom I will have much to say later. I will never forget that one of our delegation's military members, Ted Rees, who retired as a three-star Air Force general, was able to escort with honor the remains of an airman with whom he had flown.

We received the remains in small metal boxes, but I urged that they be placed inside flag-draped caskets when they were unloaded in Hawaii and military officials of course accorded this sign of respect for the fallen.

We stayed in the old French compound in Hanoi. Henson Moore, the congressman from Louisiana, and I had a big building, two residences apiece, and Sonny Montgomery was in another one. One evening, we all met and were joined by a very attractive Red Cross lady who I think was from Switzerland. Sonny, being single, was quite the ladies' man, and he was trying to get her to go to dinner with him. But she wouldn't do it. Then Sonny met her again, I think in Paris, a year or so later, and she told him the reason that she didn't do it was that we were being listened to in the common room. We were wired by the Vietnamese military. He did finally get to take her to dinner, by the way.

Sonny got a dinner out of the trip, but the rest of the Congress got something as well. One of the Air Force escorts, Doug Roach, then a colonel, later joined the Armed Services Committee staff and served until his death in 2013 as the expert in military procurement.

Another trip opened my eyes to the realities of the post-Vietnam military. I went aboard the carrier USS *Saratoga* in 1978. My escort was a Navy captain and friend from Lexington, Ray Miller. After chow that night, I met with a number of sailors in sort of a town hall meeting, and all I heard was a very negative discussion. They were all unhappy with their careers, their leadership, their equipment, and the lack of support they felt from the American public. Every one of them was getting out of the Navy except one man who had been in for nineteen years. He was going to stay in for twenty, and that was it.

When you talk to the troops today, the change is profound. They're proud of what they do. They'll tell you all about what they've done. They'll tell you about home and their families, not the negative comments I heard aboard the *Saratoga* that night. You can say that with a volunteer military, they're there because they want to be, but that was true in 1978 too. Back then, the Congress evidently wasn't giving them very much in the way of support. At least that's the message I got.

Some of my friends were Boll Weevil Democrats, conservative Southern Democrats with an emphasis on fiscal responsibility, not unlike today's Blue Dog Democrats, except there were a lot more Boll Weevils back in the day. I did not join the Boll Weevils, but many of my votes were parallel to theirs, in line with my rural, somewhat conservative district. Many of the Boll Weevils eventually left the Democratic Party and went to the Republican Party, including my great friend Andy Ireland.

Another friend, Tom Carper, was a member of the House of Representatives and served in the Navy Reserve. Tom later became the governor of Delaware, and now he's the senior senator from Delaware. Tom's job in the Naval Reserve was as aircraft commander on a P-3 sub hunter. He invited me one weekend to join him in looking for Soviet submarines, so we flew to Bermuda on a Friday evening and spent all day Saturday in the P-3 looking for Soviet subs. We think we found one. But what was also memorable about the trip was that I had a Marine escort with me, a major. I told him I try to go to church every week, and he found an 8 A.M. Anglican Communion service, so I said, "Let's go, because we're going to leave by ten or eleven." We went, and there were a total of seven of us in the church. It was an old church, with memorials from the 1700s and 1800s all around the walls. He and I were sitting toward the back, and the Anglican priest went through the homily and invited everyone up to take Communion. I sat there, but the major said he was Episcopalian and was going to take Communion, which I didn't do. He said, "Let's go," and I said, "No." He said, "Oh, come on." So I walked very slowly up to the altar, where everyone was kneeling. I went to the far left and knelt down at the end of the altar. I kept looking to my right to see what people were doing. They were taking a wafer and drinking out of the chalice. The priest got to me and gave me a wafer and a drink out of the chalice. So when we were walking back down the aisle, I said, "Major, Major! Do you know what that was? That was Harveys Bristol Cream Sherry!" I'm sure that the old codger bought a bottle of Harveys and gave everybody a sip of it, and then he got the rest for himself. There's no way of mistaking Harveys Bristol Cream Sherry. You cannot.

By the way, this was the only foreign travel for which I ever recall being criticized, probably because Bermuda was involved. Of course, most of my trips were to war zones to spend holidays with the troops, so those trips probably didn't seem too glamorous.

After the 1980 census, the boundary lines of congressional districts were re-drawn, as happens every decade. Because of population declines, Missouri dropped from ten congressional representatives to nine. In the 1982 election, I was thrown into a race in a newly merged district with a freshman Republican from southern Missouri. It was one of just two congressional races in which I remember feeling less than charitable toward any of my opponents, the other one being a 1996 contest. Through redistricting, the Fourth District lost and gained several counties through the years. Between Congress and the Mis-souri state senate, I was privileged over the years to represent fellow citizens stretching from Macon County in northeast Missouri to Webster County close to the Arkansas border.

In achieving that representation, I had the benefit of smart, tough, dedi-cated campaign advisers and workers. The man who handled my polling, Mi-chael Rowan, first worked for me in 1975 as I prepared for the 1976 race. From 1976 through 1994, I was helped by the late, brilliant political consultant Tony Schwartz, who had an ability to analyze political messages that was uncannily on target. Tony was best known as one of the creators of the highly controver-sial television ad for Lyndon Johnson's 1964 reelection campaign that showed a small girl plucking petals from a daisy as a chilling voice counted down to a nuclear bomb detonation. That ad appeared just once, but there was such an uproar that it made political history. But it reinforced the intended effect—cast-ing Republican nominee Barry Goldwater as untrustworthy to put his finger on the nuclear trigger. (Once I was in Congress, I enjoyed working with Senator Goldwater on the defense reform legislation that was named in his honor, the Goldwater-Nichols Act.)

A lot of people today denounce the idea of "negative campaigning" that was so embodied in Tony Schwartz's ad against Goldwater. I don't care for negative campaigning at all. I would prefer that candidates talk about themselves and their ideas, and let the voters decide which plans they like better. But there is no doubt that negative campaigning can be effective—even though it backfired when it was tried against me a couple of times.

One was in 1982, after the 1980 redistricting, when that Republican incum-bent who was thrown into the same race as me failed to disavow one of his top campaign officials' personally disparaging comments about my polio-weakened arms. The rotten rhetoric backfired—I won with almost 55 percent of the vote.

The other time was in 1996, when my Republican opponent tried to insinu-ate that I was associated with organized crime because I had received support from hard-working labor union members. That backfired too—I received more than 65 percent of the vote. My GOP opponent had relocated from Texas to enter that congressional race. It was said that when it came to caring about Missourians, my 1996 opponent was "all hat, no cattle."

In contrast to those nasty races, more than once, my Republican opponent was a former state senate colleague, James Noland from the Lake of the Ozarks area. We always got along well, and Jim was always very sincere, telling his audiences and me that he ran to make sure voters had a choice in November.

But in 1980, those races were in the future. Seniority counts in Congress, and as a junior member, it was hard to get much attention or traction, but I was never discouraged and kept up my practice of working hard. Then I found the opportunity for which I'd been waiting and training for most of my life—to serve America's military.

BUILDING A MORE EFFECTIVE MILITARY

MY EARLY CONGRESSIONAL service on committees on agriculture and small business served the Fourth District very well. In 1980, when I joined the Armed Services Committee, I was finally in a position to begin fulfilling my childhood dream of assisting in keeping America safe—and benefiting my beloved Missouri.

My seat on the Armed Services Committee came about through the good offices of my friend Dick Bolling. Dick was a veteran, even having served as an aide to Douglas MacArthur, and was very pro-military. In 1980, a death created a vacancy on the committee. Dick pushed me to take it, which I did. Then he used his position as chairman of the Steering and Policy Committee to put me on as a permanent member the following year. I had finally reached my lifelong goal of serving the nation's military, but like any new recruit, I had to start from the bottom rung.

Even for a junior member of the committee, there was no lack of things to do. The early 1980s were marked by dramatic American military actions. Unfortunately, two of them shared a common failing. The unsuccessful raid to free American hostages held in our embassy in Iran was blamed in part on poor coordination among the military services, while the ultimately successful action in Grenada was made much more complicated by the same flaw.

Today's younger generations may not recall how the Iran hostage crisis gripped America's attention, frustrating our best strategists and painfully tarnishing our image around the world. To some, that mocking image was of an impotent super-nation. We seemed to some to be paralyzed, powerless, outmaneuvered by thugs who brazenly seized our embassy and held our people for 444 days, from November 4, 1979, until the final hostages were freed on January 20, 1981.

The Iran hostage taking was a diplomatic crisis, to be sure, but the failed attempt to rescue the hostages by military means indicated to me a far deeper crisis in the need for concerted, integrated action among the services—what the military calls "jointness."

Once negotiations to free the hostages had proved futile, the U.S. military mounted a secret rescue called Operation Eagle Claw. But Eagle Claw was aborted in the blowing sands of the desert on April 24, 1980, when three helicopters malfunctioned due to mechanical reasons. As the stealthy rescuers converged to begin their operations outside Tehran, the rotor of a Navy helicopter sliced into an Air Force transport plane. In mere seconds, there were fiery explosions that killed eight men before the operation could swoop in to extricate any hostages. The TV news images back home showed scorched ground and shattered aircraft, an image of unmitigated disaster.

Popular reaction to the failed Iran rescue attempt, at a time when Vietnam was still fresh in memory, prompted some to question whether our military was still the world's most capable or best equipped. The popular if uninformed questions were about basic competencies. But I never questioned the devotion or spirit of service in our military personnel. I believed then and I know now that the real issues behind the failed rescue arose from the lack of jointness in executing such a complex and challenging mission. At the most basic points in its concept and evolution, there had been too little coordination of the mission's training, oversight, and execution.

As a result of the disaster in the Iranian desert, conversations about improving military jointness intensified. But they were still only an intermittent part of a much larger dialogue in the early 1980s about America's standing in the world and the readiness of our military. In this dialogue, I stood firmly on the side of favoring the most up-to-date military, with joint training to make the most of our services' united strength. It was not a majority view.

The conversations regarding the need for jointness gained more urgency as we moved further into the new decade and a new presidential administration. President Jimmy Carter, whose single term was dominated by the anguish of the Iran hostage crisis, left office at the very hour on January 20, 1981, when the last of the hostages went free and Ronald Reagan was sworn in as his successor. President Reagan ran on a platform of military strength, and although we were from different political parties, I admired and supported much of the Reagan military agenda. I also liked the man personally, and he showed great kindness to Susie and me.

Then two major international events in a single month, October 1983, illustrated that while supporting the military was a national priority, there was urgent need for greater collaboration, communication, and jointness among the armed services. On October 23, 1983, the quietude of a Sunday morning in America was rocked by the news that suicide bombers had plowed an explosives-packed truck into the U.S. Marine barracks in Beirut, Lebanon. The barracks attack killed 241 Marines. The dead had been housed in one building that was devastated by the sudden blast attack.

I was part of the Armed Services Committee investigation that retraced the steps which had led to the horrible bombing and loss of life. Several of us arrived in Lebanon soon after the attack, while they were still digging out remains of bodies. We spoke at length with the Marine colonel in charge and others up and down the chain of command. The chain of command was remarkably cumbersome; it involved twenty-two persons, all the way down to the guards who were laboring under rules of engagement that hampered them from firing on the terrorists barreling toward the fences, resulting in the largest single-day death toll for the Marines to that point since the World War II Battle of Iwo Jima.

The sentries in Beirut were hampered because the rules of engagement kept their weapons unloaded. When we asked who gave those orders, they weren't sure, so we began backtracking up the chain of command. There was conflicting guidance for staff and inconsistent orders for barracks security. There were clearly clogs in communications that contributed to the disaster.

Faulty communications of a different sort would figure significantly in a series of military events in the Caribbean taking place during the same days as the events in Lebanon. Militant Marxists had staged a coup on the island of Grenada on October 12, 1983. The militants ousted a government of Marxists deemed somewhat more moderate than themselves and eventually murdered several of its leaders. The United States had multiple interests in these events, not least concern for the instability and unrest in the Caribbean but also for the lives of several hundred Americans attending medical school on Grenada.

In the first major action by U.S. military forces since the war in Vietnam, an invasion called "Operation Urgent Fury" commenced on the morning of October 25. The mission was to safely evacuate the American students. But as in the Beirut Marine barracks disaster just days earlier, issues arising from the lack of military jointness and communications—this time in planning and executing the invasion—slowed and confused the situation as U.S. troops arrived on Grenada.

The National Security Council had ordered planning for a joint task force in Grenada including all of the military services. But the operation's jointness did not and could not live up to its intent, and with little wonder; basic communications issues confounded the military's ability to operate as one joint force.

For some seven thousand U.S. service personnel in the Grenada operations, there was little or no technical ability to communicate among the different services. I was told of one soldier who used his own telephone calling card to put in a call to the Navy at sea in the Caribbean by patching the call through the Army's Fort Hood in Texas. We also learned of military orders having to be physically flown out to the ships at sea. There were famous stories of troops moving on the ground having to rely on commercial tourism maps rather than professionally designed military maps.

The U.S. military action in Grenada was completed by December 1983, and, in contrast to Vietnam, it was hailed as the military victory that it was, achieving its goals while limiting U.S. casualties to nineteen deaths. But the conversations about jointness were also renewed because of the shortcomings that may have prolonged the Grenada operation and certainly stymied it at certain points. Those conversations only intensified following our analysis of the Beirut Marine barracks bombing.

The follow-up inquiries on Beirut and Grenada revealed essential communications issues. There was a clear need to streamline the chains of command, increasing not just the clarity of communications but also accountability for actions.

Today's joint military training, collaboration, planning, and execution in the field among the service branches seems so natural and smart that it's hard to believe this coordination was not always the case. But the joint services' march on Baghdad in 2003 truly began with baby-sized steps decades earlier. I consider those who often worked fruitlessly in their own times for jointness between military service branches—Air Force General David Jones, Army General Maxwell Taylor, and Admiral Harry Train, among others—to be heroes. Their visions have been vindicated by our recent victories in the air, at sea, and on land.

For most of our young nation's history, the service branches were distinct in purpose, preparation, and execution of missions. Obviously, in the early days of America, the basics were driven by the places of battle—either at sea or on land. America's service members of old were foot soldiers, artillery, or horseback cavalry on land, or they were sailors aboard vessels that evolved from wooden ships. Airborne forces, nuclear weapons, massive bunker-busting bombs, unmanned aerial drones with attack capacity—all were the stuff of fantasy. But with the inexorable passage of time, the evolution of technology, and the enduring global realities of war and peacekeeping, America's military services grew in number, scope, abilities, and expertise—and in entrenched defense of their own prerogatives, turf, customs, systems, and culture.

To understand this, think of each distinctive military service branch as a length of sinewy fiber. Then imagine a thicker length of rope composed of these separate strong fibers. To attain peak strength, these separate lengths of fiber must be intertwined. That just makes practical common sense. So, too, with the military service branches combining into a united, jointly coordinated fighting force.

But some entrenched opponents of military jointness were more interested in protecting the power, perks, and turf—represented by the distinct decorative service braids on their own uniforms—than in braiding their strong but separate branches into much greater unity of American force and purpose.

Fortunately, not all of our top military leaders were so narrow or parochial in their outlook. One of my personal heroes in this regard, who became a much-respected friend, was the late General Maxwell Davenport Taylor. He rose to serve as chairman of the Joint Chiefs of Staff under presidents Kennedy and Johnson.

General Taylor's native roots, like my own, were deep in rural Missouri. He was a native of Keytesville, about a ninety-minute drive through the rolling northern Missouri farm country from my boyhood home in Lexington. He loved the excitement of the military, thrived on its history, and could speak at some length about the military philosophies of Clausewitz and Julius Caesar. The future general was quoted as saying that he made a lifetime decision at age five: He would attend West Point.

He graduated from Northeast High School in Kansas City at age fifteen and then enrolled at Kansas City Junior College, where he took entrance exams to attend both West Point and the U.S. Naval Academy at Annapolis. He flunked the Navy exam, quipping later that if he had fared better on the geography portion of the exam, he might have been an admiral instead of a general. That would have been odd, because in background, education, and culture, General Taylor was all Army from his cadet years at West Point to his eventual super-intendency of the U.S. Military Academy. On D-Day, General Taylor arrived by parachute in the earliest waves of Allied troops at Normandy, leading the 101st Airborne Division. Known as "Mr. Attack," he was, indeed, an Army soldier through and through. That is why it is somewhat ironic to me that General Maxwell Taylor, an Army man and personal commander of boots on the ground, became one of the foremost apostles of a flexible national defense.

In our conversations during the mid-1980s push toward military reforms, General Taylor, then in retirement, agreed that achieving the greatest flexibil-ity meant increasing joint training, preparation, planning, and execution of missions engaging all of the service branches. General Taylor understood that getting there meant easing old service rivalries—literally changing a culture which was so entrenched that respected military men defended it as if they were defending a mountaintop fortress. But General Taylor was no stranger to being a dissenter when it came to internal debates regarding military policy. He was often the odd man out among members of the Joint Chiefs of Staff during the Eisenhower years, because General Taylor didn't follow the military establishment's prevailing orthodoxy that the main focus of strategic defense should be nuclear weapons. As the *New York Times* reported in General Taylor's obituary, he "became one of the main architects of the modern Army. It was his belief that the infantryman was indispensable in the atomic age, especially for fighting small-scale conflicts." "Air power is our initial line of defense," General Taylor once conceded, "but no one has proved to my satisfaction that we will have only world wars to be settled only by big bangs. Specific cases have a way of differing from expected patterns, in many ways, but infantrymen at one time or another become indispensable. Nothing we have discovered or expect to discover will reduce the need for brave men to fight our battles. The atom bomb is no weapon to counter a coup d'etat. Airborne troops appear to be an ideal force to police the free world."

General Taylor knew from his own experience that the often polarized and insular interests of the service branch chiefs, with the resulting pabulum passing for unified decision making was not serving the president or the nation well. The *New York Times* reported, "It was General Taylor's view, which he expressed with increasing frustration, that the nation's military policy should be based on 'flexible response.'"

By the 1980s, General Taylor, then retired but still sharp of mind and spirit, was one of my sources of inspiration and wise counsel as we renewed efforts to make jointness among the service branches a reality. In my endeavors toward achieving joint service, training, and missions, I stood on the shoulders of not only General Taylor but also many other dedicated proponents, including Texas Congressman Dick White.

Richard White chaired the Investigations Subcommittee of the House Armed Services Committee. I had joined the larger committee in 1980 as a two-term member of Congress, and Dick and his successor as Investigations Subcommittee chairman, Bill Nichols of Alabama, were real mentors and great friends to me.

Dick, who was from El Paso, was a believer in military reforms. He served in the U.S. Marines as a rifleman during World War II and was awarded the Purple Heart for his wounds received in the Pacific. That type of background can give you some perspective on the kind of "battles" we have in Washington. But although our foe wasn't armed, it was almost as implacable—three times we passed House military reform legislation, and it was thrice blocked in the Senate.

In 1982, Dick White's greatest asset as subcommittee chairman was the singular legislative staffer Dr. Archie Barrett. For members who have to rush from issue to issue and are fortunate to master one or two disciplines, congressional committee staffs provide expertise, background, and continuity. Many of the Armed Services staffers have long military experience. Yet even in that company of experts, Archie, a retired Air Force colonel who flew fighter jets in Vietnam, stood out. Together, he and Dick White held a series of excellent hearings on the lack of coordination between the services, and they put together some fine legislation—which didn't go anywhere in the sense of becoming law, running into opposition from not just some military leaders but some veteran lawmakers as well.

By 1982, I'd been in the House for five years. Missouri had a Senate seat coming up, and I thought about running for it. About this time, John Danforth and I were getting sworn into the Bar of the U.S. Supreme Court, and we found ourselves sitting next to each other. Jack turned to me and said, "You gonna run against me?" I think my answer was, "I don't know." But after thinking about it for a very short time, I decided the place for me was in the House, not in the Senate. I think I probably would have run a good campaign. At that time, Missouri was Democratic, although it was slowly turning Republican. Jack Danforth actually was the first Republican olive out of the bottle.

My colleague Dick White didn't run for reelection in 1982 and returned to Texas to practice law. He died in 1998 and was honored with interment in Arlington National Cemetery. His successor as Investigations Subcommittee chairman, Bill Nichols, was a true gentleman from rural Alabama who proved his iron courage in World War II combat, losing a leg to a land mine explosion while serving with the Army in Germany.

William Flynt "Bill" Nichols was first elected to the Congress in 1967 and died in office in 1988 while serving his eleventh term. He was a popular member, a soft-spoken Southerner with a spine of steel. Bill's word was good, and he had respect on both sides of the political aisle. When I sought to continue attending the subcommittee's hearings on military reorganization, even though I was not a member of the panel, Bill welcomed my participation, including opportunities to inquire of generals, admirals, right up to the secretary of defense.

The Investigations Subcommittee became a lively venue for discussion of military reforms, along with some dramatic proposals. One of the first things we did was write a bill to abolish the Joint Chiefs of Staff. After introducing that legislation, it didn't take long for me to learn that not one member of the Joint Chiefs had a sense of humor.

With tutelage from my good friend Archie Barrett, I became knowledgeable about the elements of jointness and the intricacies of making joint training and missions a reality. I'm not sure he understood my interest at first; I wasn't even on the subcommittee at the time. In fact, Archie has pointed out more than once that defense reform has probably never gotten any congressman a single vote. Archie has also kindly referred to me as the fellow who, with the blessing of Bill Nichols, picked up Dick White's commitment to reforms and ran with it. It all culminated in that bill I introduced in 1983 to get the attention of the service chiefs and let them know the House was serious. The bill's title declared it was to "amend Title 10, United States Code, to abolish the Joint Chiefs of Staff and establish a single Chief of Staff for the National Command Authorities, to establish a National Military Council, and for the other purposes." But our real purpose was to change the way America prepared for war and, when necessary, fought.

I had no cosponsors. But still the bill's filing got the attention of the military—and Bill Nichols loved it, because it was a strong yank on the reins at the Pentagon. We soon had a subcommittee hearing on the legislation, and while a public debate raged, it couldn't compare in intensity to the arguments behind the scenes. I knew that the prospect of bringing separate services together under one commander would, in the Pentagon phrase, "upset a few rice bowls." I really hadn't realized how much these chiefs liked their rice.

But it was all uphill when we got our legislation to the Senate. One barricade to reform was Texas senator John Tower, chairman of the Senate Armed Services Committee and a former chief petty officer in the Navy Reserves who wanted no part of jointness. But Senator Tower very much wanted the title of secretary of defense as his career capstone, and he was not of a mind to alienate the service branch chiefs and old Pentagon hands who could either help smooth his way or derail him. I vividly recall one example of Senator Tower leading his members in a conference with our House Armed Services Committee. Tower did such a masterful job of stalling consideration and working the rules and the chairman's prerogatives to his advantage that even the ultra-cool, dauntless, and thoughtful scholar Archie Barrett was the very face of frustration and defeat.

Although our House allies—our able staff as well as the members—had advanced the discussion of reforming the Joint Chiefs to a conference committee, a long and edgy negotiating session ended with us holding far less than half a loaf. Some would suggest we had mere crumbs. Still, despite John Tower and his unified committee, we had achieved a few advances toward reform. Archie Barrett and many others saw these as mere slivers of what we hoped to achieve. But I saw progress in that more-than-incremental step, and I told Archie so.

Archie looked at me in disbelief when I called it a victory. But I meant it. After all, this was the first time both chambers had advanced any meaningful reforms of the military command structure in more than a generation. To be sure, this was a skirmish in a much larger campaign that would take years. However, we had the forces of reason, a growing number of influential voices on our side, and indeed some recent battlefield experience behind our viewpoint. And now we had something on the table, which was motivation enough to keep going.

Not all of the wise military men were against true jointness. In fact, Air Force General David Jones, chairman of the Joint Chiefs from 1978 to 1982 when I was a relatively new member of Congress, went public in the early 1980s to say the chiefs could only provide the president and the Congress with watered-down advice because every chief had to agree, which meant each one had veto power. Of course, that led to every recommendation representing the lowest common denominator. And that meant pabulum advice, which helped no one. I was a junior member of the Armed Services Committee and I did not know General Jones very well, but his points made simple good sense to me. And they helped propel my introduction of the bill abolishing the Joint Chiefs.

General Jones's arguments included that during the Vietnam War, each of the service branches considered the conflict their own, to the exclusion of sharing planning, strategies, responsibilities, and execution. Obviously we now realize such shared planning, objectives, and execution would have improved matters, but at the time it was simply a bridge too far to span. Make no mistake, I think it's important that there be a great distinction between each service because along with that comes special knowledge, special missions, and also special pride in that particular uniform. But the services had to learn to get along and work together, just like getting along with brothers and sisters, which is what people in the other services are. And history shows that it has worked.

I was learning the ways of the House, making some close relationships, and beginning to take an active role in making new legislation happen—including my first tentative steps into parliamentary procedure. These efforts came together in 1984, early in my time on the Armed Services Committee. I was then serving on the Personnel Subcommittee with one of my closest friends, G. V. "Sonny" Montgomery of Mississippi. Sonny was a very lovely human being who never achieved through political ends what he could accomplish with charm. For example, during the military base closure processes in the 1990s, many towns feared and resented the visits from the commissioners reviewing the bases. But Sonny took a different tack. He arranged parades, with the commissioners on the backs of convertibles while bands led them through cheering crowds showing their community spirit. And it worked, too.

In 1984, Sonny was nearing the end of a long fight to pass a bottom-up overhaul of the G.I. Bill of Rights. The previous G.I. Bill, passed after the Second World War, created a series of benefits for veterans, especially in education. After the Vietnam War, returning military personnel were not treated with the same respect and gratitude as their forebears. So Sonny wanted to update the benefits to fit a new era and recognize a new generation of veterans. Although he was chairman of the Veterans' Affairs Committee, Sonny needed the legislation to also clear Armed Services, but the Army in particular was opposed to the bill because of its cost.

That's where I stepped in—and almost stepped in it, if you will. The bill's opponents had done their work well, to the point that despite Sonny's best efforts, there weren't enough votes in favor to even get the bill out of the Personnel Subcommittee. So I offered an amendment that bridged the gap. I was so proud when it was adopted and the G.I. Bill passed out of the subcommittee. I felt I was really getting the hang of making Congress work and, even better, making a mark for veterans and on my friend's bill, too!

You can imagine my surprise when Sonny was upset with me for daring to amend his bill. "Ike," he said, quite clearly aggrieved, "I wouldn't have done that to you!"

"Sonny," I replied, "you wouldn't have gotten the bill out of committee without it!"

Well, after he calmed down, I think he saw the sense in that. In fact, I know he did, because when he introduced the bill at the full Armed Services Committee, he called it the "Montgomery-Skelton bill"—a magnanimous gesture from a very sweet man. Sonny passed in 2006, and our country is the poorer for it.

1984 also marked the one hundredth anniversary of Harry Truman's birthday. I introduced legislation to have a joint session of Congress in tribute to President Truman that passed the House and Senate, and thanks to Senator Tom Eagleton, I was elected to chair the committee to plan and conduct the joint session.

I called President Truman's daughter, Margaret Truman Daniel, who was living in New York. She had become a friend of mine, even having appeared at a fund-raiser for me. She was deeply appreciative of the idea of honoring her father with a joint session, because he always fondly recalled his service in the Capitol.

But Margaret told me with a directness that proved she was indeed the heir to Mr. Truman that she didn't want Congressman Claude Pepper of Florida to have any role in the recognition. This astounded me, because Claude Pepper was on the joint session planning committee, and I told her that. Still, she said, "I don't want him to have anything to do with the ceremony." She recalled that during the 1948 Democratic National Convention, Claude Pepper had led an unsuccessful insurgency against the renomination of President Truman—and boy, did she remember!

On May 8, 1984, we had the joint session honoring the centennial of President Truman's birth. I spoke, and so did former Missouri senator Stuart Symington, and then Margaret spoke. It was a wonderful occasion, but as we were walking off the podium, here came Claude Pepper making a beeline for her. He said, "Wonderful speech, Margaret," and without looking at him, she said a curt "Thank you" and kept walking. That treatment may sound harsh, but Margaret shared two qualities with her late father: loyalty, and a long memory.

Meanwhile, the fight to increase military jointness continued. We received two boosts in 1985, and I had a little bit to do with one of them. At the time, the chairman of the Armed Services Committee was Mel Price of Illinois. Now, Mel was a wonderful guy, don't get me wrong. But for whatever reason, he was not running the show at the committee at the time. I was talking with the committee's staff director, John Ford, and he told me that he was making decisions that no non-elected person should be making. I appreciated his candor, because power is seductive and many staff would really have relished the chance to exercise the privileges of a committee chair without actually having to run for office. But John knew that wasn't how things should be.

At the time, one of the brighter members of Congress, Dave McCurdy from Oklahoma, was on the Armed Services Committee. Dave and I decided that we really ought to run someone to challenge Mel Price and make the committee work. The question was, who? Who would be better, who would be willing to challenge a sitting chairman, and who had the seniority to pull it off? (Just to be clear, that left me out; I was still too green in congressional terms, and this wasn't about any ambition on my part.)

Well, everyone loved Bill Nichols, so I asked him first. He understood, and said, "Let me think about it." Bill called me a day or so later, and he said, "Ike, you know, when I go to heaven, the good Lord isn't going to ask if I were chairman of the Armed Services Committee. I just can't do it."

Word apparently got around that Dave and I were looking for a candidate, because Les Aspin came over in the House chamber one day and asked, "What about me?"

This was a real stroke of luck. There are sixty-two members on the House Armed Services Committee today and twenty-six on the Senate counterpart; the committees were a bit smaller then, but you could still count the number of members who really focused on defense on one hand. Most are there because they have a base or a factory in the district. But Les was a real defense intellectual. He cared about the whole range of defense issues—personnel, procurement, nuclear weapons—and he was a real idea man. Also, he was from Wisconsin and more liberal than some on the committee, so there was a real prospect of support across the Democratic caucus. It wasn't a slam dunk by any stretch, because while Les was on the top row of the committee, one of the more senior members, he wasn't next in seniority at all. So we would not just be replacing the sitting chairman, but jumping over a few others who had been waiting their turn.

But Les was too good a candidate to pass up. So McCurdy and I started putting together support in the Democratic caucus. We actually got a real crew of liberals, and others. There was a lot of affection for Mel, and I shared it. But he wasn't running the show, and we knew Les Aspin would run the show.

When the time came to choose chairmen for the Ninety-Ninth Congress, as expected, the Steering Committee nominated Mel Price. Of course, Tip O'Neill and all the warhorses supported the seniority system. I'll admit, the more seniority you get, the better it looks. But we nominated Les from the floor during the organizing caucus. It was a close vote, but Les won, and just as we had hoped, he really took charge of the committee and made it a force in the defense debates.

We had to fight for Les again two years later when a bunch of liberal members got upset with him because he chose to compromise with the Reagan administration on deployment of the MX missile, the system that's now called Peacekeeper. Les also had supported arming the Nicaraguan rebels, which was pretty much a litmus test back then. He actually had the chairmanship taken away briefly, and in 1987, at the beginning of the One Hundredth Congress, Marvin Leath from Texas ran against Les for chair. The caucus sent Les a pretty strong message—Les won by only 17 votes out of 249.

Part of the challenge was that Les wasn't a natural campaigner. He wasn't really what they call a "people person." One day, when he was being challenged by Marvin Leath, I made Les stick his arm out and crook it a little bit. I said, "Just walk up to people and put your arm around them just like that." But

Les was good to work with. He gave me my head in whatever I wanted to do, especially when he named me chairman of a panel on professional military education, which I'll tell you more about in just a little bit.

The other real boost to our efforts to make the military work better came when John Tower left the Senate. Tower was later tipped to be defense secretary, his long-coveted goal. But revelations about his personal behavior ultimately denied Senator Tower the position he had longed for throughout his life. Barry Goldwater of Arizona succeeded him as Senate Armed Services chairman, and Senator Goldwater's ranking Democratic member was my good friend Sam Nunn of Georgia, then as now a true defense expert.

Senator Goldwater came to understand the good sense of jointness, and he was a man disposed to cutting to the heart of the matter. From the obstructionism of Senator Tower to the military reform convictions of Barry Goldwater, there was a sea change in how the Senate approached the issue. That change didn't come overnight, but once it came, the pace quickened noticeably.

Again, there was strong opposition. In May 1986, the Joint Chiefs of Staff had about half a dozen of us over for a breakfast, and the coffee had barely been poured and was still steaming when they started in with bitter criticism of the reform legislation we had proposed. Finally, in a fit of emotion, the Chief of Naval Operations, who shall remain nameless out of my own sense of charity for the misguided, declared, "What you are doing is downright unpatriotic!"

There was tense silence. Then Bill Nichols, the Southern gentleman, broke the silence. Bill, who had left his foot in a German forest during World War II, made it clear he resented being called unpatriotic. Breakfast was quickly adjourned.

We went back to the Capitol more determined than ever to achieve reforms. Not long after that tense breakfast, Congress passed a major reform bill that became known as Goldwater-Nichols. The legislation encapsulated the results of Dick White's and Archie Barrett's work and my hearings under Bill Nichols to mandate jointness between the services. It specified that the chairman of the Joint Chiefs of Staff rather than the entire staff is the principal designated military adviser to the president and the secretary of defense, and it created a vice chairman of the Joint Chiefs of Staff, in part to oversee and coordinate cooperation among the services. Goldwater-Nichols also created a set of regional commands, each with its own commander-in-chief responsible for operating American forces in that region. Instead of each service running its own show under its own commander, American forces would operate as a joint team under the command of someone familiar with the region and with personal ties to the local Allied forces and their commanders. And it required officers headed for flag rank to serve in joint billets during their career in order to understand how the counterparts in other services thought and what tools each could bring to the fight. The ideal of Goldwater-Nichols was a single, unified

American military pulling in the same direction regardless of what uniform any individual service member wore.

One of the tougher issues to resolve was whether the Joint Chiefs of Staff should have a vice chairman, and I was adamantly in favor of it. Before this, the service chiefs got to be acting chairman on a rotating basis if the chairman was out of town, and they wanted to keep it that way. In my office one time, my friend Admiral Bill Crowe said, "I'm going to the mat against a vice chairman." And I said to myself, "I'm going to the mat to get one." When we reached that issue, which was the last issue to be decided in conference, Sam Nunn asked for a recess. After talking through the recess, we got a vice chairman with limited powers, which was OK because we changed it a couple of years later and gave the vice chairman full powers. That's how Congress works best—making progress a step at a time instead of insisting on a full loaf. So many of today's fights come about because one side or the other wants it all now instead of compromising, getting a little of what they want now and later coming back for more.

Although members of Congress got the most credit (or blame, from those who opposed it) for the bill, it bore the fingerprints of retired General Maxwell Taylor. I had dispatched Archie Barrett and my trusted staffer Tom Glakas to meet with General Taylor and solicit his ideas for this latest charge against the barricades. General Taylor was pleased to oblige us, and he was very generous with his time. When I sat down with him at his apartment for sessions sometimes lasting several hours, General Taylor provided notations to the bill, line by line, written in his own hand in pencil, as when he edited the student newspaper as a West Point cadet.

Then General Taylor, a trusted adviser to presidents who had generously provided us with his unvarnished advice, came over to the Capitol to deliver his personal testimony in support of the sweeping reform legislation. He remained realistic based on past disappointments. He confided that this was a fine proposal—but added that it probably would never come to pass. Happily, he was wrong.

General Taylor died the following year. While the nation lost a great general, a patriot, and a hero of military combat, I lost a much-respected friend, a fellow Missourian, and a personal mentor in military reform. But General Taylor's advocacy of military jointness lives on in Goldwater-Nichols, and those reforms may be the most lasting part of his rich legacy of service. I know that I consider their enactment one of my most rewarding moments in Congress.

A lot of people commented on the draft Goldwater-Nichols legislation, but aside from General Taylor, nobody gave it as detailed a look as then-Secretary of the Navy John Lehman. I had given him a copy and said, "Tell me what you think." I didn't hear from him for a long time, and I figured he'd gone on to other things. Then Lehman asked me to come out and speak at the recommissioning of the World War II battleship the USS *Missouri* in San Francisco. And as we were in the captain's cabin, getting ready to go out to the podium, Lehman handed me the bill—all marked up. You could barely see the original text.

Among the ways Goldwater-Nichols sought to create jointness was through improvements to professional military education, and in 1987, as I mentioned, Les Aspin appointed me chairman of a panel on that subject. We investigated all of the military war colleges, including the Army War College in Carlisle, Pennsylvania; the Naval War College in Newport, Rhode Island; and the Air War College at Maxwell Air Force Base in Alabama. We held twenty-eight hearings, received testimony from forty-eight witnesses, and interviewed more than a hundred retired and active-duty personnel. Our research and hearings on professional military education led to a number of recommendations, the most important of which called for stressing renewed academic rigor in all of the war colleges. In the words of Sir William Francis Butler, "The nation that will insist on drawing a broad line of demarcation between the fighting man and the thinking man is liable to find its fighting done by fools and its thinking done by cowards."

Between the First and Second World Wars, America experienced a golden era of professional military education. We had outstanding military leaders lecturing as professors and teachers—for example, thirty-one of the thirty-four corps commanders in World War II had taught at one time or another, earlier in their careers, at war colleges. We were concerned that changes in faculty qualifications and curriculum meant that the next generation of leaders might not be as well served.

America's war colleges emphasize understanding the levels of warfare: tactics, operational art, and strategy. Tactics means, for example, taking a hill, or crossing a river. Operational art means theater warfare, such as decisions on whether, in World War II, the Allies should invade France by way of Calais, or Normandy? Strategy in that same World War II context would be the big picture, such as whether we go after Germany first or Japan first. And of course diplomacy is another type of strategy, and it works alongside our military preparedness.

In 1987, with big changes in the international situation looming and with the very real prospect of the bipolar Cold War world giving way to some new paradigm, we asked: Where are tomorrow's strategic thinkers, the military men and women who will have to make sense of the new world? How do we develop the leaders whose vision will lead us into the future? Those questions are why, for more than twenty years, I made professional military education a specialty of my work on the House Armed Services Committee.

I believed the war colleges should be a prime source of outstanding global strategic thinkers, and that these men and women are priceless assets in human capital. It is up to our leaders to utilize these diverse wellsprings of strategic thought. President Dwight Eisenhower knew the power of reaching to the wisest thinkers when he commissioned the Solarium Project during the Cold War. His directive was clear and brilliant: three teams of the best minds would be assembled to separately research and then advocate with intellectual force the competing views about possible future U.S. policy.

Extreme views such as adopting one-world government or preemptive nuclear strikes were off the table, but the participants were given free rein to sort and re-sort other views, including long-held and comfortable assumptions. Then the three teams reassembled in the White House solarium with President Eisenhower and his top advisers as their attentive audience. When the teams' individual presentations were finished, frank discussions ensued with probing questions informed by recent memories of world war and the dawn of the atomic age. Then the president made his decision, which largely sustained and continued the policies of President Truman, but with the satisfaction that the policy had received fresh review by leaders of conviction and experience.

One way military professionals build and develop their skills is through war games and exercises. But although practice during drills is important and such exercises can be a very useful tool, a professional military education is incomplete if it does not include serious historical study of past conflicts. I have come to believe that a dedicated student of military history can benefit from some three thousand years of fighting experience at the price of time spent reading and analyzing the whispers of warriors past. Historical precedents can help guide us into the future. Every war or conflict may be examined as if it were a petri dish for learning from previous situations. This isn't a matter of simply memorizing names and dates and geography.

To make the best decisions, professionals in all arenas need the capability to move beyond dealing with the crisis at hand. They must be able to create a vision for future action. They must call upon past precedents and insights. A general of genius is one who can exploit his instincts and knowledge of the art of war, interpret the signs correctly, and then mobilize the material, human, and intellectual capital to win the next war.

Deep study of the past allows students to synthesize what they have learned, so that they can use these lessons to prepare for future conflicts and not just prepare to fight the war that was just fought—which is a trap that many leaders and national military establishments have been caught in throughout history. Simply put, we found that it should be part of the military's mission and vision to ensure that members of the American military know their history better than anyone else. Following our hearings, this renewed emphasis on professional military education, including the instruction of history, became essential to career advancement in the military.

And we built the education reforms in a spirit of jointness as well. A team of military officers was on temporary assignment to my staff on the Armed

Services Committee during my intensive work on professional military education: Air Force Colonel Mark Smith, Army Colonel John McDonald, Navy Captain Robert Natter, and Air Force Colonel Don Cook, whom I collectively called the "Dawn Patrol," because to me they were as dashing and dedicated as the British World War I pilots in the 1938 movie of the same name. They have all retired now, but not before Bob Natter made admiral and Don Cook general. They say they wouldn't have made flag rank but for the fact that I wrote their fitness reports, but I know better. And after the year was up and the panel was dissolved, I got a picture of all the members of the Dawn Patrol from the movie, had it framed, and gave one to each of them.

As these reform processes were going on, I was given a classified briefing in 1983 about an unconventional-looking airplane that was being built. I asked, "Does this thing fly?" I was told that it would indeed fly, and more: it would fly right over the enemy without their knowledge. The black triangular aircraft was like nothing I had ever seen, employing the latest masking technology to avoid radar detection in delivering its payloads. I knew this real-life "bat plane" would need a home, and I began a very quiet campaign to have the classified aircraft put at Whiteman Air Force Base. The story of how the B-2 came to call Whiteman home is one of bipartisan cooperation and steady community support for this vital element of our national defense.

The base now known as Whiteman—the Sedalia Army Air Corps Base of my youth—has had a long history. By the time I got to Congress in 1977, it was the coordination point for an array of Minuteman missiles located in underground silos, which appeared as pinpoint dots on a map of western Missouri. The Minutemen were aging and on the road to being phased out, and I was in search of new priority missions for Whiteman.

There were three major arguments in my case for bringing the B-2 to Whiteman:

1. It is located in the heart of our country, making attacks on the base harder and making the B-2s roughly equidistant from trouble spots in the Middle East and Asia;
2. The base was long established, with an existing runway and ready for specialized facilities to support the B-2; and
3. There was critical in-state support for the base, its staff, and their families in the surrounding communities. (This support remains in place today.)

I was at Offutt Air Force Base in Nebraska in 1984 and met my old friend Air Force Major General Jim McCarthy—later a four-star–for a midnight snack of milk and cookies during the base visit. I meticulously made my case for Whiteman, and Jim was in a favorable position to give me some help and advice.

We kept up the campaign for Missouri to host America's newest example of superior air power. It was not an easy fight, as there were vociferous critics of the B-2's cost (eventually more than $2 billion per plane) and its capabilities, including many critics from my own party. I never let up, however, and in 1986 I received a call from then-Defense Secretary Caspar Weinberger, a stalwart advocate of upgrading and modernizing America's military defenses. He asked for a private meeting at his Pentagon office.

I met with Secretary Weinberger and his deputy, Will Taft, and Secretary Weinberger gave me the great news: "Ike, since you worked so hard to get the stealth bomber for Whiteman, we're going to put it there. We'll let you announce it." We made the formal announcement in January 1987—the B-2 would call Missouri its home.

When the first B-2 flew into Whiteman on December 17, 1993, a palpable shiver of awe ran through the crowd as that magnificent plane appeared in the wide Missouri skies, landed, and taxied to a stop.

We have built twenty-one B-2 bombers, and they bear names such as *Spirit of Missouri,* which was the first of the contingent to arrive at Whiteman. The B-2 mission, as carried out by the 509th Bomb Wing, saved the base. I'm convinced that without the mission, Whiteman would have fallen victim to subsequent waves of base closings. Instead, the B-2 mission has strengthened Whiteman's place in our national defense, and the neighboring communities have provided a warm and continuing welcome for the men, women, and families who serve there.

The B-2 has a crew of two. The plane was originally conceived at the tail end of the Cold War to carry nuclear weapons, and it still has that capability. But over time and with the latest technology, its flexibility has been demonstrated with deployment of conventional weapons. In its first major campaign, over Kosovo, the B-2 carried global positioning satellite–controlled "smart" bombs with tremendous accuracy. After the September 11 attacks, the B-2 was used in the opening hours of war in Afghanistan and later in Iraq.

The slogan of the B-2 crews is, "We kick in the door," meaning they are the forceful first wave that gives real meaning to "shock and awe." Enemies never knew the radar-evading B-2s, which look like a huge bat, had visited until they were long gone and the bombs were going off. Just as impressive has been the length of nonstop flights using aerial refueling, including round trips from Missouri to the Middle East and back again.

Back at home base in Missouri, the B-2 crews and their families have become active and involved members of the neighboring communities. And those communities have responded with formal support groups for the Whiteman families, providing a welcoming sense of home and caring for their neighbors who serve America. But that's nothing new for Missouri.

MISSOURI AND THE MILITARY

THROUGHOUT MY TENURE on the Armed Services Committee, while we were working to improve the nation's defense, I was mindful of how Missouri could continue contributing to the effort. My home state is the birthplace or chosen home of famous military heroes, including Mexican War fighter Alexander Doniphan, Union General Ulysses S. Grant, Confederate General Sterling Price, World War I Allied Expeditionary Force commander John J. Pershing, and the first chairman of the Joint Chiefs of Staff, General of the Army Omar Bradley. Missouri saw statewide conflict during the Civil War, when our state was divided in sympathy between North and South. Missourians take a lot of pride in the rich military heritage of our Show-Me State, and I have done my part in Congress to build on that heritage.

At the time I left office in 2011, there were three major military installations in Missouri's Fourth Congressional District—Fort Leonard Wood in south-central Missouri, one of the Army's largest posts; Whiteman Air Force Base in west-central Missouri, home of the B-2 Spirit stealth bomber; and the Missouri National Guard Headquarters and Training Center in Jefferson City. I am so proud of the work I did, with much help from citizens and colleagues on both sides of the political aisle, to keep these important installations thriving as key elements of our national defense and Missouri's economy. Every member of Congress has to continually maintain a balance between serving the best interests of the nation and properly representing the people back home who trust you to put their interests first. So it's terrific when the two can go hand-in-hand as well as they did in reinforcing Missouri's support of the military.

I've told the story of bringing the B-2s to Whiteman, and the way the community adopted the base, and of how they both flourished together. It's the same story around Fort Leonard Wood in the Missouri Ozarks next to the communities of Waynesville and St. Robert. Fort Wood was first established in 1940, and in 1941 it was named for General Leonard Wood, a great hero who was famously associated with Theodore Roosevelt's Rough Riders, served as Army chief of staff, and for a time in 1920 was heralded as a presidential candidate.

Fort Wood has always had a central role for basic Army combat training. But today it is a prime example of what we worked for in the hard-fought Goldwater-Nichols Act, which required joint coordination, training, and missions by the various service branches. Its mission as an Army engineering school has been strongly enhanced by educating Marines, Coast Guard, Air Force, and Navy personnel.

The momentum from serving as a model of joint training has helped place additional missions at Fort Wood. Today some twenty-three thousand civilian and military personnel are around Fort Wood on a daily basis, providing an enormous positive economic impact for the state and region while preparing our men and women in many different uniforms.

A major development for Fort Leonard Wood came in 1999, when the Army's military police and chemical weapons centers and schools were transplanted from now-shuttered Fort McClellan in Alabama. The move represented a more efficient use of taxpayer dollars, consolidating training and research and eliminating duplication. And here I must note the key role of a Missourian and a great personal friend of mine in bringing these missions to Fort Wood.

S. Lee Kling was a St. Louis banker and insurance executive known not only for his remarkable business savvy but also for his warm and wise manner. Lee liked to tell his life story simply. I can still hear him saying, "I got out of the Army and went into accounting. Then I bought a bank. Then I had five banks," as if it was all a miracle and required no effort on his part. But make no mistake, Lee was a worker. At the same time, he was one of the friendliest and most approachable men I have ever known, and he never sought the spotlight for himself, which made him even more attractive as a confidant for U.S. presidents and top leaders of government. For example, President Carter dispatched him as a special envoy for business relations in the peace talks between Egypt and Israel.

In 1995, President Bill Clinton appointed Lee Kling to the Base Realignment and Closure Commission, known by the acronym BRACC. The commission had a tough job—reviewing all the military installations that the Department of Defense wanted to close to determine whether the department had correctly gauged the bases' relevance, cost, and future roles, if any, in defending America. It was a thankless task, and commissioners were subject to enormous pressure and often barbed criticism for making tough decisions, whether those decisions supported the department's wishes or went against them. By June of 1995, the commission had visited more than seventy military installations and conducted multiple hearings around the country.

Lee Kling understood the capabilities, capacity, and usefulness of Fort Leonard Wood as an outstanding point of consolidation for joint operations. And he made enhancing and expanding Fort Wood's missions a priority. While the commission ultimately recommended to President Clinton the shutdown of some seventy-nine bases and realignment of about two dozen others, with a projected savings of more than $19 billion over twenty years and the loss of some ninety-four thousand jobs, Fort Wood was not only spared but actually benefited from the expanded missions that were moved to Missouri.

I give Lee Kling enormous credit for his relentless advocacy of Missouri and Fort Wood. Lee passed away in 2008 at age seventy-nine, and Missouri lost a great statesman and I lost a great friend. But his legacy in support of Fort Leonard Wood and his home state is substantial and should never be forgotten.*

Thousands of Missourians also support the military through the National Guard. I have long advocated better relations and familiarity between the military and civilian populations, and there are no finer ambassadors for this work than the men and women of our National Guard units. They are, after all, our neighbors in civilian life, attending school meetings and church services, operating farms and businesses, and unselfishly devoting their time to training, service, and, in recent years, long months of military deployments, not just in overseas war zones but also in response to disasters and crises at home.

Support of the National Guard and Reserves was naturally one of my top priorities in Congress, and I was able to help manifest this in substantial funding for local armories and for the National Guard Headquarters and Training Center at Jefferson City. Enabling the Guard's mission was my mission, undertaken just because it was the right thing to do. So I was never more humbled than when the Guard informed me of plans to name the Jefferson City headquarters after me.

My connections to the National Guard go way back, and here I must speak in appreciation of another longtime friend and supporter, the late Major General Charles Kiefner. When I served in the Missouri state senate, then-Governor Kit Bond appointed Charlie to serve as his adjutant general of the Missouri National Guard. It was a somewhat controversial appointment, because Charlie was only a lieutenant colonel when he was nominated, and it got mixed up in politics between a young Republican governor and old bulls who ran the Democratic-controlled Missouri senate.

It was noted that Charlie, at age forty-two, was the youngest adjutant general in the nation at the time, and he was certainly the youngest man to hold the post in our state's history. But Charlie was dedicated and had come up from the Guard, so he knew its members as colleagues and fellow citizen-soldiers. When it came time for a floor vote on his confirmation, I was proud to cast the deciding senate vote in favor of Charlie's appointment. Charlie never forgot this, and I will never forget the ways in which we worked closely to improve the Guard and services for its members.

---

* Today, there is a building at Fort Leonard Wood named for Lee Kling.

I joined the House Armed Services Committee in 1980, after Charlie had been replaced as adjutant general due to a change in gubernatorial administrations. When Kit Bond was reelected as governor in 1980, he reappointed Charlie as adjutant general, and Charlie remained in that top post for the entire eight-year administration of Governor Bond's successor, John Ashcroft. Charlie served one of the longest tenures as a state adjutant general, and he was instrumental in helping establish a unified Guard lobbying presence on Capitol Hill through the years.

Charlie Kiefner began his Guard service in 1947 and retired as adjutant general in 1993. As I noted in a speech on the House floor, Missouri lost a true leader with Charlie's passing in 2007. He embodied the best of us, and the best of the concept of the citizen-soldier.

I dedicated my congressional service in advocacy of our military forces. In so doing, I thought not only of the men and women who proudly wear the uniform, but also of native Missourians like Lee Kling and Charlie Kiefner, who worked so passionately to build and preserve their presence in our state.

INTO A NEW WORLD

ONE OF THE features I cherished in life as an attorney was learning. Lawyers are required to take continuing education to stay current on changes in the law as it evolves. Of course, in Congress, I was part of making those changes happen. But after ten years there, I wanted to update my skills and knowledge to better deal with the issues that came before us. At the same time, democracy movements around the world—and especially behind the Iron Curtain, in Eastern Europe and even the Soviet Union—were changing what had been a familiar world landscape into uncertain territory. So, to try to anticipate the future and help Congress move into it sensibly, I sought a knowledgeable tutor on world affairs.

I asked for a meeting with former President Richard Nixon. Today, perhaps, meeting with a senior member of the other political party—especially one with a cloud attached to his past—might be seen as foolhardy. And few American politicians (save perhaps Aaron Burr, who killed Alexander Hamilton) carried with them a darker cloud than Nixon, who had resigned from office rather than endure an almost certain impeachment following the Watergate affair. (Incidentally, I believe Gerald Ford would have beaten Jimmy Carter in the 1976 election but for his pardon of Richard Nixon after Watergate, although to my mind, history tells us that it was the right thing to do.) But Nixon, with the aid of his close adviser Henry Kissinger, had been a very impressive and visionary president when it came to foreign policy. He negotiated the opening to China when it was still a politically distant and openly hostile state, a move that facilitated the transition to détente with the Soviet Union and eventually led, in my view, to the failure of the Warsaw Pact and the broad decline of communism. I knew that I might not agree with everything Nixon said or certainly that he had done, but I believed there was much to be learned from him.

Nixon graciously agreed to meet, and on May 12, 1989, my close aide Tommy Glakas and I sat with the former president. Over the course of half an hour, Nixon displayed an insightful knowledge not only of the Soviet Union and world affairs, but even of my district and background. He had clearly done his homework, even just for a short meeting with a Democratic congressman of middling seniority. He was pleasant and cordial, and I do not recall his once alluding to the difference between us in party allegiance except to note the value of bipartisanship. Nixon thought bipartisanship was essential in advancing foreign policy goals, because many Democrats didn't like offering military aid and many Republicans didn't like spending money on other countries, so to make anything positive happen, it had to be done cooperatively and from the center. Considering the 1960 presidential election, I was a bit surprised when Nixon described how, as senators, he and John F. Kennedy had worked together to advance foreign policy.

Nixon was pessimistic about the chances for restructuring, or perestroika as the Russians called it. He urged me to go to the Soviet Union to meet the Russian people firsthand, saying that I would find them gracious and warm—even though the government would make sure to show me only the very best of the country, including "Potemkin villages" set up to show an idealized version of life there. He also didn't think that then-divided Germany would successfully reunify and noted candidly that the Russians would be "scared s—less" if Germany did come back together.

It was clear from our discussion that Nixon was tremendously bright and still very engaged in world affairs. I was reminded of something I'd seen so often as a prosecutor—that no one aspect of a man, good or bad, can tell you everything about him. But of course time has not borne out all of his predictions.

The questions I asked Nixon were part of trying to figure out the map of the world after the Cold War. The fall of the Soviet Union led many people to question the need for the United States to maintain strong military forces and to preserve its military abroad. With the United States' largest competitor gone, they asked, where is the enemy? And why would we need to spend so much money on defense when no single powerful foe or group of foes can easily be identified to defend against?

Over time, an answer became clear. The enemy was not any single country or entity; it was instability itself. By dividing the world into two camps led by two strong patrons, the Cold War gave structure and a perverse sort of power balance to international affairs. In the multipolar world that followed the demise of the Communist bloc, there was no natural balancing force, nor a restraint on many nations from aggressive actions that would in the past have been suppressed by Moscow. Civil war in the former Yugoslavia, famine in North Korea, and tensions between Taiwan and the People's Republic of China are but a few examples of the problems that continued then—and in at least two of those cases, continue today—to threaten the peace.

In the Cold War world, we understood our adversary and its capabilities and interests. That made defense planning comparatively easy. In the world that followed, though, threats to the United States could take many forms and appear in many locations. We needed a greater flexibility in our military forces to meet whatever challenge arose. This meant a military that had different capabilities from its predecessor but was not necessarily any less expensive to procure and operate.

Looking at America's commitments around the world, I became quite concerned that what's called "end strength," the number of people in the services, was too low. This was echoed in testimony by then-Lieutenant General Ted Stroup when we were just going into Bosnia, and it turned out that sadly I was right. The military was too small.

Acts of terrorism challenged us as well in the years after the Cold War. Just as Operation Eagle Claw highlighted flaws in military jointness, terrorist attacks pointed out another possible shortcoming in America's security posture. Deadly attacks were taking place, in particular the bombings of U.S. embassies in Kenya and Tanzania in August 1998, which killed about 250 people. But nothing unifies Americans on the role of government as much as when we are attacked. I had been studying the issue of terrorism and U.S. preparedness for some time and commissioned four reports by the General Accounting Office (now the Government Accountability Office) detailing U.S. efforts to combat terrorism. The reports revealed that more than forty federal agencies were working on federal antiterrorism and counterterrorism initiatives, together spending upward of $7 billion a year. That sounds reassuring. But I was concerned that with so much going on, the left hand may not have known what the right hand was doing. After the embassy bombings, terrorism became a much more significant focus of our work on the Armed Services Committee; indeed, for a time it was renamed the National Security Committee to reflect its engagement in the full range of security challenges to our nation. But it would take a much more dramatic and costly attack a few years later to finally consolidate the government's national security structure.

I got to see the complicated world of American overseas commitments and the consequences of our end-strength reductions firsthand during visits with the troops. I went out into the field as often as I could. As I was a member of the Armed Services Committee, and certainly when I was its ranking member and chairman, the military was only too happy to present any kind of information I might want. But even the most articulate general officer can't give you the same perspective that you get from a recent enlistee overseas for the first time, or from that staff sergeant who knows the reality of dealing with the population—and his young charges—on a daily basis. As often as possible, I spent holidays with American forces forward—and in the 1990s, that meant Eastern Europe, where American troops were part of a NATO force trying to stabilize what had been Yugoslavia following war among Serbs, Bosniaks, and Croats. This war—including the related conflicts in Macedonia and Kosovo—was a tangible example of the unpredictable instability America's military had to be ready for.

This wasn't glamorous travel; these weren't the junkets of old, when the press focused on tales of representatives and senators on fact-finding tours of sunlit islands with lots of tennis courts. Some of it could get downright gritty. But I believe that it is vitally important for members of Congress not only to understand the world, but to see firsthand where we are asking American personnel to go, what we are asking them to do, and how our money is being spent. A sheet of paper with numbers on it doesn't tell you how attitudes change by our simply connecting a village to clean water or ensuring that children can attend school safely. And it also can't show you the looks in the eyes of the people we are there to help—the wary, the angry, the grateful.

When less than a quarter of sitting congressmen have ever served in the military, and when a significant number don't even hold passports, I get concerned. How well can you make decisions about how America is to succeed in the world if you haven't seen the world? How well can you decide on whether an American involvement overseas should continue if all you see are the press reports and official statements? I don't think America can—or should—expect Congress to be both wise and insular.

I will admit that what I heard in the field from a junior enlisted soldier or a petty officer on his or her first deployment often carried at least as much weight as a briefing from the service chief of staff. Those kids speak from their hearts, and they give it to you straight. That doesn't happen often enough in Washington. And, of course, if they happened to be from Missouri, their word was gold.

One type of travel of particular interest to me was the privilege to join military tours of famous battlefields, called staff rides, led by respected historians who know their stuff—the lay of the land, the conditions of the days and weeks of combat, the factors seen and unseen that only unblinking and thoughtful reflection and analysis can put into proper historical context.

To see where history happened is to put yourself in the shoes of the people making the decisions about how the battles were fought. Some battles are complicated, in terms of geography and troop placement and other factors. So it takes study to understand the decisions that made these places of historic importance, places where men triumphed and men fell. Visiting these places and learning the background of what happened there is important—it makes you consider what caused certain commanders to make certain decisions, whether they were good decisions or bad ones.

The name "staff ride" comes from the old custom whereby those who fought a battle over a certain terrain would take younger officers on horseback and tell them this is what happened here, and this is what happened there. But although they are called "staff" rides, they are great tools for the strategist, the tactician, and the historian, and I don't know if anyone in Congress has had as many as I've had.

Some of my dearest friendships arose from these staff rides, with experts such as now-retired Major General Bob Scales, former commandant of the U.S. Army War College in Carlisle, Pennsylvania, and a Vietnam veteran, whose perspective has been so important to me. He personally led staff rides around the Civil War battlefields at Gettysburg and Antietam. Another great friend is retired Army General Montgomery Meigs, who led us on a three-day staff ride studying the Battle of the Bulge in the dead of winter. And retired Army General Jack Galvin, who headed our European Command, spoke with great scholarly authority during our staff ride analyzing the Battle of Waterloo.

When my friends visit my hometown of Lexington, I conduct my own staff rides along the battlefield where in September 1861 the Missouri State Guard, fighting for the Confederacy, defeated Union forces. At Lexington, the State Guard prevailed by soaking hemp bales from a nearby rope factory in the water of the Missouri River to use as shields against the flaming Union ambuscade. Methodically rolling the wet bales up the hill, they cut off and captured the Union high ground.

As a boy I played on this battleground. As a military academy cadet I studied it more carefully, gaining appreciation for the various stages of battle and the decisions behind them. I still pause and imagine the history that happened there as brave men died on both sides of the conflict.

One particularly memorable staff ride was at Iwo Jima, where over 6,000 Americans were killed and 19,000 wounded in the Second World War. I was accompanied by a Japanese captain and an American Navy captain. When we landed at the little airport there, the two captains were at the foot of the steps. The Japanese captain stepped forward and said, "Welcome to Japan." Even though Iwo Jima had been returned to Japan in 1972, it was a shock to see the Japanese flag flying over the little headquarters. We rode the narrow, twisting path to the top of Mount Suribachi, past the open pit still emitting sulfur fumes.

Two other memorable trips were to the Normandy American Cemetery and Memorial in France, which was the first U.S. military cemetery on European soil in World War II. The graves of more than nine thousand of our fallen warriors line up in now-peaceful symmetry at Normandy, a sight that moves and stirs every patriotic heart.

I was honored to attend the fiftieth anniversary commemoration of the D-Day invasion at Normandy. At the time I felt additional pride in the service of our son Ike, who was stationed in London doing public affairs work for the Navy and who helped stage a commemorative ceremony at London's Grosvenor Square during that anniversary.

After the Normandy ceremony we went to the VIP tent, where I met Patricia Neal, the famous movie actress. At one point I was standing by myself, and in walked a familiar face with an Eisenhower jacket on, with sergeant's stripes, faded Silver Star, and Purple Heart with a cluster. It was Dr. Tommy McDonald from Marshville, Missouri, a very, very good friend. He had to be the most popular person in that county, a Democrat that always got reelected to the Missouri legislature. Tommy says he brought half of the county into the world. "Ike, Ike, I found it, I found it!" he said. I said, "Tommy, what did you find?" Well, he had found the place where he was positioned when he was a sniper on D-Day, and he wanted me to go out and look at it. I was afraid the bus would leave me, so I didn't do it. Looking back, I wish I had.

Mike and Bettie Boorda were also in the tent. Jeremy Boorda, although everybody called him Mike, was at one time probably my closest military friend. For some reason, he and I hit it off quite well, and I traveled with him quite a bit. I saw him conduct a town hall meeting with the sailors on the stern of a ship in Pascagoula, Mississippi. He was really good with the sailors, which wasn't surprising, because he'd been one of them. Mike was a mustang, which is the nickname given an officer who started out as an enlisted man and worked his way up. And boy, did he—all the way to Chief of Naval Operations.

I didn't get acquainted with Mike until he was a one-star. He was later, as a three-star, the head of Navy personnel, and became the four-star in charge of European Command. When I was with him over there, with or without Susie, we stayed in his house. That day in Normandy, he was early into his term as CNO.

A decade later I was back at Normandy with the D-Day survivors for the sixtieth anniversary commemoration at Normandy. But the ranks of the living heroes being saluted anew were of course thinned by the peacetime attrition of old age. If we remain steadfast, their contributions and sacrifices will never be diminished.

One hero missing from the sixtieth anniversary ceremony was Mike Boorda. In late April or early May of 1996, Mike invited Susie and me over to dinner with a few other folks. Representatives Norman Sisisky and, I think, Owen Pickett, both of Virginia, were there too. Before dinner, we were all sitting in the living room of the Tingey House, the Chief of Naval Operations' official residence, where Mike and Bettie lived. And Mike said, "I just wanted to have my good friends over tonight." I didn't think much about it.

After dinner, Mike and Susie and Norm Sisisky walked together outside in the yard for a while. I was inside talking to somebody. When Susie and I got back to our townhouse, she said, "Did you notice anything different about Mike tonight?" I said no. She said, "There's something different about him." She had noticed it during the walk outside. She didn't elaborate, but Susie had a sixth sense about her, and she must have picked up something.

Two weeks later, Mike was gone of a self-inflicted wound. He had been the focus of a controversy about whether he was wearing a combat decoration he hadn't earned, the V for valor. I understand what that means; my son Jim has the Bronze Star with a V. Although there was a fair case to be made that Mike had earned his, it was nonetheless a real mess in the press and inside the Pentagon. The whole thing was very sad.

After Mike passed, I learned that he had told people I was his closest friend in Washington, which is a humbling honor. One of his sons, Bobby Boorda, has stayed in touch pretty well through the years. Now and then, I've talked to Bettie. I've always felt bad that with the exception of Susie and me going over to the dinner, I didn't see an awful lot of Mike for two or three months. I just thought, "Oh, he's busy. I don't want to bother him." And I should have, looking back, especially when he was catching hell about wearing the combat V. That's the kind of time when a man needs his friends.

Mentioning my son reminds me that I had to tone down my proud-papa routine a bit when I was on the Armed Services Committee. Not that I was any less proud of my boys, you understand. But my two sons in the service didn't need that association, or any notion that they were different or should be treated differently because their father was on the committee that authorized their service's budget. Other members were in the same situation. Even before we became chairman and ranking member, I would confer often with Duncan Hunter, who became a very good friend. His son, young Duncan, joined the Marines right after 9/11 in 2001 and served for four years in the Marine Corps, and has since succeeded his father in Congress.

Of course, try as one might, it's not always possible to keep the secret. My son Jim did a very good job of making his own way. He had it down to an art. People would say to him, "Skelton, Skelton, are you . . ." and he'd say, "Yes. Kin of Red Skelton."

When Jim was serving in the headquarters in Iraq, he briefed the commander, General David Petraeus, from time to time. But one day, Petraeus came to see me—and he was onto it. He said, "Your son, Jim, tried to be incognito, but his nametag and his height gave him away." Not much we could do about that, I suppose.

A few years after the fiftieth anniversary of D-Day, I was able to give back a small homage to my friend and mentor Harry Truman. On July 25, 1998, a Saturday, the U.S. Navy commissioned its newest aircraft carrier, the USS *Harry S Truman*. Of course, I felt a personal tie to that ship thanks to my family's friendship with the Truman family. But I had also urged the Navy for many years to name an aircraft carrier after President Truman.

In the end, the naming of the *Truman* was part of a great political compromise. After Ronald Reagan was reported to be ill, Republicans in Congress had pressed for a carrier to be named after him. President Clinton finally acquiesced—with a hidden catch. Although he agreed to name a carrier for President

Reagan, he didn't agree to name the *next* one for him. So he announced that the carrier known as CVN-76 would be named for Reagan—but its predecessor, CVN-75, would be named for Truman.

To the student of history, this introduced echoes of the past. Until being named for Truman, CVN-75 was expected to be called the USS *United States*. The last time a carrier had been proposed to carry that name was in the 1940s, when, under Truman, the Navy proposed the first supercarrier, the USS *United States*. Overruling his secretary of defense, James Forrestal, Truman canceled the *United States*. Forrestal resigned and died not long after. When a new carrier was finally built to replace the *United States*, it was christened the USS *Forrestal* in honor of the late secretary. So just as the previous *United States* gave way to a ship named for Truman's secretary of defense, this new one gave way to Truman himself.

But the connection didn't end there. After the USS *Forrestal* was retired in 1993, a number of parts were removed for later reuse. Obviously, the more technology-intensive items were long obsolete. But the relationship of inertia and mass hadn't changed. So the *Forrestal*'s two main anchors went back to sea—as anchors aboard the *Harry S Truman*.

Another opportunity to pay tribute to President Truman came on September 22, 2000. I went to the State Department that day to witness the fulfillment of another of my legislative initiatives—the naming of the State Department headquarters building in honor of Truman. President Clinton and Secretary of State Madeleine Albright were there, along with cosponsor Roy Blunt of Missouri, and the event was made all the more memorable by the master of ceremonies, James Earl Jones. That man could read a feed store catalog and make it sound wonderful.

I told the audience the story of how my father had met Mr. Truman at the dedication of the Pioneer Mother Statue—the Madonna of the Trail—in Lexington. And I noted that it was especially appropriate that the State Department bear his name, since it was Harry Truman who guided the United States away from our established pattern of peacetime isolationism in order to assist European economic recovery and security, creating the Marshall Plan and NATO. This was but a small part of repaying my debt—and America's—to that great Missourian.

Given our mutual love of history, I think Mr. Truman would have been pleased.

As the years went on, the political center—at least in Congress—dwindled, and the competition between the parties changed. I was increasingly asked what government was for. A lot of people came to see government as an enemy, an impediment. To my mind, though, government has a real purpose. It's there for when bad things happen, like tornadoes, floods, and other natural disasters, because government can do real good helping people in times of severe trouble. That's part of the security that America owes its people—not just national security, which is military, but safety, whether it's rebuilding levees, paying for damage, home crops, or helping rebuild a community. For example, when Stockton, Missouri, got hit by a tornado that walked right down Main Street, FEMA (the Federal Emergency Management Agency) did a very good job helping to stabilize and rebuild the town. That's the kind of thing government should do.

Similarly, government has a role on a daily basis in securing America, whether at the borders or against crime with agencies such as the FBI and Alcohol, Tobacco and Firearms, or with other agencies that protect people, like the Coast Guard. Another big role is protecting people's health—food safety, disease control. There's no other entity to do that. And I think Social Security has been a huge success; in fact, I'm not sure that the writers of the Social Security Act knew how much of a success it would be. Government takes a role ensuring employment because people have to feed their families. And government research and pricing policies keep the best farmers in the world in business.

In late 1998, the House became subsumed by a drama that did little to strengthen the political center or improve public perceptions of government. President Bill Clinton stood accused of misleading a grand jury by making false statements about his relationship with a White House intern, Monica Lewinsky.

Like many, my first real exposure to Clinton had been at the Democratic National Convention ten years earlier in Atlanta, where, as governor of Arkansas, he made a stultifyingly long speech after which everybody said, "This guy's career is over." I remember sitting through that speech . . . and sitting . . . and sitting. To this day, I have no idea what he was talking about. His speech was so long that when he said, toward the end, "And in conclusion," people started cheering. But even then, it was clear Clinton was a very bright guy, and a very nice guy.

One way you could tell he was smart is that he took a shine to Susie. When we'd go to the White House for dinners, he'd have Susie sitting next to him and I would often sit next to the First Lady, Hillary Clinton. When all this stuff came out about Monica Lewinsky, Susie refused to believe it at all because she was very fond of President Clinton. So we went over there to a reception during this era and he was in the receiving line. Susie and I went through the line, and he saw her and he hugged her and held up the whole line talking to Susie! They were seriously good friends. When they were done, we both turned around and walked away, and then she wheeled around and walked back to him. Susie just shook her finger in his face and said, "Don't you let me down!" Then she and I walked away.

Well, a week later Clinton fessed up, and Susie went off: "I'm through with him; I don't want anything more to do with him." She was very angry at him, and she remained angry. Several weeks later we went to a Democratic retreat down in Greensboro, North Carolina, as I recall, and he was the guest speaker at the dinner. We decided that maybe we ought to go speak to him. And of course all the members of Congress were shaking hands with the president, so we waited till the very last. Everybody was gone except Jerry Nadler, the congressman from New York. They were going on and on with each other, so Susie and I walked up there because we'd been waiting a while. When Clinton saw her, he reached over and grabbed both her hands while still talking to Jerry Nadler. He held her right there until he was done, and then he turned to Susie and they chatted a while.

And right there, he got her back. I don't know what he said. Just by being nice to her, I suppose. But person to person, he was good. He was that good.

However, his getting Susie back didn't help me much, because I was going to have to vote once or twice on Clinton's conduct. It was clear that the Republicans, who had the majority in the House then, would force a vote on whether to refer the matter of impeachment to the Judiciary Committee for a formal inquiry. If the committee recommended articles of impeachment, which seemed likely, then I would have to vote on those.

One concern about authorizing the Judiciary Committee inquiry was the potential for a drawn-out, political investigation. As an alternative, the Democrats offered provisions for a time-limited investigation by a committee of the whole House, and I would have preferred that had it been a viable option. But I put on my former prosecutor's hat and did my homework, and after thoroughly reviewing the allegations contained in the independent counsel's report, I concluded that it would be in the best interest of the nation for the Judiciary Committee to be given the authority to begin an impeachment inquiry. I wasn't convinced that the president had done anything impeachable, but I wanted the American people to see the system working—especially with only the second presidential impeachment in history on the line.

The Democratic leadership made clear that while they had a preferred position on the issue, this was a free vote, to be cast as each member's conscience dictated. So I (and thirty of my Democratic colleagues) voted for a full investigation—it turned out about as I thought it would, which meant actually having to vote on articles of impeachment.

And on December 12, 1998, I did. I voted against impeachment.

I know that many Americans believe there are too many lawyers in Congress, but this was one time that my legal training and experience was a significant asset in reaching a sound decision on a vote. I studied the Constitution and the facts of the case and, without getting into too much detail here, concluded that even if all of the allegations in the Judiciary Report were true, President Clinton's actions did not constitute impeachable offenses under the Constitution. There was just no evidence that permitting him to stay on would

INTO A NEW WORLD

cause great or serious harm to our system of government. I believed that the Congress should censure him strongly, but that impeachment was simply not warranted by the facts.

Of course, a majority of the House disagreed, and the president was impeached. He went on trial before the Senate, defended by the formidable debater Dale Bumpers of Arkansas, and was acquitted.

By the way, I think that trial was one of the better parts of televising Congress's proceedings. Live television of legislative business came to the House in 1977, and while it certainly added transparency for the people, I think as a whole it hurt the institution. Not because the world could see what we were doing, but because we could see it ourselves—from our offices.

Back in the day, members would hear that a respected orator, like Dewey Short from Missouri, was going to speak, and they would go to the floor. Not only would they hear the arguments propounded by whoever was speaking, but they would talk together, work out compromises, and get to know each other.

Congress is a place of relationships, and you don't have relationships unless you're with people. You don't have relationships through a television set. But if you're sitting over in the House chamber visiting with members between votes or during votes or listening to the proceedings, you have the opportunity to get to know someone and get to make good friends. That's where decisions are made. That's where compromises are made, because you get to know someone and you trust them. You can't make a compromise unless you trust someone. You get to know people, and there are strong friendships, usually, brought on by trust.

Nowadays, every office has the television on and at least the staff is watching it all the time. If something comes up, the staff will say, "You should go if you want to speak on this," or, "They are getting ready to vote on this, and you'll want to get there before the vote is called." The House chamber thus becomes a drive-through when it should be a place to spend time and build the relationships that make Congress work.

Today, the only way you end up spending a lot of time on the floor is when you're managing a bill, and then you're too busy to be socializing. And you're one of only a few on the floor at the time; the speakers come and go. They get a call in their office: "You have five minutes to get over here." You go over and you speak for your five minutes and you go back to your office, and you're not sitting there making friends.

Electronic voting doesn't help either. The House used to have a teller vote system, where you had to be there front and present and go through a different line for yea or nay. Through all this you would be talking to people and meeting acquaintances and friends. We went through teller votes for a period of years, and then it all became electronic and they would string all the votes together, five, six, seven votes back-to-back. And the individuality of each vote somehow slipped away.

When the House was first going to be televised live (the legislative business, that is; Harry Truman did a State of the Union live in 1947), we knew it was coming several days ahead of time. No one much thought about giving the first speech, except Al Gore. That's why Al was on the floor and gave the first televised speech in the House of Representatives. I don't recall what he talked about, but he was the first one there to take advantage of it. He was always thinking ahead.

I think another thing that has hurt comity and the work of Congress is the fact that most members now, particularly the younger members, go home every weekend. As I recall, we used to be budgeted to go home once a month. That meant the weekends were other times that we could get to know our colleagues and do things together as families. I think that helped forestall a lot of the rancor you see today.

Susie and I decided early on to bring our family to Washington. Those three-out-of-four weekends that I was in Washington with my boys, we were tourists. We got to see Washington, D.C., and the boys seemed to enjoy it. Jim always wanted to go down to Georgetown to Sunny's Surplus, which is an Army store, and I don't know what all they sold there, but they sure sold it to my sons!

In March of 1999, the B-2, which I had done so much to bring to Whiteman Air Force Base, saw its first action. Now, if you'll recall, I noted that I first heard about the B-2 sixteen years earlier, in 1983—which points up one of the paradoxes of defense procurement.

People complain, and justly, about the cost of defense systems. We buy the best, there's no doubt about it. But they're like life insurance—you want to buy a good policy, but you don't ever want to use it. I'm reminded of the B-36, the huge bomber from the 1950s that went through its whole life without ever being used in anger. I would call that a success—nobody wants to fight a war, and to me the best military system is one that so intimidates the enemy that they never attack. But some people look at that and see waste: "Why did we buy that if we're never going to use it?" They said the same about the B-2, which was the most expensive airplane we ever bought. I hear it about the F-22 today.

Then in 1999 we began an air campaign in support of Operation Allied Force, NATO action in the former Yugoslavia. The B-2s flew nonstop from Knob Noster, Missouri, to Europe, put their ordnance on target, and flew all the way home. That precedent would be followed in even more far-flung missions over Iraq, Afghanistan, Libya, and elsewhere.

I know we can't deter every enemy, but it's good to know that we have the right tool for the job when deterrence fails.

Along those lines, over time, I became increasingly concerned about the size of the Navy. No, Missouri isn't on an ocean, although there are large anchors displayed at Whiteman Air Force Base and Fort Leonard Wood—just as little reminders of the need for jointness. In June 2000, I gave the commencement address at the Naval War College. The president of the college at the time was Vice-Admiral Arthur Cebrowski. Cebrowski was a big thinker, a Billy Mitchell type who wasn't afraid to advocate unorthodox solutions even if the Navy didn't particularly like them.

In our talks before and after the speech, Admiral Cebrowski spoke enthusiastically about a class of small, fast ships that he envisioned for the future Navy. They would be very flexible, capable of operating close to shore as well as on the open ocean, and relatively inexpensive. He called them Streetfighters. I was intrigued by this idea and sent my Armed Services staffer J. J. Gertler back to Newport to follow up and learn more. Admiral Cebrowski and his staff were so persuasive that he wound up enrolling in the college!

I knew that the chance of the Navy embracing smaller ships was pretty remote, especially if they were to operate in what sailors call the "brown water" close to shore. But two things caught my interest. The first was the prospect of keeping the number of ships in the Navy up. Since President Reagan had advocated the six-hundred-ship Navy in the early 1980s, the actual number had slipped to about half that. I was intrigued by the possibility of less-expensive ships of the line, perhaps based more on aircraft technology than traditional naval architecture.

But I also really liked what these ships could do for America's forward presence. I mentioned the idea that the best military system was one that deterred an adversary. But I also believed that an American ship showing the flag at a foreign pier makes friends, warns enemies, and ultimately reduces the need to send many more ships out on the ocean. We have made the difference by our presence in keeping Taiwan separate from China. And if you don't have presence that is serious, you lose credibility. The first question that gets asked when problems happen is, "Where are the American ships, where is an American presence?" If we're not there, confidence in America slips. Our allies trust us. For instance, Singapore, at its own expense, built a huge dock to accommodate our aircraft carriers. They want us there, they want our presence. The pending reduction in ship numbers meant that we could not maintain the same presence overseas. I hoped that new, smaller ships would allow a big enough fleet to be wherever American power was needed when it was needed there.

In October 2000, the House passed the defense authorization bill for the 2001 fiscal year. To be sure, there's a bill every year—in fact, the defense bill is one of the few that has actually passed every year, a record of which we on the Armed Services Committee were proud. But the Fiscal 2001 bill made a significant change.

In February of 2000, Gene Taylor of Mississippi, Neil Abercrombie from Hawaii, and I had introduced legislation expanding military health care, most notably extending its most important provisions to retirees. As with all legislation, it was trimmed and modified on its way through the process, but the most important points stayed in, resulting in significantly improved access to health care for those who had served America. I was and am as proud of that achievement as anything I accomplished in Congress.

Then came several terrible shocks. First, on October 12, 2000, terrorists supporting al Qaeda struck the destroyer USS *Cole* in the harbor of Aden, Yemen, killing seventeen sailors and injuring thirty-nine. I have great admiration for the professionalism of the crew of the *Cole* in tending to the wounded and taking care of their ship. But there was no mistaking the message that al Qaeda would take the fight to U.S. forces wherever they might be found. And I was struck by how the attack symbolized the strategic situation of the post–Cold War world; instead of being damaged in an engagement with an opposing naval fleet, our ship of the line was attacked by a man in a skiff with a bomb. Coming so soon after my advocacy of naval presence, the attack was a sobering reminder that not everyone welcomed the United States.

Less than a week later came more personal and difficult news. Mel Carnahan, Missouri's excellent governor and a friend of many years, was killed along with his son Randy and his close aide, Chris Sifford, when their airplane crashed in Jefferson County while he was campaigning for the Senate. For me, as for many Missourians, the echoes of Jerry Litton's 1976 crash made dealing with Mel's loss even more difficult.

I was very fond of Mel. He had a very simple, no-pretense air about him, and people were just naturally drawn to him. I can't think of anyone who really disliked him, even those who disagreed with him. I know I disagreed with him on any number of occasions, but he got along well with people. Mel campaigned on being a straight arrow, and he was—but he wasn't boring. He was a clean-cut, nice guy, attentive. I think he would have gotten elected on anything he ran for.

His funeral was probably the largest Missouri has had in years. We marched from the governor's mansion down the hill to the Missouri state capitol where we had the ceremony outside. His passing was a real loss to Missourians and the country.

Mel won the election posthumously and his widow, Jean, took his seat for a term. I see Jean occasionally. Their son Russ is a very good friend, and he was an able member of Congress. But I still miss Mel.

February of 2001 found me back in the Balkans. I had spent Thanksgiving with troops there, as was my custom. But the U.S. involvement in helping NATO quell some ancient rivalries over there had become controversial, and a group of members wanted to see what was going on and hear from the troops on the scene.

The Balkans had been a mess for centuries. As I reported to the House on February 27, "Broadly, Serbs inside Kosovo are afraid of the Albanian majority, while those Albanians are afraid of the nation of Serbia next door. These two groups have one thing in common: they are both glad the U.S. and European troops are there to protect them and provide stability."

And make no mistake, those American troops—who were only 18 percent of the NATO force, by the way—did just that. I asked soldiers of all ranks what would happen if the United States pulled out of the Balkans. One said it best in a simple word: "Boom." Those great American kids stopped the boom.

About this same time, a debate was going on as to whether we should still have forces in Europe, then fifty years after World War II. I was in Mons, Belgium, having lunch with the NATO commander, Wes Clark, and his German four-star deputy, just the three of us. Wes had to get up to answer the telephone. The German general and I were sitting there chatting, and he said to me, "You know, it's important that you Americans be over here because you know how we Germans are." I know exactly what he meant.

The debate had taken place around the presidential election of 2000, which had been as contentious and complicated a saga as I ever hope to see. In the end, of course, after all the recounting and a visit to the Supreme Court, George W. Bush was declared the winner over Al Gore. A lot of people thought that a Republican administration heralded a return to big defense budgets, although in truth, both candidates had advocated greater defense spending. As I said in the House on March 22, 2001, "If we can keep our promises to the troops and maintain an effective defense, I don't care if the money comes from Democrats, Republicans, or Martians."

I should have voted for the Martian. Boy, did we get a surprise when the first Bush defense budget came down.

To be sure, President Bush's defense budget for 2002 asked for about $311 billion for the Department of Defense. That's a whole lot of money. But after adjusting for inflation and retiree health care, the actual increase in the defense budget was $100 million from what President Clinton had proposed.

Because $100 million is a nice, round number, it lets us take a look at defense spending. Sometimes the numbers get so big that it's hard to put them in context. If you or I won that much in a lottery, we'd be rich. But in the Defense Department, I asked the House, what does $100 million do?

At the time, $100 million was enough for a pay increase for every soldier of one dollar and eighty-five cents per pay period.

Or it's 1/45th of an aircraft carrier.

Or it runs the ballistic missile defense program for six days.

Or it's one and a half F-15 fighters.

You pick whichever you like, because for that money you only get one.

So often today, I hear members of Congress—especially the newer members, and particularly those affiliated with the Tea Party, the right wing of the

Republican Party—talk about how big the budget numbers are. But I hear a lot less about what you get for that money. That matters too. It's making hard choices like what you do with the budget you have that make the job challenging—and worthwhile.

But money wasn't all that was at stake. After terrorist incidents overseas, plus the bombing of the Murrah Federal Building in Oklahoma City and the attempt to destroy the World Trade Center with truck bombs, it was clear that the chance of a major attack inside the United States had to be taken seriously. In March of 2001, I introduced a bill to require the development and implementation of a national homeland security strategy, similar to the already required National Military Strategy that focused on external threats.

We had brought jointness and interoperability to the military, but there was little to no coordination for either planning or incident response among the federal, state, and local government entities that would need to work together to provide homeland security. Congress and the administration were in the process of throwing money and missions at various homeland security entities before, in my view, understanding either what the threats were or what assets we had on hand to combat them. But it seemed clear to me that trouble was on the way. I wish I'd been wrong about that.

That March, the Armed Services Committee lost Norm Sisisky. Norm had made his money in the soft-drink business, and he brought that same businessman's eye to the business of the committee. He was fearless and didn't suffer fools—well, at all. He was a good man to have by your side in a debate. But at the same time, Norm had a twinkle of mischief in his eye. He went too soon.

You might imagine that as the chairman or ranking member of the Armed Services Committee, you get to see a lot of secrets. That's true. But an awful lot of them are things you saw in the newspaper that morning, and a lot of the rest just aren't that interesting. You don't get many dramatic nighttime phone calls from the president or the secretary of defense reporting some surprising development. The day of Norm's funeral, though, was one of the exceptions. I got a call informing me that one of our surveillance planes, an EP-3, had been in a collision with a Chinese fighter. It wasn't clear whether it was an accident, and the damaged U.S. plane managed to land safely on Hainan Island. But it took us ten days to get the crew back, and the Chinese charged us for their room and board! They also gave that EP-3 a pretty good going-over.

Not long after Norm Sisisky passed, in August, Floyd Spence died. Floyd was then the chairman of the Armed Services Committee. Although he was a Republican and from South Carolina, we had an important thing in common: he had also been born and raised in Lexington, just, as I told him, the wrong one. He was a real gentleman.

Floyd's passing meant that from my position as ranking member, I would be working directly with my first friend in Congress, the new chairman, Bob Stump of Arizona. I knew our dealings would be fair and equitable.

Not too long after this, I received a surprising inquiry from the White House, although it came through an intermediary. Would I be interested in becoming secretary of the Army?

I don't mind telling you that the idea was intriguing. After being so focused in my youth on joining the Army, here was a chance to get in as close to the top as a civilian could get. And I wasn't blind; I knew as well as the Republicans did that my district had drifted to the right over the years, and that if I took the Army job, my seat was very likely to go to whatever Republican ran. I'm not sure they really wanted Ike Skelton. But Ike Skelton's seat—now, that was worth something to them.

In the end, I could do more for the military as the ranking member on the Armed Services Committee, so I turned the offer down. (And that didn't stop them from coming back with the same offer a couple of years later when the sitting secretary was having some trouble.)

A little later that year, I put out a long essay on strategy. It seemed to me that the military was being sized and prepared for the wrong tasks. I recommended an increased focus on homeland security, on the Asia-Pacific theater, on cyber security, and on presence, including those small Navy ships I found so interesting. All in all, it was not so different from the strategy the Department of Defense unveiled . . . in 2012.

What we didn't know was that the world was about to change.

It was September 5, 2001.

President Jimmy Carter signing the Agriculture Bill, with Congressman Tom Foley, the author, and Secretary of Agriculture Bob Bergland looking on, 1977.

Congressman Leon Panetta, Secretary of Agriculture Bob Bergland, and the author, 1977. Skelton's Family Collection

Senator Thomas Eagleton and the author conducting an open forum, 1978.
Skelton's Family Collection

Returning American remains from the Vietnam War. Air Force officers Doug Roach (second from left) and Ted Rees (third from left) escort members of Congress: (from left) the author, Sam Hall, Henson Moore, Jack Murtha, Tony Won Pat, George Danielson, Jim Broyhill, and G. V. "Sonny" Montgomery, 1978, Hanoi, Vietnam. Skelton's Family Collection

Good friends—Sheriff Gene Darnell and the author, 1978.
Skelton's Family Collection

The author (second from left) with, to his left, congressmen Dick Gephardt and Richard Bolling, 1978. Skelton's Family Collection

The author visiting with Vietnamese children, 1978. Skelton's Family Collection

The Skelton boys, Ike, Page, and Jim, and their father meeting comedian Red Skelton, 1979. Skelton's Family Collection

The author with Anwar Sadat and Speaker Tip O'Neill, 1979.
Skelton's Family Collection

The author with Tip O'Neill and Menachem Begin, 1979. Skelton's Family Collection

The author being greeted by President Ronald Reagan, 1981. Skelton's Family Collection

The author with Army troops, 1981. Skelton's Family Collection

Participants in a joint session of Congress commemorating the one hundredth anniversary of Harry S. Truman's birth. Left to right: the author, Clark Clifford, Senator Stuart Symington, and Margaret Truman Daniel—May 8, 1984. Skelton's Family Collection

The 1982 election victory with Ralph Soule of Lexington, Missouri.
Courtesy of the *Kansas City Star*

The author and Susie Skelton with President and Mrs. George H. W. Bush, 1990.
Skelton's Family Collection

Larry McMullen introducing the author as commencement speaker for the University of Missouri School of Law, graduation, June 1992. (Dean James Westbrook in the background.) Courtesy of Larry McMullen

The author's appearance at the national prayer breakfast, with President George
H. W. Bush and Mrs. Bush looking on, 1992. Skelton's Family Collection

The author at the American Cemetery, Normandy, France, 2004.
Skelton's Family Collection

The author and General David Petraeus. Courtesy of the Truman Library Institute; Bruce Mathews, photographer

Granddaughter Sarah Skelton shoveling dirt on grandmother's memorial tree on U.S. Capitol Grounds, 2007. Reprinted with permission from the *Kansas City Star*

The author meeting Pope Benedict XVI at the Vatican, 2008.
Skelton's Family Collection

The author and Patty Skelton, wedding, 2009. Skelton's Family Collection

Skelton speaking at Warm
Springs, Georgia, 2009.
Courtesy of Roosevelt Warm Springs
Institute for Rehabilitation

The author with former secretary of defense Donald Rumsfeld, 2010.
Skelton's Family Collection

Armed Services Committee subcommittee chairmen (left to right): Gene Taylor, Solomon Ortiz, the author, Ellen Tauscher, Neil Abercrombie, Adam Smith, Marty Meehan, and Vic Snyder, 2010. Skelton's Family Collection

The author accepting the Sylvanus Thayer Award at West Point, 2012.
Photo by A. Battista; courtesy of the U.S. Military Academy at West Point

ATTACK ON AMERICA

ON THE MORNING of September 11, 2001, I was having breakfast with my longtime friend the federal judge Ortrie Smith and his wife, Kris, in the members' dining room along with Jack Pollard, my chief of staff. During our breakfast one of my staff told me that Susie had called with news of an explosion at the World Trade Center, and that an airplane had flown into it. I remembered a similar incident many years before at the end of World War II when a B-25 had flown into the Empire State Building. It had been bad, but it did not cause the building to crumble.

Before we left the dining room, we were made aware that the second tower had also been struck by an airplane. One airplane could be an accident, but that second plane changed everything. That was the moment we knew America was under attack. We went back to my office in the Rayburn Building to follow developments on CNN. About 9:45 another staffer rushed into the office, switched the channel, and said, "Ike, they've hit the Pentagon." And we heard later about the airplane that ended up in the field in Pennsylvania.

Shortly thereafter we were all ordered out of the Rayburn Building, and staff and members gathered in the street and the park behind the office buildings. Then the policemen told us to get out of there and start running because another plane was headed for the Capitol. At the time, seeing all these people gathered outside, I thought that this might be a perfect target. Fortunately, we all ended up over at my aide Whitney Frost's house nearby. That evening I went over to the Pentagon, where the fires were still burning. I got a briefing on what happened from three Navy officers and thereafter I went on home.

The next day I went to the floor of the House and spoke. I'm not sure I can say it any better today.

> Yesterday, people touched with evil brought hate and darkness
> to a land of light and freedom.
> I need not recount the details of their crimes. Those will forever
> be too familiar. I saw some of the damage firsthand at the Pentagon

last night. But the lives that they took, structures that they damaged, were not the true target.

Here is what they attacked:

The idealist nation that guarantees all of its people equality in law, and enforces it in deed.

The determined nation that time and again deploys its finest men and women to restore peace where it does not exist, and to maintain peace where it does.

The generous nation that gives more selfless support to other countries than any other in history.

The steadfast nation that is the first one called when disaster strikes, when tragedy erupts, when fortune's heart turns cold.

That is what they attacked.

They killed many Americans. But they did not kill—they could not kill our idealism, our determination, our generosity, our steadfastness.

They could not kill what makes America America.

Shortly after Pearl Harbor, the commander of Japanese forces, Admiral Isoroku Yamamoto, mused, "I fear we have roused a sleeping giant and filled him with a terrible resolve."

Those who assisted in perpetrating this deed should take those words to heart. Because resolve, too, is in our national character, as Admiral Yamamoto learned to his eternal regret.

We do not go weeping through the streets. We do not wail and beat our breasts. We just set about, methodically and with great certainty, to bring justice.

To those who devised and plotted this attack, I say: You will not find haven in the world of decent men and women. And the hearts of many others will be turned against you. If you believe, as the attackers did, that your own life has no value, America will be glad to cash that check. And any country that dares harbor you will pay its due.

At the same time, I hope that all Americans will remember another lesson of the Second World War: that not everyone who looks like our idea of the enemy actually is the enemy. Tragedy is no excuse to create new injustice.

Let me extend my sympathies and those of the Congress to all the families of the victims, and particularly those who were killed or wounded while responding to give aid to others. I ask prayers also for anyone with a loved one in uniform. Indeed, if there is a positive to be found in all of this, it is that Americans may rediscover their respect for our military forces.

Toward that end, and as a sign to our attackers of their futility, I ask that every American who has an American flag take it outside and fly it. And if you don't have one, I hope you'll get one.

We have been in a quiet war against terrorism for some time. The difference today is that now everyone knows it.

As today's debate will show, anyone hoping to sow discord or to profit from political division will be disappointed. There are no Republicans or Democrats today. There are only Americans; proud, somber, resolute, and looking forward.

I am proud to say that it was true—that our Congress and nation were as united then as at any point in my lifetime. And I am sad to say that the political unity did not last as long as it might have.

That incident changed America in many respects. First, it was obvious that we should have known a terrorist attack was going to come to pass. George Tenet, the CIA director, was quite concerned about it, as was Richard Clarke, the National Security Council expert on terrorism. After all, this was the latest in a string of attacks on Americans. It began with the 1993 attack on the World Trade Center by the blind cleric Omar Abdel-Rahman and his followers, who were captured and convicted. After that came the Khobar Towers in Saudi Arabia in 1996 and the twin embassy bombings in Africa in 1998, then the USS *Cole* in Yemen in 2000. As I said in my speech, our country had been in a quiet war against terrorism for some time. The difference on September 11 was that now everyone knew it.

None of this should have been a surprise, but frankly it changed America in many respects. It changed America visibly by causing us to think more and do more about security. For instance, you now see police officers with shotguns and automatic weapons on Capitol Hill as well as elsewhere. Twenty-two agencies were combined and put under a new department known as Homeland Security. There are stricter requirements for getting on an airplane, and security became a part of the American life, particularly if you were a traveler.

But more than that, I think it changed the attitude of Americans in many respects. It caused Americans from all backgrounds to realize that we're all on the same team, the American team, and I think to a great extent it helped eliminate feelings of some Americans being hyphenated Americans first— Irish-Americans, Italian-Americans, German-Americans, and the like. We became just flat-out Americans. I think that still continues today, and if anything can be called a positive effect of 9/11, I think that is it.

When asked how America has changed as a result of 9/11, I'm reminded of Chinese premier Zhou Enlai's comment when he was asked by Henry Kissinger, "What do you think about the French Revolution?" His answer was, "Too soon to tell." And we may find it still too soon to tell about the effects of 9/11. In my opinion, the best change is the increase in security and the way of thinking. It changed the notion of invulnerability that we have had for so long. America is no longer an island nation.

I am old enough to remember Pearl Harbor. Right after Pearl Harbor, everyone was willing to fight and to accept the rationing, the need for war bonds, and the importance of service in the military. I remember very well, along with everybody else in my fifth- and sixth-grade classes, having war stamp books. For each quarter, we would buy a stamp and put it in the book. When you got to $18.75 you got a $25 war bond. That was a big deal. Everybody did something to help. That attitude seems to have faded this time around.

A week or so later, I visited the scene of what had been the World Trade Center in New York City. It was an absolutely unforgettable and sad experience. About one hundred people were in the congressional delegation that visited the site. We took an Amtrak train from Union Station in Washington, D.C., to Penn Station in New York City. From there we took a bus to a ferry, which took us to the site near Battery Park at the southern tip of Manhattan Island. We could see the Statue of Liberty in the distance.

The destruction in lower Manhattan was unfathomable. Pictures from television and newspapers did not begin to do justice to the extent of the disaster, particularly with the knowledge that thousands of people had perished in the attack. One nearby building had parts of the World Trade Center stuck into its side like arrows.

I was impressed by Mayor Rudolph Giuliani, who took the delegation through the site and briefed us on the recovery efforts. Seeing the World Trade Center site in person prompted an indescribable anger, and I don't think there was a member of Congress there who didn't resolve to work, as a nation and with our allies throughout the world, to confront the terrorists and those individuals and nations that supported them.

I do want to say a word about the allies. They really stepped up. People question NATO and what we get out of it, but the first time they ever invoked Article 5 of the NATO Charter, to come to the mutual defense of a member, wasn't for a fight in Europe, but when we were attacked.

Government changed a lot after September 11. National security, a subject that had become a province of specialists and that received only occasional attention in the press, was suddenly the prime topic of conversation—and funding. An accompanying new phrase appeared: "Homeland security." It referred to the efforts to keep Americans safe inside our country, although it seemed to me that if the national security apparatus did its job, the bad guys wouldn't get close enough to require homeland security.

September 11 at least did allow us to begin to address the military end-strength problem. We didn't know where the fight against terror would take us, but we did know that if America's military was stretched to take care of Kosovo, then a global war on terror would require more troops. Earlier in the year, I had visited the USS *Harry S Truman* in Norfolk, the USS *Peleliu* in San Diego, Fort Campbell in Kentucky, and Whiteman Air Force Base. At each stop, I heard that our current forces were being pushed to their maximum and our military personnel and their families were strained. So I introduced a bill to increase the authorized level of manning for the services. The result was 4,800 more people for the Army, 3,757 for the Navy, and 1,795 for the Air Force. In addition, the administration had requested and received 2,400 additional Marines.

One of the singular aspects of the Armed Services committees is that every year since 1947, when the Department of Defense was created, Congress has successfully passed a defense authorization bill. That may sound like pretty inside baseball, but to my mind, if a committee isn't passing legislation pretty regularly, then you have to wonder about its effectiveness and whether it's worth serving on.

That isn't to say it's always easy. The Fiscal 2002 bill proved that. Most of the differences between the Senate and House versions of the bill had been resolved through the conference process, when the two committee staffs and then the members get together to make the necessary compromises to craft a single agreeable bill. The really hard issues wind up in the laps of what's called the "Big Four"—the chairmen and ranking members of the two committees.

In 2001 the bill was hard fought, and we nearly didn't get one. It even got physical. The chairman of the Senate Armed Services Committee, Carl Levin of Michigan, had what's called a "hideaway"—a little office in the Capitol that some senior members get. The Big Four were meeting there to resolve those final items on the Fiscal 2002 bill. At one point in the negotiations, not for the first time, things got a little heated. This was Bob Stump's first bill as chairman, and he took it seriously. At one point, Bob got so riled over being asked to compromise on some provision that he leaped from his chair and headed for the door. Senator John Warner, the ranking member, as courtly a man as you'd ever want to know, grabbed Bob by both arms, gently, and eased him back into the chair. Half an hour later, we had a bill.

The ranking member—the senior member of the minority party on a committee—doesn't always have to get physical to make a difference on a bill. But ranking members do play a vital role in conference. The chairmen of the respective committees are bound to defend the bill their committee crafted. Although each bill is created in partnership with the respective ranking member, the "rankings" are also the loyal opposition. So they have more flexibility in building bridges and helping to make compromises; they are in a real sense the swing votes in the Big Four. I enjoyed being ranking member and got real pleasure working with not only three different House chairmen but also our opposite numbers in the Senate, Carl Levin, John Warner, and John McCain. They were men of very different backgrounds and temperament, but completely devoted to our nation's defense.

In 2002, Congress took up the idea of creating a Department of Homeland Security, bringing together agencies scattered among government departments as far-flung as Customs, Transportation, and Treasury. At its core, the idea to bring these departments together echoed my earlier writing on homeland security consolidation. The problem was that the entities were being merged under a single management, but without an overarching strategy. It was as if we had decided to build a house and started pouring concrete and cutting lumber before we had the blueprint. In fact, when talking about the new department, I used the carpenter's adage, "measure twice, cut once." Without an overall strategy to guide our efforts, I thought we were cutting without even measuring once.

Don't get me wrong; there was no way DHS wasn't going to happen. I just thought that perhaps we should take a moment from the passions of the day and think about what we were doing before we did it. Like any of us, Congress works best when its brain is engaged before acting.

In President George W. Bush's State of the Union address in 2002, he made reference to an Axis of Evil, the axis being Iran, North Korea, and Iraq. Afterward, I went back to my office and told my staff, "That's a declaration of war against Iraq." The public discussion of Iraq continued, and the evidence of its alleged connection with the al Qaeda terrorist group was discussed openly. I was invited with a few others to the White House, where President Bush spoke to us about the "threat" of Iraq. It was pretty clear that he intended to act. Following the briefing, I asked the president, "What are you going to do once you get it?" He said, "We've been giving some thought to it." So had I. In response, I sent President Bush what has since become probably the most widely quoted letter of my career.*

I was concerned that we go about intervening in the right way, mindful of the lessons of history and the possible consequences. In the letter, I set out four issues that I thought essential considerations in resolving our issues with Iraq. My concerns were to emphasize multilateral action, understanding the implications of using military force for the United States' role in the Middle East and in the world; to have a plan for the rebuilding of the Iraqi government and society if armed conflict was necessary; to ensure that America's commitments to the war on terrorism and to other missions throughout the globe would be upheld; and to acknowledge that any occupation would require money and troops for many years to come. But the part that caught public attention was my questioning of whether the planning had included what we would do with Iraq after the United States' likely victory: "I have no doubt that

---

* The full text is in Appendix D at the back of this book.

our military would decisively defeat Iraq's forces and remove Saddam. But like the proverbial dog chasing the car down the road, we must consider what we would do after we caught it."

I take no joy in looking back at that statement—or the fact that the failure to plan for the aftermath made Iraq a quagmire that kept U.S. forces in the country through 2011, followed by an exit that didn't resolve the issues bedeviling that poor country. The U.S. withdrawal from Iraq reminded me of Santayana's aphorism that "Americans never solve their problems; they just amiably bid them good-bye."

I should say that the concerns so many members of Congress and others expressed about Iraq did not apply similarly to operations in Afghanistan. We knew that Osama bin Laden had trained there, with the acquiescence of the Taliban government. We had to get rid of al Qaeda, and if the Taliban were still around, they'd help al Qaeda breed again. We knew that a number of terrorist training camps remained there. And with Afghanistan's tribal structure, there wasn't the same question about what might happen if we successfully chased the Taliban from power. History did not favor the success of any outside power in Afghanistan, but at least it looked like we wouldn't have to prop the country up after we were done there. In Iraq, the military or government functionaries might have been able to keep the central government running, had we let them. But it didn't look like we would (and, in the end, we didn't.)

By the way, my letter did not get an answer from the White House—unless you count the National Security Council staffer who told me, "Well, Congressman, we really don't need your vote. We've got the votes."

And, in the end, they did get the votes. The House voted to authorize military action in October 2002. In speaking from the floor, I told the House that this was the third time I had stood at that podium with the question of military action in the balance. I noted that Winston Churchill's book *The Gathering Storm*, which detailed the world's slide into the Second World War, was subtitled, "How the English-Speaking Peoples, Through Their Unwisdom, Carelessness, and Good Nature, Allowed the Wicked to Rearm." Having defeated Saddam Hussein's Iraq once after its invasion of Kuwait, I was determined not to allow that particular evil regime to rearm with what our intelligence suggested were weapons of mass destruction. I ultimately supported authorizing action, noting that despite reservations, the question before the House was, "Shall we stay the hand of the miscreant? Or permit the world's worst government to brandish the world's worst weapons?" To me, based on the intelligence that was presented to us, the answer was a no-brainer. It was only later that we found out some of the intelligence wasn't so intelligent.

To be fair, Iraq was a hard nut to crack. Over the course of years, the U.S. intelligence community had moved to rely more and more on technical means of gathering intelligence and had deemphasized human intelligence, the often contradictory and laborious process of talking to human sources—people—who have seen what you want to know about with their own eyes. Not only did we not have that much human intelligence in Iraq, but some of the people we did rely on turned out to have their own agendas.

Another part of the Iraq problem was that for years, the U.S. military had deliberately configured itself to fight wars successfully, but not to manage their aftermaths. Post-conflict activities, what the military calls "phase four," were the target of considerable criticism from Congress and others in the 1990s. Post-conflict work came to be called "nation building" with some derision, as if it were below the dignity of the military and not in America's national interest. Our plans left such activities to our allies; the United States would fight the war and then leave the cleanup to others.

To me, this argument missed a significant point of history. What did the United States do in Germany and Japan after the Second World War? That was nation building of the most basic sort. It was in our national interest that those countries become both strong and friendly, and we were highly successful in that regard. We not only got them on their feet but also made them world leaders. We did that by occupation and encouragement and giving them our know-how, and we created alliances that have lasted more than sixty years. So to me, the lack of preparedness for Iraq, for what we would do after we caught the car, was another consequence of insufficiently studying history.

Another initiative that I thought overlooked history was President Bush's proposal to cut taxes during the war. His thought was that even though fighting the war was expensive, tax cuts would stimulate the economy and the postwar economic recovery would fill in the shortfall in revenues. That may make sense as far as it goes. But here's what it missed: A little while back, I asked the Congressional Research Service to give me a list of major American military deployments just during the time I had been in Congress. At that point, in about thirty years, there had been twelve major deployments. That's a military crisis about every three years. If you think you're going to have a financial recovery without another military conflict coming along, you're betting against history. But history has the house odds on its side, so one had best pay attention.

To help remedy that shortcoming for the future, I combined my love of reading military history with my passion for education by releasing a National Security Book List in 2003. The chiefs of the military services traditionally put out such a list each year, but they tended away from jointness as a subject, and some seemed short on history to me. So I assembled a list of fifty books that I had found tremendously useful in thinking about military subjects.[†]

Compiling that list, and especially reading all the books through the years, had led me to thinking about a lot of subjects to do with military history and

---

† You'll find that list at the end of this book, in Appendix B, so you can impress your friends with your expertise.

jointness. I enjoyed discussing those topics with various members of my staff and some of the military fellows who were assigned to my office from time to time, and some of them turned those discussions into essays. I was very pleased and gratified in 2004 when, to my surprise, the National Defense University published twelve of those essays as a book entitled *Whispers of Warriors*. Lieutenant General Mike Dunn was the president of NDU then, and he passed copies out to his students. It still gets cited in a lot of essays by students at the war colleges.

In September 2003, I went to Iraq with Gene Taylor, John Spratt, and a few other colleagues. This was one of the first congressional trips after the fighting had settled, and it came in that relatively brief calm before the Iraqi insurgency really got started; we could meet with Iraqis in the streets and move about without body armor or in fear of improvised explosive devices. Within a couple of months, that wasn't the case. That's part of why the House Armed Services Committee led the charge to acquire mine-resistant trucks and body armor for the forces in Iraq, often over the Pentagon's objections. It's an initiative I'm particularly proud of. I'm sure it saved countless lives.

Anyway, during the September trip, our group met with the American governor of Iraq, Paul Bremer. His official title was "Presidential Envoy," but whatever you called him, he was the man in charge. Bremer was accompanied by the military commander, Lieutenant General Ricardo Sanchez, who sported a spiffy pair of pearl-handled revolvers. We went into that meeting pretty open-minded. But we came out mad.

Bremer laid out the situation as he saw it, and it was going reasonably well right up until he got to the military part. Then I realized that he was discussing "acceptable American casualties," and it sure sounded to me like he considered the lives of American troops to be just part of the cost of doing business. It was just shockingly callous.

I am a respectful and civil man, and some of my colleagues would tell you I may usually be too much so. But I took him to task on that. And not just me; he pretty much lost the whole delegation at that point, Republican and Democrat. Moreover, it was obvious that General Sanchez didn't approve of what Bremer was saying—these were his kids that Bremer was talking about "acceptably" losing. But Sanchez sat there with his arms folded and didn't say much of anything.

I don't blame Sanchez much for what went on over there; I think he tried his best. But he was pretty new as a three-star, and he didn't know the Middle East well. I think whoever put him in charge either wanted someone that could be bossed around or was not the best judge of what the job needed.

Not too long after I got back, in 2004, a military reporter for the *Washington Post*, Tom Ricks, rode with me around the Fourth District to hear what Middle

America was thinking about, especially regarding Iraq. He sure got an earful, and overall I think he heard a lot more skepticism than he expected. That skepticism didn't translate into votes; in the fall, President Bush got 64 percent against John Kerry. But I got 66 percent, which showed that the people of the Fourth knew how to split a ticket.

Then my world fell apart. Just days following her sixty-ninth birthday, Susie suffered a sudden heart attack at our home in Lexington. She passed away at Research Hospital in Kansas City on August 23, 2005. Bill and Hillary Clinton were among the first to call. Her funeral was held at Wentworth with an overflowing turnout of mourners in attendance—the Joint Chiefs, quite a number of my congressional colleagues, former staffers, friends—and she was laid to rest in Machpelah Cemetery in Lexington.

Susie was the essence of a full life partner, the indispensable rock for generations of Skeltons while I was practicing law and politics. Susie was always patient as she was frequently thrust into family decision making for both of us—and what beautiful spirit, constant wisdom, uncommon sense, and unfailing love she brought to my life. She also enriched the lives of my colleagues and their families in the nation's capital, immersing herself in activities for legislative spouses and in service to Missourians.

After her death, Speaker Nancy Pelosi arranged for a tree to be planted on Capitol Hill in Susie's memory. Congressional Club friends attended and noted, among other things, that Susie presided over one of the largest memberships in the organization's history. And the *Kansas City Star* ran a beautiful article about Susie and the day, which is reprinted in the appendixes to this book.

Nor were those the only tributes. A garden was planted in her honor at the University of Missouri. The Air Force named a child development center at Whiteman Air Force Base for her. The sign in front of our church announcing each week's sermon was christened in her honor. And her name titles the award given to the outstanding female cadet at Wentworth.

For Susie, it was all just a matter of being a good neighbor, whether in Washington or in Missouri. She was a popular speaker at orientation seminars for new members of Congress and their families, served in Congressional Families for Drug-Free Youth, and was president and vice president of International Club II, which is an organization of the spouses of lawmakers and ambassadors.

With all of these "official" activities in Washington, Susie considered Lexington our real home. She played in a hometown bridge club, volunteered with community organizations, and served as both an elder in the First Christian Church of Lexington and as a Cub Scout den mother.

Susie added her own style as the official sponsor of the nuclear-powered attack submarine the USS *Jefferson City*. This role meant providing support for the vessel, including nice furnishings and gifts for the benefit of captain and crew. Susie christened the submarine with the traditional bottle of champagne.

She had considered using a bottle filled with Missouri River water to add a Show-Me State touch, but regulations didn't permit the substitution. She stayed in close touch with the *Jefferson City*'s plank-owner captain, Daryl Caudle, over the years, and he was a pallbearer at her funeral.

One of our very good hometown friends, Laveda Cross, told the *Kansas City Star* upon Susie's passing, "She always took time to check on several older residents who were 'less fortunate' . . . she never met a stranger. She was always so gracious, and she would stop and visit with everyone."

Our forty-four-year marriage had been absolutely heaven on Earth, at least for me. But one anecdote may sum it up best.

One time I bought a small sailboat, and we kept it up on Lake Jacomo in Jackson County. Susie and I had a lot of fun sailing that boat, but one day when we were heading for the other side of the lake, the wind died and we couldn't quite get there. So Susie climbed down and walked along the lake bottom pulling it by a rope, with all of these people standing on the shore staring at us. We made it to dry land and safe harbor, thanks to Susie. It was so symbolic of the heavy lifting that Susie did for our family throughout our marriage.

CHAIRMAN

IT WASN'T LONG after Susie's passing that I went to Iraq and was involved in the truck accident described at the beginning of this book. There is an amusing note to go with that story, though.

Much of the time, when congressmen travel, the committee staff member responsible for the subject we're learning about goes along too, both to learn and to provide expert insight. On this trip, a staffer named Miriam Wolf had been riding in a different truck in the same convoy.

After Tim Murphy and I had been loaded into the ambulance, she came up to the back door, put her hand on Tim's foot, and said, "Congressman Murphy, I want you to know I'm praying for you." Then she turned around and walked away.

I called out, "Hey, what about me?" Nope, she had already gone.

I teased her badly about that afterward, and she took it well. In response, she came by my office one day and gave me a framed picture of Pope Benedict.

That wasn't the only support I received. After Susie died, my colleagues Jo Ann Emerson, Diana DeGette, Carolyn Maloney, Ellen Tauscher, and Darlene Hooley took it upon themselves to form a sort of Ike Skelton Caucus, going out of their way to chat and look after me. It was very good of them, and did make things easier.

It was an election year in 2006, and the public was growing unhappy. The wars in Iraq and Afghanistan were showing no signs of ending, and the economy, which had been pretty strong, was starting to weaken. That summer, home prices dropped for the first time in ten years, and gasoline was steadily over three dollars a gallon for the first time. Come election time, the voters decided that twelve years of Republican control was long enough. Democrats took thirty-one Republican seats, enough to create a Democratic majority in the House.

Most press coverage focused on what this would mean for the president and that it would likely result in Nancy Pelosi becoming the first female Speaker of the House. But it also meant that I would become chairman of the Armed Services Committee in the 110th Congress.

I have to tell you, my emotions about that were pretty mixed. Of course, I had looked forward to the possibility of becoming chairman for many years, and particularly since I had become ranking member. I knew there was a lot we could do to strengthen our military. At the same time, I had seen just how much of a chairman's life was taken up with the mechanics of running the committee—overseeing staff, dealing with the committee members and the party leadership, and running hearings. It was clear that my accustomed luxury of thinking big, strategic thoughts would be challenged by the demands of the clock.

Hearings proved to be an even bigger change. Some members show up with a list of written questions, read the ones they have time to get through, and leave. I was accustomed to real give-and-take, asking questions, listening carefully to the answers, and using my prosecutorial experience to devise new questions to follow where the answers led. As chairman, though, there was a lot of business to do while the hearing was in progress. The committee counsel would advise me when a speaker was running over time, or which member should be recognized next. Staff would bring notes advising of calls from senior military and defense officials or the vote schedule on the floor of the House, which was no respecter of committee hearings regardless of their importance. Many times we convened a hearing on a matter of some significance, only to have six or seven floor votes gut the attendance and the time available. I knew that I could rely on my able staff, and the staff director, Erin Conaton, was first-rate. But for all its attractiveness, the chairmanship would not be without its complications.

Nonetheless, on January 4, 2007, I was proud to accept the chairmanship of the Armed Services Committee. Duncan Hunter, who was making the no-less-difficult transition from chair to ranking member, was unfailingly gracious and supportive. Duncan and I complemented each other well; he had a strong interest in hardware and technology, while I focused on the troops. I knew that together, we could do great things.

When I accepted the gavel as chairman, America's military faced several significant challenges. The wars in Iraq and Afghanistan were wearing our people and equipment out at a stunning rate. National Guardsmen and reservists, whose roles had previously been as a strategic reserve to be called upon in a prolonged, large conflict, were instead being used as an operational force and were rotating through the war zones as often as the active troops. That put a great strain on families as they sought to adapt to their service member's frequent, extended absences. Because a high proportion of Guardsmen and reservists are in public safety professions in peacetime, their home communities had to adapt as well.

At the same time, hardware, especially the Army and Marine Corps' helicopters, trucks, and Humvees, was wearing out at what the services estimated was five to nine times the peacetime rate. In particular, the fine sand in Iraq just abraded mechanical parts away. So at the same time that the services needed more money for all the extra people they were using, they also needed to rebuild or replace lots of equipment.

But money was an issue. The Department of Defense steadfastly refused to put war costs in its budget, preferring to use what's called supplemental funding to bill for operations in arrears. The advantage of supplementals was that because of accounting rules, the supplemental money was essentially off the budget—it didn't count against the DoD total when they went to budget for new planes or submarines, and it also didn't count for purposes of calculating each year's government deficit. But the actual dollars had to come from somewhere, and with the United States bringing in less money than it was spending, that money had to be borrowed, often on the international markets. The situation was exacerbated by the Bush administration's decision to cut taxes during a war, forcing us to borrow even more.

The tax cut was actually one part of a larger problem. Our country was at war, but Americans—aside from those in the military—weren't being asked to sacrifice. Quite the opposite: we were being told to shop and go about life as if nothing were different—oh, and in many cases, to pay even less in taxes. That all sounds pretty cushy, but it meant that for most people, the war was largely out of sight and mind, which meant that public understanding of and support for the military budget was much less than in past conflicts, and certainly less than those of us who support the military would hope.

On that note, I should point out that especially on the Armed Services Committee, but also in Congress as a whole, the divide on support for the military was much less a function of party than one of familiarity with military matters. It seemed to me that the more members knew about how the military worked, the more likely they were to support defense spending. There were more objections to the defense budgets from members sensitive to deficits and spending levels than from more liberal members.

As if that all weren't enough, the military was struggling with the implementation of the "Don't Ask, Don't Tell" rules governing troops' conduct. When President Clinton moved to open the military to acknowledged homosexuals, Congress was ready to go to war against the idea. I had had a hand in crafting the compromise that—imperfectly, to my mind—allowed gay Americans to serve, but the arrangement had come under increasing criticism and there were strong calls to do away with the rules. I understood the other side's arguments, but thought the disruption to our military in the middle of two wars would be too great to make that big a change at this time.

Each of these concerns, in its own way, contributed to problems with the military's readiness—the measure of how well the armed services are manned, trained, and equipped to complete the full range of missions necessary to defend our nation. In the fall of 2006, I had spoken on the floor of the House on just that subject, noting that the ground forces and their reserves faced a crisis with manpower and equipment shortages. Because of the high usage rates, DoD was having to cannibalize the equipment of nondeployed units and the National Guard. This cannibalization of equipment had left the Army without a single combat brigade in the continental United States ready for all of their wartime missions. Simply put, the war in Iraq was breaking the Army.

The Armed Services Committee had taken some steps in the Fiscal 2007 defense bill to help solve the problem, but it was really just a down payment on what the Army and Marine Corps estimated to be more than a $29 billion bill to repair or replace equipment damaged in Iraq and Afghanistan. And now that problem was right in my lap.

On top of all that, the administration wanted to send even more troops to Iraq. This "surge" seemed to me an extra burden on an Army and Marine Corps already stretched to breaking, and there hadn't been a good explanation of the military mission the extra twenty thousand troops would carry out.

I believed that we should have had far more troops at the beginning of the mission, as Eric Shinseki, the Army chief of staff at the time, had said, but that ship had sailed. Instead of increasing troop strength too late, we should have been undertaking some redeployment out of Iraq to show the American people and the Iraqi government and people that we were not there to stay forever, so the Iraqis would step up and take control of their own country.

Shinseki's successor as chief, Pete Schoomaker, testified before our committee that accelerated deployments decrease the amount of time available for forces to recuperate, train, and replace equipment. And that was a prescription for further lowering readiness. But I could see that like the situation in Iraq itself, the debate over the surge would be a long fight with a pretty good chance of ending poorly.

Not too long after that, I mentioned to a reporter from the *Kansas City Star* that since becoming chairman of the House Armed Services Committee, I seemed to be much smarter and much better looking. Of all things, he printed that! So I guess it must have been true.

While Iraq was getting all the headlines, the fight in Afghanistan was a forgotten war. We had underresourced that war for too long. In some ways, it was a tougher fight, and we knew that the real bad guys of 9/11 were probably still there. And having convinced NATO to join in the action there, it seemed to me a folly not to do a proper job. Our readiness problems could not be resolved as long as we continued to deploy in excess of one hundred thousand troops in Iraq. I advocated redeploying some of those troops home and putting others to work in Afghanistan, where they could do some real good. To me, that was a win-win proposition.

Strategically, I was concerned that all the attention to those wars might take our eye off the real long-range issues, China and Iran. China was clearly bidding to take the crown of global leader from our heads, as we had done to Britain early in the twentieth century, and Iran was, then as now, pursuing nuclear weapons pretty single-mindedly. When even the people charged with long-range strategic policy at the Pentagon and State Department were fixated on the sandy areas, I was quite concerned about the conflicts that might follow. About that time, speaking to students at Westminster College in Missouri, where Churchill had made his "Iron Curtain" speech, I noted:

> *Great leaders like Winston Churchill, or Harry Truman, were*
> *recognized as extraordinary not only because they led their nations*
> *through war, but because they mobilized nations, economies, and*
> *peoples. If the United States is to continue to be a great nation, we*
> *must attend to all the elements of that greatness. We do not wish*
> *to be consigned to the dustbin of history, after all. It has been said*
> *before the United States is the indispensable nation. That is so, and*
> *I believe that we should aspire that it remains so. History has shown*
> *us what happens when we disengage from the world. It took us two*
> *world wars to learn that lesson, but we understood it well enough to*
> *win the Cold War.*

"Attend to all the elements of that greatness." To me that included the economy, yes, and a ready military—but it also meant unifying our nation behind the war effort and requiring sacrifice of our people. As I see it, if the nation isn't willing to make some small sacrifices for a given cause, then we have little business asking our troops to risk the ultimate sacrifice.

Unity of purpose is a central element of American greatness. By that, I don't mean that we all have to agree on everything; healthy debate is essential to the success of a democracy. But I do believe in the motto "E pluribus unum," "From many, one." The goal of our debates should be to unify, to reconcile and reach a consensus on what to do. Increasingly, I see debate being used for the opposite effect, to drive wedges and widen fissures in the body politic. History does not show us many examples of divided nations succeeding. As I told the student body of the University of Central Missouri when they were so kind as to confer on me an honorary doctorate of laws, my friend, the late Congressman Fred Schwengel, told me about meeting then-Senator Harry S. Truman when Fred was a college student. Senator Truman told him, "Young man, if you want to be a good American, you must know your history." Amen.

Meanwhile, the readiness issues in the overburdened Army continued, with some deployed units not receiving significant items of military equipment until several weeks after arriving in the combat theater. That's why we focused on readiness in the Fiscal Year 2008 bill, with the usual bipartisan cooperation that marked the Armed Services Committee. Yes, we added substantial amounts of money for readiness, although funding is a short-term solution and more in the bailiwick of the Appropriations Committee. What an authorizing committee like Armed Services could do—and, in this bill, did—was to address some of the underlying structural issues that we believed were hurting our nation's readiness.

Chief among those was the enforced myopia of the budget process. Congress deals with one year's worth of money at a time, and readiness issues, as I mentioned, were mostly dealt with at that time through the supplemental funding process, which is to say in arrears. In short, we could pay to fix the problems that had popped up, but we didn't have a way to look forward and prevent them from happening in the years ahead. So we created a Defense Readiness Production Board to advise the secretary and the Congress on how to make significantly greater efforts to identify and fill critical readiness requirements across all of the military services. And, as importantly, we gave the Department of Defense resources and authority to act on the board's recommendations.

That August, I went to China. It was a very interesting trip, both for what we did and what we heard. Before going, a few of us had lunch with retired Major General Johnny Alison, who had been one of the Flying Tigers, the American volunteers who flew fighters under General Claire Chennault in China during the Second World War. One of the stops on the trip was to be Kunming, the Tigers' old base, and we wanted to hear firsthand of the American experiences there and meet the Chinese who had been such a part of the team. General Alison was an outstanding fellow; very humble, very gracious. Sadly, he passed away in 2011.

I remember hearing about Kunming in news reports during the war, and I very much looked forward to seeing it in person. When we got to Kunming, four of the Chinese who had worked with the Tigers met with us, and I thanked them for their contribution toward winning the war.

I'll never forget that scene—the whole area where we were meeting was covered in rose petals. (Kunming is the flower capital of China.) In the light rain, my colleague Randy Forbes and I planted a tree to commemorate U.S.-Chinese cooperation and to honor those on both sides who had fought to defeat tyranny. Listening to the Chinese officials' remarks, I noticed that when speaking of the Second World War, they never said the words "Japan" or "Japanese"—it was always "the aggressor." It was obvious that great animosity still existed between the two countries, which made me all the more interested in helping to craft a proper role for the United States in Asia.

In my remarks I saluted the Tigers and the American aid that flowed into Kunming from pilots flying over "the Hump"—the Himalayas. And I referred to the "spirit of Kunming," meaning a time and place when Americans and

Chinese worked together for a common goal. Well, the Chinese certainly took to that idea. I felt that we really understood each other there. I referenced the "spirit of Kunming" a few more times that trip, and every time, it delighted the Chinese in attendance.

In turn, they also mentioned some things at our various stops. In fact, this provided a contrast to a later trip to China. On this trip, although our hosts were friendly, the official Chinese remarks at every stop sounded like they came from the exact same set of points. Over and over, in very formal language, we heard about the Chinese attitude toward Taiwan, about China's peaceful intentions, and about how their country deserved the world's respect as an equal power. Someone had clearly decided that this was China's chance to introduce itself to the new chairman of the Armed Services Committee, and they wanted no ambiguity about who they were and what they wanted.

That suspicion was borne out on the later trip, when the uniformity of message disappeared. They had made their point; they guessed by now I had either understood it or was never going to. So things were much more informal and cordial the second time around. They even let us visit the Second Artillery Division, in charge of the Chinese strategic rocket forces and nuclear weapons. Those folks really rolled out the red carpet for us. We were briefed by a two-star general, which didn't bode well; our experience with Chinese officials was that they could dodge and deflect questions pretty adroitly. But this general politely answered every question put to him. That whole visit was quite unusual; as I found when I signed their guest book, the only American to visit previously was Secretary of Defense Donald Rumsfeld.

We had a more typical experience aboard a Chinese destroyer. The U.S. delegation sat on one side of the wardroom table, with the Chinese on the other. I asked the ship's captain how many destroyers the Chinese navy had. He looked at the political officer, then turned to me and said, "I don't know."

Two other stops on the itinerary provided impressive examples of modern China; one was expected, the other wasn't. The first was a shipyard where the Chinese workers produced a new container ship—every week. The other was a Christian church in Beijing. I was astounded by the sheer size of the congregation; there were at least a thousand worshipers there. Through the translation, I couldn't tell much difference between their service and what I was accustomed to in an American church. Afterward, the minister and assistant minister took our delegation out to a very fine restaurant, which seemed to be stretching the notion of a church supper somewhat.

I also accompanied Nancy Pelosi on her first trip as Speaker to visit American troops in Iraq and Afghanistan. She took the chairs of the relevant House committees: Jack Murtha, David Hobson, Tom Lantos, and Nita Lowey. Although congressional travel can be a heady experience, traveling with the Speaker adds a bit of formality and deference—from many people. One who clearly didn't subscribe to that idea was President Pervez Musharraf of Pakistan. We arrived for an 8 P.M. meeting. He let the delegation cool its heels for half an hour . . . then forty-five minutes . . . then an hour. Word has it that's a long-standing custom among Pakistani presidents, but if he was hoping to send us a message, it backfired. I never got the message, and he got a meeting with a bunch of peeved congressmen.

Speaker Pelosi had not been very directly involved in defense and foreign affairs before winning the Speakership. But on this trip, she showed a keen curiosity and asked a lot of good questions. She clearly understood the importance of the war effort and its effects on the American people and the Congress, and wanted to learn its full scope. In meetings, she showed deft diplomatic skills—which she also needed within her delegation. Jack Murtha, who ran defense appropriations, had already come out against the war in Iraq and had submitted a resolution to withdraw troops. Others of us supported the war effort, or thought that now that our forces were engaged, they deserved our backing. As when we were back in Washington, Nancy had to reconcile these views into coherent statements and policy, and it was fascinating to watch her do so on the fly and while learning the nuances herself.

To enhance her knowledge of military matters, I had already taken Speaker Pelosi on a separate trip to Whiteman Air Force Base; in fact, I think that was her first visit to a military base as Speaker. She did very well, both with the uniformed personnel and the local officials, and again showed a knack for asking the right questions. She may have been from California, but she understood the concept of "Show-Me."

Of course, American servicepeople understood "Show-Me" too. That was made plain on a trip I took to the Balkans, where American forces were helping to keep the peace in Kosovo and the former Yugoslavia. During a stop in Macedonia, my friend Gene Taylor, who always had an ear for enlisted troops and knew where to find them, tried to get into the small beer hall on the U.S. post. A young soldier denied him entry and groused that the place was shut down because some congressional delegation was visiting. Gene announced, "I *am* that delegation," and before long the doors were open and he was playing pool and lifting beers with the troops.

On another trip to Kosovo in 2008, I brought along fifty Missouri country hams. The Missouri National Guard was there in force, and their deputy commander, Colonel Randy Alewel, was part of a family in the country ham business, Alewel's Country Meats in Warrensburg. I spent a day with the Missouri Guard, but Colonel Alewel was nowhere to be seen . . . until suppertime. It turned out that because of his family background, he had taken charge of preparing the fifty hams himself. When I finally saw him, he was in an apron carrying the fruits of his labor. Now, that's a citizen-soldier.

But back to Washington. I mentioned earlier Bob Stump's experience with his first bill as chairman. My first one wasn't a whole lot easier, although that didn't have so much to do with the bill itself.

Congress had been looking at the issue of hate crimes for some years, and the House had passed a bill in 2007 adding attacks based on a person's sexual orientation or gender to the list of what could be considered hate crimes. President George W. Bush threatened to veto the bill if it came to him. Similar legislation died in committee in the Senate that year, so it looked like the president wouldn't get a bill to veto.

Then Senator Ted Kennedy proposed adding the hate crimes provisions as an amendment to our defense authorization bill, knowing that would put the president in a bind. Would he really veto the whole defense bill over this provision?

It looked like we'd find out. In September of 2007, the Senate voted to attach the hate crimes legislation to the defense bill—and sure enough, the president threatened a veto. Now, I wasn't opposed to the content of the hate crimes bill. I had voted for it in the House. And I understand the motivation to attach it to a bill that is usually pretty popular. But I thought it was wrong to attach it to our bill. It muddies the debate; you don't know if the bill is being passed on its own merits or just because it is attached to a more popular vehicle. And, of course, having the hate crimes language attached to our bill led to another contentious conference and made the prospect of a veto all the more real. I hadn't become chairman to make history by failing to pass a defense authorization bill for the first time in sixty years.

Ted Kennedy came and talked to members of the House committee about the hate crimes language. The passion he felt on the issue was clear. But in the end, the veto threat worked. The House leadership counted votes and realized that between members opposed to the hate crimes language and members opposed to the defense bill, there weren't enough votes to pass the conference report. So the hate crimes language was dropped in conference. (It passed two years later—yes, again attached to the defense bill—after the composition of the House changed.)

Also that September, the Senate Foreign Relations Committee held a series of hearings on Iraq. The main witness was the commander there, General David Petraeus. The content of the hearings was dramatic. But I also thought that they represented a breakdown in the acceptable roles and norms of civil-military relations. Congress had required the general to report publicly on the progress in Iraq, which I believe was appropriate. However, in the weeks leading up to the report, the president indicated that he would wait until the general's testimony to Congress before he would announce the next phase of his Iraq War policy. That hung General Petraeus out to dry. If the president's policy was going to be based on Petraeus's testimony, then that placed the burden of making U.S. war-related policy on the shoulders of a serving military officer. If it wasn't, then the president could announce a different path and render Petraeus irrelevant. Either way, the general was in a fix.

What should have happened? The president should have received General Petraeus's report in private first, and then issued his policy for the nation. It would then have been more than appropriate to hold a hearing with General Petraeus to determine if that civilian-determined war policy was supportable by the facts presented in his report and by his professional military judgment.

My thoughts on civil-military relations were compounded about this time by reports that retired General Ricardo Sanchez, the former commander in Iraq, had criticized the administration's policy in that war, calling it "a nightmare." That seemed odd to me, given General Sanchez's role in initially shaping the occupation of Iraq. But it also concerned me because of the specter of a military officer—even a retired one—criticizing his commander in chief.

Polls tell us that the American public holds the military in higher regard than any other profession. The people believe our military officers to be professional, competent, and trustworthy—because they are. We should regard anything that would threaten that perception as unwise.

Looking back in history, it was a defining moment in our Republic when General George Washington took off his uniform after the Revolution and resigned his military commission. That example gave the message to future Americans that the military is subservient to civilian authority. That's a lesson that stands with us today.

It is interesting to note that some generations of our military never participated in the political process; that is, they never voted in a political election. General George C. Marshall followed that standard, as did many for decades before and after he lived. However, there also have been elections in this country in which the military vote turned the political tide. For instance, the overwhelming soldier vote of 1864 reelected Abraham Lincoln for a second term.

Congress also holds the military in high regard. When we see a military uniform, we see a professional, and we have no reason not to expect that the call of duty is paramount within that individual when they appear before us. We are realists as well, and we understand that military officers are responsive to their chain of command, and that the chain of command extends to the commander in chief. But the execution of Congress's duty under Article I, Section 8 of the Constitution requires Congress to raise and maintain the military and exercise appropriate oversight, including oversight of the whole chain of command. That structure puts our most senior military officers in the middle of the tension between the executive and legislative branches. It seemed to me that in this case, though, Dave Petraeus had been unfairly thrust into that gap to put a respected, uniformed face on a policy that should have been led and defended by a civilian—the president of the United States.

In June 2008, that principle of civilian control was made starkly evident when Defense Secretary Gates fired the military and civilian heads of the Air Force. It was the first time that both leaders of a military service had been removed simultaneously. Of course, I knew both men. Air Force Secretary Mike Wynne had served in a number of senior positions and was a smart, big-picture thinker. General Buzz Moseley was an even more familiar face, as he had run the Air Force's congressional liaison office for a few years before becoming chief of staff. Buzz had been instrumental in working with the Base Closure and Realignment Commission to preserve the 131st Wing of the Missouri Air National Guard. At his initiation, the 131st converted from F-15 fighters to become the first Guard B-2 wing, in the process moving from St. Louis to Whiteman Air Force Base. Missouri owed him a lot.

Buzz and Mike were and are good men; you won't find two nicer guys. But a disturbing series of errors had happened on their watch, particularly concerning the Air Force's stewardship of nuclear weapons—a most grave and solemn trust. It culminated in an Air Force bomber flying over the United States with live nuclear weapons on board, something that should never happen. Worse yet, the Air Force didn't know where those weapons were when they were being flown around, and losing track of nukes is something no country can afford to do. There were enough black eyes to go around that I don't remember any of my colleagues objecting to Gates's action or casting it in any partisan light.

Of course, 2008 was also a presidential election year. Perhaps not surprisingly, given our relationship, I had decided to back Hillary Clinton, and when I told her so she seemed quite pleased. I thought her tremendous experience in the White House and the Senate would stand her and the country in good stead. She had been a good, centrist senator who got along well with people, contrary to some of her public image. By contrast, Senator Barack Obama came in not knowing that many people in Congress, particularly in the House. My district voted heavily for Hillary in the primary, so I knew I was on the right track. I think she would have been an outstanding president, although it certainly wouldn't have been easy; she would have still been a lightning rod to a number of the people who act so disagreeably toward President Obama, because she is a woman and her last name is Clinton.

At first, when Obama became the nominee, I didn't think he was going to win. But as his campaign went on, it was clear he was on a roll. On the other hand, John McCain, who had been my opposite number as ranking member of the Senate Armed Services Committee, had some rough going. His choice of Alaska governor Sarah Palin as a running mate didn't help. I'm still not sure why he chose her, other, perhaps, than for ideological balance, but almost no one knew her. She was a blank slate and didn't automatically bring along a bunch of votes. I think the election was up for grabs for a while, but Obama had a steamroller going. He hit the same responsive chord I had seen in the Fourth District—the desire for change. Of course, the idea of what change was needed differed widely from voter to voter, a fact that would come to haunt Obama after the election—and me two years later.

Once Senator Obama had secured the nomination, the Clinton supporters and staff seemed to fold into the campaign pretty well. As a result, the president had some pretty good people around him. And I thought it was a masterstroke that he was able to retain the services of Defense Secretary Bob Gates, who had done such a good job for President Bush.

I had occasion to join Secretary Gates and his wife, Becky, that September for a day filled with memories of my father and Susie. The Navy had decided to name its newest submarine the USS *Missouri*, like four ships of the line before it—including my father's battleship in the First World War. I reminded the audience in the yard at Quonset Point, Rhode Island, where the latest *Missouri*'s keel was laid, that Secretary Gates had served as an airman at Whiteman Air Force Base, and I was able to advise Becky Gates on the thrilling role of a ship's sponsor based on Susie's having done the same on the USS *Jefferson City*.

In late 2008, our nation was being rocked by a major upheaval unrelated to military affairs. The collapse of the home-mortgage and derivative markets had led to some spectacular failures on Wall Street and endangered the whole banking system. I wasn't much inclined to help the financiers who had staked ordinary Americans' financial security on high-risk and shady investments. But it seemed clear that if we did nothing, a serious recession was inevitable—if not a depression. A lot of the farmers in my district depended on credit for tractors and seed at planting time, to be repaid at harvest time. Their livelihoods were at stake. But for many of them, credit had already become almost impossible to get. I wasn't going to let Main Street crash because I was unhappy with Wall Street. So I supported the financial bailouts that restored stability to the markets. I took some heat for that in my campaign in 2008, but the voters came through once again.

Early in 2009, I turned my attention to strategy. Like most countries, we have a bad history of preparing for the last war rather than the next war. In my time in Congress, the United States fought in twelve conflicts, four of which I'd call major. And that's in thirty-four years. So we know another conflict is coming. We just don't know what it is. I wanted to practice as I preached and make sure I not only paid attention to the day-to-day details of the current conflicts in Iraq and Afghanistan but also looked ahead at America's coming challenges.

To me, it looked like a pretty daunting list:

- Restoring America's credibility in the world;
- Redeploying responsibly from Iraq;
- Renewing focus on Afghanistan;
- Restoring military readiness;
- Recruiting and maintaining a high-quality force;
- Dealing with the looming defense health care crisis;
- Striking a balance between near-term fixes and long-term modernization;
- Improving nonproliferation efforts;
- Developing a more comprehensive counterterrorism strategy;
- Reforming the interagency process (by which the various parts of government coordinated their work to achieve a common end);
- And, at the very top of my list, developing a clear strategy to guide national security policy in addressing all these other tasks.

It seemed to me that the new administration had a pretty full plate right there. I had recommended to President Obama that he convene a group of experts with differing views, as President Eisenhower had done with the Solarium Project, to develop a comprehensive strategy. The good news was that President Obama, Secretary Gates, and the national security adviser, General Jim Jones, understood the need for such a strategy and were at work.

Of course, at the same time that we faced all those challenges, U.S. forces continued to fight wars in Iraq and Afghanistan; the security situation in Pakistan was uncertain and troubling; pirates off the coast of East Africa posed a new threat not just to the United States but to commerce of all nations; oh, and the global economy was in some real hurt, causing hardship for millions of people. Nobody ever said it was easy being president.

Looking beyond Iraq and Afghanistan, it was clear to me that future American security interests would center on Asia. Madeleine Bordallo, the delegate from Guam and a member of the Armed Services Committee, and her predecessor, Bob Underwood, who had become president of the University of Guam, invited me to their island, which had grown in importance to the United States as an outpost from which to monitor and, if necessary, counter threats in the Pacific.

It seemed to me that the rise of China and the simultaneous emergence of India, coupled with a reemergent Russia and shifting internal politics in Pakistan and Bangladesh, gave the United States an opportunity to engage with these nations rather than just to see them as implacable rivals. Some of my colleagues in the Congress had been arguing for a retreat, a focus on the American homeland and domestic interests at the cost of our engagement overseas. But it seemed to me that the surest way to keep your home safe was to be on the best terms possible with your neighbors—and in a world connected through finance, information, and non-national threats, every country was in our neighborhood. No part of the globe could truthfully be said to be beyond the sphere of America's national interest. As I told my audience on Guam, *U.S. world leadership should be earned by virtue of the esteem other nations hold for us, engendered by our productivity and moral leadership, and not through a self-justifying hegemony which views the peaceful rise of other nations as an inherent threat.*

We also needed to maintain our strength. Particularly in the Pacific, that meant naval forces. But the U.S. Navy had shrunk to the smallest fleet since my father served aboard the *Missouri*, and I hadn't noticed the oceans getting any smaller. The class of smaller ships that I had advocated had evolved into the Littoral Combat Ship program, but none of those had yet made it to sea.

I have heard it said that the United States may no longer need to maintain a fleet to guarantee freedom of the seas. After all, the argument goes, when our nation was a massive manufacturing power and net exporter, our economy depended on being able to ship goods to hungry markets overseas. But now that the United States is a net importer, freedom of the seas is far more important to nations like China. An interruption in the sea lanes might crimp America's supply of cheap toasters, toys, and televisions, but it would cause those exporting nations real harm. So why should we foot the bill?

I believe that a viable fleet is part and parcel of being the world's indispensable nation. As I said, America has national interests everywhere in the world; that means we need to be able to project American power anywhere, at the time and place of our choosing. From an economic standpoint, the flow of oil alone, on which so much of our economy depends, is sound reason to maintain freedom of the seas. Iran's periodic threats to close the Strait of Hormuz are just one example of how the world community sees the flow of oil as essential not only to the United States' economy but also to its standing in the world. They see the value of command of the sea. I believe we should too.

While this was going on, I had the committee revisit one of my favorite subjects, and one that I had led in examining under Les Aspin's chairmanship: the professional education of our military. At my urging, Dr. Vic Snyder of Arkansas, the chairman of our Oversight and Investigations Subcommittee, convened a twenty-years-on review of how the military incorporated the committee's earlier work. This became a comprehensive series of hearings looking at the missions of the service schools, their curricula, the quality of faculty, students, and staff, and the resources available to keep providing exceptional leaders to America's military.

I know that to a lot of people, the subject of professional military education is as interesting as paint drying, and sitting through hearings on it may be worse. By having the subcommittee undertake this review, I hoped to expose a younger generation of members to the importance of the issue and have them carry the banner forward. Also, the full committee deals with broad strategic issues, and while it may get into details as need be, it's the subcommittees that focus on mastering arcane issues. I had some really sharp subcommittee chairmen, and I liked to let them run in their areas of expertise.

Overall, though, I wanted the committee to focus on the troops. The military is made up of people. We have to make sure they are high-quality, that they are trained well, and that they are led by good officers who have been exposed to strong, creative thinking. What use would it be to have the finest weaponry in the world and to be led by a group of second-raters?

Of course, it's easier to maintain a top-notch corps of leaders if there are more qualified candidates to choose from. As a subcommittee chair in the 1990s, I had pushed to open more military specialties to women and led the legislation that placed women aboard ships. I continued that push as chairman. Interestingly, when I got out to the field to speak with enlisted male soldiers, sailors, airmen, and Marines, they seemed to accept serving alongside women. It was the brass who more often made a fuss.

Another issue that provided constant controversy during my chairmanship was the question of how to handle and prosecute detainees captured during the wars in Iraq and Afghanistan and in other anti-terror engagements. The issue wasn't what to do with ordinary soldiers, but rather with those we believed to be involved with al Qaeda and its various plots against America. The military prison at Guantanamo Bay, Cuba, was the focus of these debates, but many were of a legal-process nature: What rights should the prisoners have? Should they be treated as prisoners of war or as criminals? Should their trials be in a military system, civilian, or some blend?

Once again, I found history to be a useful guide. In 1942, four Germans left a submarine and landed on Ponte Vedra Beach, Florida, which at that time was an isolated area. Another four landed on Long Island. All eight were arrested and put on trial. A reserve Army colonel named Carl Ristine was recalled to active duty and assigned to represent one of the Germans, George John Dasch. I was quite familiar with the case because at the time, Ristine was a prominent attorney in—you guessed it—Lexington, Missouri, and my father spoke well of him.

President Roosevelt established a military commission to hear the cases of the eight Germans. Six were sentenced to death; Dasch and one other instead received long prison sentences in recognition of the fact that they had turned themselves in. But what seemed most on point to me is that the Supreme Court, in a case called *Ex parte Quirin*, held that the military commission was a constitutional venue in which to try these crimes. It described the difference between uniformed military and those who seek, in civilian clothes, to destroy the life and property of those they consider enemies. To me, this set a strong precedent for military commissions to try al Qaeda terrorists. Although we addressed this issue in more than one defense authorization bill, the debate continues today, as do the trials.

We also undertook a review of acquisition. The Pentagon is famous for the complications in its weapons programs, and one can understand that stretching technology to get the ultimate edge can yield surprises and difficulties. Increasingly, the process of acquisition was interfering with getting anything new into the field. And over the years, Congress had actually cut oversight and eliminated a lot of positions for experienced professionals to make the process work. I asked Rob Andrews, from New Jersey, to head up a panel to review acquisition and make real changes. The result was the Weapons Systems Acquisition Reform Act of 2009, and although it's still early, I believe we made a significant improvement on the hardware side to complement our focus on the troops. The signed front page of the bill hangs on my wall at home today.

During a return visit to Warm Springs in August 2009, I was privileged to sleep in the bedroom of the first cottage President Roosevelt called his home away from home there. A push-button to signal for assistance that was installed for the president still rests on the bedside table. This cottage was the filming location for the award-winning HBO movie *Warm Springs*, which is about Mr. and Mrs. Roosevelt's life-changing experiences in the community where their memories are still revered.

I have been a frequent visitor to Warm Springs through the years, returning for medical checkups and for fund-raising events. Strolling through the Foundation grounds, my memories come flooding back—I remember the events, people, and places that were instrumental to the recovery of a teenaged Missourian who arrived shattered in both body and spirit. Even with society's eventual medical victories against polio, it makes me so proud that the Institute continues its mission of physical rehabilitation, so that other patients today may benefit from the Warm Springs experience.

Today the Little White House is still a much-visited shrine to President Roosevelt. Visitors may walk the same floorboards upon which his special wheelchair rolled along, while he trailed a plume of smoke from his cigarette held aloft in its jaunty holder. They may stand on the back terrace, which has the feel of the jutting bow of a battleship, and still see the narrow wooden shelters where Marine guards stood at attention beneath security floodlights mounted high in the pine trees.

It was during that same visit that the Warm Springs Foundation honored me by placing a brass plaque bearing my name on one of the white columns lining the pleasant strollways leading from the main lobby in Georgia Hall. I was able to stand with two of my sons and two granddaughters at a place where I confronted the most serious challenge of my young life.

It all started with that man with a positive outlook, Franklin Roosevelt. In Warm Springs, what seemed a ridiculous dream to some was seen by President Roosevelt as an achievable goal—giving hope to the hopeless. He carried that same strength of vision to the unprecedented burdens of his presidency in peace and war.

In that dusty corner of rural Georgia, where others saw only a dilapidated resort, President Roosevelt saw and built medical facilities. Where others saw cripples and expressed pity or cruel indifference, President Roosevelt saw beautiful people full of life and potential to be fulfilled. His positive outlook and faith in his mission pervaded the place long after his passing.

When I visited President Roosevelt's Little White House as a teenaged Warm Springs patient, I noted the framed display of an unfinished speech he was to have delivered on April 13, 1945, at an event honoring the memory of Thomas Jefferson. The speech was typed, but President Roosevelt's handwritten edits were scattered throughout the text.

I laboriously copied the speech in longhand on a Big Chief tablet, only to learn later that the printed text was for sale in the gift shop. At the speech's conclusion, added in Mr. Roosevelt's own hand, was the distillation of the very spirit of Warm Springs, and of the America that President Roosevelt would not live to see after the guns of World War II fell silent:

> *The only limit to our realization of tomorrow will be our doubts of today. Let us move forward with strong and active faith.*

And it was with a strong and active faith that I prepared to once again go before the voters in 2010.

TUESDAY TSUNAMI OF 2010

I BRIEFLY CONSIDERED not running for an eighteenth term, but with my unfinished work as Armed Services Committee chairman and the ongoing severe conflicts in the Middle East, I did not feel it was time to abandon my efforts to support our troops and our strategy. So I decided to run once again in the 2010 general election.

Unquestionably, I knew times were hard for Missourians because I was back in the Fourth Congressional District several times every month and I stayed in touch, though political critics blasted me with accusations of not listening. In truth, I listened closely—but I was never one to stage a three-ring circus for the TV cameras when a quiet one-on-one conversation could allow me to hear, think, and try to find ways to help.

Traveling the Fourth in 2009, I found anger simmering and sometimes flaring at the Democrats who had won total congressional and executive branch control in Washington the previous November with bold promises of change. The people were impatient to have change for the better, change they could see, change that would ease their anxieties, put them to work, and restore their faith that brighter days were ahead. Such positive change couldn't happen overnight, but the people were in no mood for excuses.

I cannot say I blame them; it was never easy to look into the worried eyes of a worker who had lost a job when a plant's payroll constricted, or of a family provider worried about health insurance and medical costs, or of the owner of a multigenerational family business who was going broke. But I did listen, and I worked hard to respond for the good of the Fourth District.

During my tenure in Congress, legislation about inflation, debt, unemployment, employment, taxes, and government spending has been enacted, rewritten, reversed, repealed, ignored, and reenacted. Much has been said about economics, and almost nothing has been said about economics that wasn't true at one point or another.

Here's one truth, in my experience: Nobody knows everything about economics, and while a few people may know quite a bit more than others, it's usually hard in the midst of economic crisis to recognize the oracles. For every economic position, it seemed through the years that there was an opposing idea or argument carrying just as much absence of proof or just as many assertions of inevitability. But we are not ignorant in terms of real-life experiences—we know our history. One truth I came to recognize from historical experience was that a strong and growing permanent military presence in Missouri meant steady incomes, stable civilian employment, and hundreds of millions of dollars in regional economic benefits, all in pursuit of keeping our nation secure militarily.

The House Armed Services Committee, the most bipartisan committee in Congress, started the 2009 congressional session with continued strong support across the board for the military, along with major weapons system reform legislation. I was now two years into the Armed Services chairmanship that I had worked an entire career to achieve. Duncan Hunter had retired at the end of 2008, and his successor as ranking Republican member, my friend John McHugh of New York, was chosen by President Obama to serve as secretary of the Army. Howard "Buck" McKeon of California, who also worked with me across party lines to sustain our committee's well-earned reputation for bipartisan results, succeeded John as ranking GOP member.

People turned out in huge numbers to see Barack Obama sworn in as president in January 2009. But for all the excitement surrounding America's quadrennial swearing-in pageantry, what marked it for me, as always, was the peaceful transition of power from one party to another, an event that sets our nation apart. I first experienced this excitement in person at President Truman's 1949 inaugural. Sixty years later, there was much optimism about the promise of the new administration and our young chief executive. Frankly, I shared that optimism because in my realm of special interest, national security, President Obama made excellent early choices in retaining Bob Gates as secretary of defense and naming his former campaign rival Hillary Clinton as secretary of state.

But the recession that began during President George W. Bush's tenure persisted, as did generalized unease—indeed, unrest—across the nation. The president recommended and the Congress passed legislation that was meant to help stabilize the economy and bring down unemployment. But the recession continued and uneasiness became the norm. Congress was the target of much of the anger, and I felt the heat.

During August 2009, after President Obama began his campaign to pass a sweeping health care overhaul, that legislation became the lightning rod for unrest, as evidenced by protests, angry telephone calls, and letters and e-mails against the proposal. My staff and I took a great deal of time to study the health care legislation pushed by my own party leadership, and I concluded it was not a good bill. So I voted against both the House and Senate versions, mainly because they stripped some $228 million from Medicare over a period of five years. I believed that would hurt Missouri's rural hospitals that relied heavily on Medicare.

Once again, I was swimming against the waves churned by my own political party, including the House Speaker and the president. Little did I realize that even though I was swimming in what I still believe to have been the right direction for my district in opposing my party's health care bill, a political tidal wave was coming. Nothing would stop that wave, just over a year later, from sweeping away congressional Democrats across the ideological spectrum, but specifically on the middle ground, which I still consider the high ground.

Two relatively well-known Republicans announced and subsequently filed for Congress in the Fourth District: Vicky Hartzler, a former state representative and a onetime teacher whose family owned farm implement companies, and Bill Stouffer, a sitting state senator and farmer. Their common campaign theme was that I was too close to Speaker Pelosi, who was carrying the water for President Obama.

Both tried to paint me as a liberal legislator, my lengthy overall moderate-to-conservative record notwithstanding. Vicky Hartzler won the GOP primary and the anti-Pelosi drumbeat continued, even though I had opposed many national Democratic legislative priorities, such as the health care overhaul, because I believed they would wind up hurting the Missourians I had long represented and cared about very deeply.

In the 2010 campaign, I had excellent assistance from seasoned campaign consultants Ken Morley and David Doak. My longtime pollster Michael Rowan assisted with speeches and research. Bright new members of the campaign team put us into the online world of social media through Facebook and Twitter. We ran thousands of advertisements. The ground game to get out the vote was primed. Red, white, and blue "Ike Skelton" signs were numerous—but we also noticed Hartzler signs in formerly friendly territory for me.

Sometimes, you don't see a loss coming. That point was driven home to me when Congressman John Murtha of Pennsylvania died in February. Jack Murtha had been a friend for more than thirty years. We didn't always agree, but you always knew that his heart was in every fight he took on. He was a bull of a man, a former Marine, and the key appropriator on defense—if you needed to get something done, Jack was the man to see. He had gone into the hospital for a relatively minor procedure, but complications arose and we lost him, just like that.

As the year went on, my attention was increasingly divided. The Fourth District race remained quite close, not only demanding my presence there even more frequently than usual but also increasing the amount of time needed for meetings and calls on strategy, tactics, and fund-raising.

At the same time, we were starting to see some real progress in Afghanistan. I had written to President Obama, urging him to adopt a counterinsurgency strategy there. After eight long years with no strategy in that conflict, Obama had adopted the recommendation, backed with some real muscle—an additional thirty thousand troops. This was different from the Iraq surge, not only because Congress had acted to fix many of the readiness issues that mitigated against the earlier surge, but also because we had already begun to reduce commitments in Iraq and, concomitantly, the stress on the Army and Marine Corps.

That comprehensive strategy was vital to preventing terrorism. Just as you cannot effectively rid your backyard of poison ivy by just cutting off all the leaves, we couldn't effectively destroy terrorist cells unless we took them out by the roots, cutting off the supply of recruits that feeds them. In addition to ramping up our missions to capture and kill terrorists, the president's new strategy also placed a greater emphasis on preventing the recruitment of violent extremists.

It's easy to look at the wars in Iraq and Afghanistan as a throwback to the manpower-intensive, foot-soldier days of the Second World War. But that would overlook a number of revolutions the United States has brought to bear in the ways it wages war.

One of those new technologies is the unmanned aerial vehicle, often called "drones." They have the endurance that manned aircraft can lack, patiently waiting for a target to reveal itself to the operator sometimes half a world away. They are operated from Creech Air Force Base in Nevada, and now out of Whiteman Air Force Base as well. I worked really hard in 2010 to get them assigned there, urging the Air Force, in particular the Air Force chief of staff, Norty Schwartz, and finally he allowed me to announce that they were coming. Whiteman will just do the control part; we won't have any UAVs there at all. But I think it's a masterstroke to be able to use them correctly, and for now at least it's an asymmetrical technological advantage for the United States. They seem to be working—in 2009 and 2010 alone, more than six hundred terrorists were eliminated through drone strikes. The technology is such that you can do great damage to an enemy thousands upon thousands of miles away, and do it very precisely, so you hit just what you want to hit. You don't have to bomb a whole block to hit one truck. I'm sure, as with any invention, that at some point technology and defenses will be found to counter them. But by then, we should be on to the next thing. That's what America does.

At times, the biggest challenge to success in Afghanistan seemed to be the Congress. As the fiscal 2011 appropriations process went on, amendments appeared that would have cut funding, troop levels, or both just when we were finally starting to get ahead, with a clear strategy and good command team. I spent a lot of time, both on the floor and behind the scenes, working to head off these ill-considered amendments. In a very real sense, I was fighting a two-front war—one in Missouri, another in Washington.

Sometimes, it seemed like even more than two fronts. In March, the House voted on the president's health care reform bill. Officially, it was called the

Affordable Care Act, although people who didn't like it tagged it with the derisive name "Obamacare." I had opposed the bill in the House, because it proposed to cut Medicare reimbursements to rural hospitals and health care clinics. But since that vote, the Senate had passed its version, which was worse, because it didn't recognize that the military health system, TRICARE, would meet the bill's minimum requirements for individual health insurance coverage. That meant that troops might be forced to purchase additional medical coverage to meet the health care bill's mandates.

I had introduced a bill to change that, declaring that the military medical system met the minimum coverage requirements. Happily, the House supported my legislation, even though it wasn't enough of a change to get me to support the whole bill.

The defense authorization bill also took an unprecedented turn when we took it to the full House in May. The bill itself was not unpopular. But a number of my Democratic colleagues cosponsored an amendment to repeal the "Don't Ask, Don't Tell" policy. The military had agreed to a thorough review of that policy, and it wasn't finished; in fact, Secretary Gates and Admiral Mullen asked Congress to defer any legislative action on the policy until they were done. This seemed a reasonable and responsible request, and I respected it. A majority of the House disagreed with me, though, and passed the amendment. That led to one of those uniquely congressional dilemmas: Should I vote for the defense bill even though it had now been changed in a way I thought ill-advised, or should I oppose a bill that I (and my committee) had labored on for months? In a time of war, I could not justify voting against funding the troops and the many other good initiatives in the bill, so I swallowed hard and voted Aye.

Back home, voter unhappiness rose, my polling leads eroded, and media analysts called the race a toss-up, just two years after I was returned to Congress with 68 percent of the vote. Less than two weeks before Election Day, the *Kansas City Star* trumpeted on its front page: "U.S. Rep. Ike Skelton is in the political fight of his life."

And I was, too. Part of the trouble is that defense, which hadn't been a seriously partisan issue before, had become very political. One sign of that came in June, when the Pentagon held a ceremony to unveil the official portrait of former Secretary Donald Rumsfeld. It turned out that I was the only Democrat present. All the rest were either military or military retirees or Republican officeholders. I sat next to former Senator Ted Stevens, who sadly was killed in an airplane crash in Alaska just a few weeks after the ceremony.

I knew I wasn't the only Democrat in the Fourth District, but the Republicans' closing-stretch message was pretty simple—I had served well, but too long. That message evidently clicked with anxious voters, even though my accumulated seniority had helped deliver vast expansions of military investment and employment across the district. I felt I had earned the honor conveyed by my campaign slogan, "The Soldiers' Congressman." That feeling was reinforced in countless campaign visits with uniformed service members, veterans, widows, dependents, civilian defense personnel, and community leaders.

From Afghanistan came word of a dark cloud that wound up having a silver lining. General Stan McChrystal, the commander there, had made some ill-advised remarks about the nation's leaders with a *Rolling Stone* reporter in the room. I thought highly of McChrystal, and I could sure understand that one can make an offhand comment in front of a reporter without thinking about it. But just as I believed civilians should respect the military, the military had to recognize civilian control—and, moreover, be seen to be doing it. So I understood when the president decided to relieve McChrystal, but I thought it was a terrible time for a distraction in Afghanistan.

The president decided to name Dave Petraeus, who had been booted upstairs to run Central Command, as McChrystal's successor. Well, Dave Petraeus was, no question, the best we had—a scholar-soldier who knew that part of the world as well as anybody. His appointment gave me some hope that for all its complications, Afghanistan would turn out well in the end.

And Afghanistan wasn't the only place where we hoped things would turn out well despite signs to the contrary. Election Day was upon us.

On my own campaign trail, Election Day 2010 started just after 6 A.M. when Patty and I voted at the Methodist Church in Lexington. Then I campaigned across the district in Marshall, Sedalia, Warrensburg, and Odessa. We found volunteers were working hard, with folks walking into local Democratic headquarters volunteering to make calls to voters.

Here I must stop for a moment and pay special tribute to Patty Skelton, whom I had married in August 2009. My dear wife knowingly married a politician, but she could not have known the arduous nature of a tough campaign. To her everlasting credit, she joined me on the trail, keeping long hours, traveling many miles, and shaking hands and chatting with voters. She was a true trouper and campaigned like an old pro—and when I was traveling many long days, she kept the home fires burning to welcome me back. I'll have much more to say about her later.

Across my native Midwest, tornado shelters—usually earthen dugouts with flap-like wooden doors that can be bolted snugly from the inside—are familiar sights in backyards and on farms. Darkening skies are one tip-off that conditions are ripe for twisters. And when tornadoes come, they travel with indiscriminate, zigzagging force across towns and pastures. The loud roaring noise like a freight train lasts just seconds, then the funnel clouds spin away. Prayerful folks eventually emerge from the storm shelters to behold destruction—and wonder why one home was mostly spared while another mere yards away was flattened.

What happened on November 2, 2010, was not just an Election Day tornado with scattered candidate casualties. It could be more accurately described as a political tsunami, stretching with particular force across the South and the Midwest, sweeping away my campaign and those of more than sixty other House Democrats from across the ideological spectrum.

The Democrats who lost races that day included ten members of the House Armed Services Committee. The Congressional Research Service reports those ten members had a combined total of 126 years of service on the House's key committee dealing with military and national security policies.

Of course the November 2010 elections were a personal and political loss for those individual members, including myself—but let us not wallow in self-pity, because the sun still came up the next morning, and as it rose around the globe, it shone on U.S. military men and women still standing as our devoted guardians at home and across faraway lands, oceans, and skies.

In my own view, of far greater significance was the loss to the nation of those Democratic Armed Services Committee members with an average service of more than a dozen years each of intense involvement with defense issues. And that doesn't count my former colleagues who chose either to retire before the election or to seek other offices.

This is not meant to question or challenge in any way the knowledge, diligence, or competence of veteran committee members from the Republican side of the aisle, many of whom I still count as friends. No—these comments are intended for my fellow Democrats who are still in Congress.

Why? Because with seniority comes more than just the ability to ask questions first. With seniority comes perspective, judgment, and experience—all of which contribute to wisdom regarding matters of our nation's security and safety. I fear that for the Democrats, Election Day 2010 dealt a critical blow to that depth of wisdom and experience. It also diminished our ability to expose as phony any perception that Democrats are weak on national defense.

The principle of governing from the center of the political spectrum also took a beating in the 2010 elections. In the House of Representatives, the political center has been hollowed out like at no other time in my memory. Just as our own houses must be built with not only right and left walls but also sturdy, load-bearing support in the center, the U.S. House needs a strong center too, but it came out of the 2010 political battles supported at either extreme but teetering in the weakened center.

The center is where we successfully govern. I know—that's hard to contemplate in this era of split-screen campaign season debates that seem to have evolved into 24/7, year-round split-screen arguments. But the center is where we find compromise. The center is where we find consensus for the American people, who put us into Congress to find such consensus and get results.

To be sure, sometimes the results are incremental, or our efforts just fall short. In their everyday lives, the people care much less about partisan ideology than about elected officials delivering results that make life a little easier—or in the case of the various legislative panels on military affairs, that make the peoples' lives more secure from military threats.

Back in Lexington, my family gathered, and after the polls closed at 7 P.M., we headed to the Victorian Peddler restaurant downtown, just across the street from the courthouse where I served in my first elected office as prosecuting attorney. When we walked into the restaurant and saw so many old friends and supporters, we truly felt that while the outcome would be close, most voters would stay with me.

But as we watched election returns coming in on laptop computers, counties across the Fourth District showed up in Republican red more often than in Democratic blue. And nationally, Democrats were losing the House majority after four years in control. When I saw that only Ray County north of the Missouri River had Fourth District results still uncounted and realized that my many friends there couldn't close the lead built up by Mrs. Hartzler, I decided to end the suspense. I called the apparent congresswoman-elect to congratulate her and pledge a smooth transition.

Then, with my family gathered around, I spoke to my supporters, some weeping, some shaken, all somewhat stunned. I began speaking, but I must confess that I was on weary autopilot after the exhausting campaign, so I will rely on the following transcript taken from KMBC-TV's video of the concession speech:

> *In 1956 a political career began. And it's been wonderful wonderful years from the time I was prosecuting attorney, practicing law, state senator, and now a member of Congress for 34 years. And I might also say that for my entire life, I have had a love affair with the state of Missouri. That love affair continues.*
>
> *I wish to tell you that I just called Vicky Hartzler a moment ago, congratulated her, and based upon the numbers that I have, she appears to be the winner of the Fourth Congressional District contest. I wished her well and I told her that I am instructing my staff to cooperate fully to make the transition smooth. That's important to her, it's important to me and it's important to all the folks of the Fourth Congressional District.*
>
> *Let me add that representing the people in this district and the State of Missouri has been the political highlight of my life. I enjoyed what I did. We still have a few days to go and I will continue my term as chairman of the Armed Services Committee, to make sure that the young men and young women in uniform will be well taken care of in their arduous task of fighting terrorism throughout the world.*
>
> *I cannot thank my neighbors, my friends, my supporters enough—they're wonderful. No one in political life has had greater friendship or support than I, and I will always be grateful.*

My friends applauded warmly, we lingered briefly to acknowledge their genuine affection, hugs, handshakes, and tears, and then we broke up the party and headed for the comfort of home on Franklin Avenue.

The phone was ringing when we walked in. We've always had a listed phone number and never used an answering machine, so our habit is to pick up the phone and say hello. On this crisp late Tuesday evening in November, the well-meaning callers were grasping for words, but their general tone was surprise and of course sympathy.

To these callers, I could only cite 2 Timothy, chapter 4, verse 7: *"I have fought a good fight, I have finished my course, I have kept the faith."*

ONE LAST VETERANS DAY SALUTE

I WENT OFF to bed on Election Night, tired, a bit sad, but comforted in another bit of knowledge that comes with experience: the sun will rise again. It did, of course, and I awoke surrounded by a loving family, and devoted friends started telephoning me before we poured the first cup of post-election coffee on Wednesday morning. I won't kid you—an election loss means the painful realization that some people who may have been friends in past years have fallen away for whatever reason, or perhaps they weren't inspired to go to the polls. But I'm not going to brood or spend much time second-guessing the voters, because what's done is done.

Besides, our nation is facing too many challenges to spend a moment fretting about a personal setback, which may not turn out to be a setback at all; many of the callers in the days after the election reminded me that multiple doors open when one familiar door closes behind you.

The Congressional Research Service reported that upon adjournment of the 111th Congress, I would mark 12,421 days in the U.S. House of Representatives, making me the second-longest-serving member of Congress—senators or representatives—since Missouri statehood. The longest tenure of House service belonged to Clarence Cannon, whose forty-one years in Congress are unlikely to be rivaled. And I managed to serve two more days than the third-longest-serving Missouri congressman, my mentor Richard Bolling of Kansas City.

In the days after the election, one former House colleague called to express concern that the Tuesday Tsunami of 2010 meant a major loss of institutional memory in Congress. That was particularly true on the Armed Services Committee, where most of the Democratic top row—the most senior members—was cleaned out. My reply is, that's why we have history books, and we must study our history and learn from it.

During the days immediately after the election, there wasn't much time to rest and regroup because the work of Congress continued, including moving out soon-to-be-former members. I was blessed that while there was immediate demand to vacate my spacious office in the Rayburn Building with its beautiful view of the Capitol, I was allowed by administrators to keep working from the considerably smaller but nobly named Truman Room in the building named for the Missouri president's favorite House Speaker, Sam Rayburn of Texas.

Once again, history was atop my agenda: my staff gathered pictures, files, and memorabilia from thirty-four years in office, most of it bound for the archives of the State Historical Society of Missouri at my alma mater in Columbia. One of the hardest items to take down was a print of the unfinished portrait of President Franklin Delano Roosevelt. It was being painted when the president collapsed and subsequently died on April 12, 1945, at the Little White House in Warm Springs, Georgia. It wasn't physically difficult to move, but that portrait is of great personal significance to me not only because Franklin Roosevelt was an outstanding president, perhaps our greatest president, but also because he was a visionary long before his White House years in establishing the Georgia Warm Springs Foundation.

On November 11, 2010, my first appearances since the election consisted of four Veterans Day speeches across the district, in Jefferson City, Tipton, Lexington, and Wellington. I told all of my audiences they must not just *think* of the men and women who serve in uniform but also should *thank* them at every opportunity. The day's first appearance was particularly meaningful to me because it was the twenty-fourth consecutive year I was honored to keynote the Lincoln University ROTC Veterans Day breakfast in Jefferson City. I looked not just into the eyes of silver-haired veterans who had served so well, but also into the hopeful faces of young ROTC cadets soon to be commissioned and deployed.

I told the young men and women preparing for lives of military service that on Veterans Day, we give thanks to those who now serve and to those who have served in the past. We give thanks for the families whose support made possible that service. We honor and remember those who lost their lives to preserve our freedoms. We honor and express our gratitude to all those who made sacrifices and bear scars, both visible and invisible, in support of this same cause. For the love of this country and their fellow citizens, our sailors, soldiers, airmen, and Marines have repeatedly demonstrated the willingness to give all that it is possible to give, and collectively we owe them a debt that can never be repaid.

Then I shared with the ROTC audience that the debts America owes its men and women in uniform had increased in personal terms for me the previous day, when I learned of the death of Marine Second Lieutenant Robert Kelly, who was killed by a roadside bomb in Afghanistan. Lieutenant Kelly was the son of Marine Lieutenant General John Kelly, who as a colonel escorted me on a number of trips to visit American troops overseas. My condolence call to General Kelly was one of the most difficult I have ever made. I was thinking of the sacrifices of both father and son on this, my last Veterans Day as a member of Congress. And then once more I recited "In Flanders Fields," the

World War I poem of honorable remembrance I learned from my father and imparted to my own sons.

We carry indelible images from childhood memories, and one of my most vivid was the sight of my best friend Don Savio's older brother Walter, on leave from the Army in World War II, arriving in his uniform to walk us home from Central Elementary School in Lexington. I'll never forget seeing Walter's gas mask slung over his uniformed shoulder in a satchel—a symbol of men in faraway conflict, an incongruous sight along a peaceful small-town Missouri street.

As Lieutenant Kelly's death reminded me, in settings of peace, sometimes we may forget about those who fought for us in war. We must not forget, because our freedom has been paid for at an awesome and dear price. My travels to battlefields and especially the American military cemetery at Normandy remind me so strongly of that.

The Normandy cemetery and the poem "In Flanders Fields" are tributes to sacrifice in pursuit of something larger than oneself. As part of my congressional service, I worked to pay other such tributes, not only among the civilian community but also for those serving in uniform, helping them appreciate the legacy they inherit and protect on behalf of a grateful nation.

For example, I initiated the naming of a new road at Fort Leonard Wood in memory of Lieutenant Hector Polla, a Lafayette County native who graduated from West Point in 1941 and was deployed to the Philippines. He was stationed on the Bataan Peninsula when the Japanese attacked there in December 1941. The courage displayed by Army Lieutenant Polla during the defense of Bataan earned him the Silver Star.

Hector Polla survived the Bataan Death March and spent nearly three years in Japanese prisoner of war camps, where survivors praised him for his leadership during brutal captivity. But he died tragically in January 1945 after the Japanese ship on which he and other prisoners were being transported to serve in slave labor was bombed by American forces. Hector Polla is remembered for his sacrifice, at Fort Wood and in Lexington.

Also at Fort Leonard Wood, I recommended naming the new headquarters building after General William Hoge, a native of Lexington whose father served as a leader of Wentworth Military Academy. A West Point graduate, General Hoge was a highly decorated battalion commander during World War I. In World War II, General Hoge directed the Ninth Armored Division in the pivotal, bloody, and game-changing capture of the Remagen bridge over the Rhine River in Germany in March 1945. This turning point allowed the Allies to immediately pour into Germany "with dry boots," as one sign at the time put it, reinforced by tanks, artillery, and supplies. General Hoge eventually retired from the service with four stars and returned to Lexington, living next door to my family and serving as a larger-than-life hero to me.

Hoge and Polla were two Missourians who served in uniform on opposite sides of the globe, but with a single mission: Allied victory. General Hoge's skill as a commander was critical. Also critical were the ultimate sacrifices of Lieutenant Hector Polla, Lieutenant Robert Kelly, and other fallen warriors who paid for our freedom today. Those warriors, and the spirit of the fallen in Flanders Fields, must never be forgotten. Nor can we ever forget or diminish our nation's appreciation of the service of those who return from war.

Just as in World War I and succeeding conflicts, we owe it to these men and women to make sure that they have the tools they need to fight effectively and to protect themselves in the field. When they have to be away from home, we owe it to them to treat their families the way we would want any of our own families to be treated. We owe them the respect that comes from knowing that our service members are volunteers who serve by choice. Their willingness to contribute to our country is precious beyond measure and must never be squandered.

I reflected to the ROTC students that during my time in Washington, I was honored to do my part to uphold Article I, Section Eight of the Constitution, granting Congress the obligation to raise and support armies and to provide and maintain a navy. It is a responsibility that all members of the legislative branch, on both sides of the aisle, must take very seriously. I noted that we worked hard on my watch as Armed Services chairman to increase military pay, improve benefits, and build modern housing for our troops and their families.

We worked to protect and improve health care for service members and their families, and we worked to improve the care we provide our wounded warriors. We increased the size of our armed forces to improve readiness and reduce the strain imposed on service members experiencing multiple deployments without enough rest and recovery time at home. And more recently, I noted, we enacted defense acquisition reforms to bring efficiencies and improve accountability for the taxpayer dollars invested in major weapons systems.

Then I shared with the ROTC audience my greatest concern that those who wear the American uniform, those who perform arduous duties, those who often go in harm's way, and their wonderful supportive families will be relegated to "out of sight, out of mind." I fear that a chasm will develop between those who protect our freedoms and those who are being protected. The reporters covering that speech on my last Veterans Day as a member of Congress caught the importance of that point about a prospective divide between the military and civilians, and it became the centerpiece of their stories, which I appreciated, because the problem is real.

In the 2010 elections, the discourse mostly did not include discussion of our ongoing conflicts in the Middle East and our fight against terrorists. I am concerned that the attacks on September 11, 2001, will fade in the American consciousness and that the purpose of our efforts against extremist terrorists will also eventually fade. It could come to pass that the American military becomes isolated from American society and that Americans may fail to consider our men and women in uniform.

This sad possibility reminds me of the poem "Tommy," by Rudyard Kipling. "Tommy" is the generic nickname of the British soldier, and the verse goes "... for it's Tommy this, an' Tommy that, an' 'Chuck him out, the brute!' / But it's 'Savior of the country' when the guns begin to shoot...."

As a nation, we need to constantly remind ourselves of those who go about their difficult duties of protecting us and keeping us safe. Without our military, we would be vulnerable to more and more 9/11s. Our ability to maintain military readiness is critical as the country deals with our ongoing challenges. There is a reasonable desire to reduce federal spending and pay down our national deficit, but there is also a constituency that believes the way to demonstrate budget discipline is by making drastic cuts to our national defense. This troubles me greatly.

While we have a duty to ensure each and every tax dollar spent on defense is spent wisely, we cannot afford to risk our national security and risk Americans' lives by shortchanging our investment in military readiness. We must have the right number of forces with the right equipment, the right training, and the right amount of time between deployments to rest, reset, and prepare for the future. There is no question we have to be ready, because conflicts can and will happen anywhere. Frequently such events have come without warning. That is why the readiness of our military—that is, the preparedness to successfully respond to any threat—is so important.

You could never realize it from the 2010 campaign rhetoric, but America is engaged in wars in two countries, near-conflicts in a dozen more, and peacekeeping or postwar reconstruction efforts in dozens more. We are so engaged for two main reasons—to defend ourselves from actual or potential attacks, and to protect our national security interests in world peace and stability.

That was borne out to me soon after, when I met with all the leaders of Israel. We had in-depth discussions with each one of them. The last one was Prime Minister Benjamin Netanyahu, whom I had met before, a very engaging gentleman. We had a very interesting conversation as to where our nations were in the scheme of things. We talked about Iran and the challenges of Israel's neighborhood, not knowing at that time what would be coming to pass in Syria. He talked a great deal about the main problems with Hamas and stressed Hamas's weapons buildup. I asked him, "At what point will Israel cease to tolerate the huge weapons buildup of Hamas?" and he said, "That's an interesting question." So I asked the question again. "At what point will Israel cease to tolerate the weapons buildup of Hamas?" He repeated his answer with almost a grin on his face. "That's an interesting question." I did not ask him a third time.

America has 4 percent of the world's people but 25 percent of the world's economy, so we are literally everywhere on the globe and are working almost everywhere for peace and stability. It is not sensible to rearm after the fact of an attack when you know from history that it has to be coming. This is why America possesses half of the world's strategic military power. And although economic times are tough, our military commitments are not likely to get lighter.

At the same time, fewer and fewer Americans have direct experience of the military. Parents used to write to me, saying, "Look after my Johnny in the service. Look after my Janie." But there are fewer and fewer Johnnies and Janies out there, and fewer parents writing. Only one-half of 1 percent of Americans are in uniform today, although a good number of them are in the National Guard and Reserve and are being deployed frequently, which brings it home to many communities. But still it's a small number. I remember very, very well how with the general mobilization in the Second World War, in Korea, and in many respects in Vietnam, the general population was touched more. In those days we all had been in the service or knew someone who was. Today, in many communities, military presence is an exception. I think we as a country lose by that, especially if it makes us less conscious of the costs of freedom.

All military missions have death and life-cycle costs. The deaths are listed on our memorials. The life-cycle costs are found in our VA hospitals and in every neighborhood across America, and this will be the case for decades to come. The human and material investments in an American warrior are made for a lifetime, so multiple simultaneous conflicts require a larger investment over the lifetimes of soldiers. We are either committed to that lifetime investment or we are not committed to our national security interests in world peace and stability, and thus in our own prosperity. In truth, we don't have a choice.

But the men and women of our volunteer military do have choices. When we shortchange them on education, training, materials, health care, housing, rehabilitation, financial support, and encouragement, we are shortchanging our own prosperity, and that is the truth. Taking their sacrifices for granted is absolutely unacceptable. And I hope that on this one issue at least, the American public and public officials from all parties can find common ground and band together so that taking care of our service members and their families remains a top priority.

This may be the best way to express our gratitude for those dedicated men and women who have served the United States so nobly.

May God bless them and keep them safe.

On Wednesday, December 1, 2010, I went to the well of the House one last time to say good-bye. I briefly reviewed my departure from Missouri in 1976 and thanked the people of the Fourth Congressional District for the privilege of representing them for thirty-four years. Other thanks followed, to family, friends, colleagues, and staff. But I wanted to leave a message—or, rather, two messages—on the subjects most dear to the nation I love.

On the need for bipartisanship, I said:

> In the past, this body has worked best after great debates, when men and women of strong principles have met and compromised on those difficult issues, which at the time could render us asunder. But through meeting in the center and solving the problems of the day, our country benefited. It was able to progress.
>
> As a result of the last election, the center has been hollowed out and more members will represent extreme points of view, which is likely to make meaningful compromise difficult, if not impossible. Once again, our system of government and our citizenry will be tested, and the outcome will determine, borrowing the eloquent words of President Lincoln's Gettysburg Address, "whether that nation or any nation so conceived and so dedicated can long endure."

And I returned to the worrisome gap between Americans and their military:

> My greatest concern is that a chasm will develop between those who protect our freedoms and those who are being protected . . . For those not in uniform or connected to the military in some way, it's easy not to relate to our service members' difficulties as they deal with the trials of war and combat, multiple deployments, family separations, missed birthdays, and other sacrifices too numerous to mention. . . .
>
> I've always considered each young man and woman in uniform as a son or daughter. They are national treasures and their sacrifices cannot be taken for granted. They are not chess pieces to be moved upon a board. Each and every one is irreplaceable. Issues of national security and war and peace are too important to lose sight of the real men and women who answer our nation's call and do the bidding of the Commander-In-Chief.

And I ended my farewell with an apt selection from Alfred, Lord Tennyson's poem "Ulysses":

> Much I have seen and known; cities of men
> And manners, climates, councils, governments . . .
> And drunk delight of battle with my peers . . .
>
> Some work of noble note, may yet be done . . .
> Come, my friends,
> 'Tis not too late to seek a newer world.

Then I left the House to the hands of the next Congress and went home.

INTO THE FUTURE

AS PRESIDENT FRANKLIN Roosevelt said in his undelivered speech of April 13, 1945, the United States has long been established as "a vital factor in international affairs." This is in large part because we represent and defend the four essential freedoms enumerated by President Roosevelt—freedom of worship, freedom from fear, freedom of speech, and freedom from want. President Roosevelt did not live to see the end of the world war he successfully prosecuted, but in the postwar decades our political, diplomatic, and military strengths have indeed kept America at the forefront of the world's major issues while protecting our essential freedoms.

I mentioned President Bill Clinton declaring the United States to be the truly "indispensable nation," a phrase I quite liked. I believe it is up to each generation to make sure that our country remains honorably indispensable. This doesn't just happen automatically or by sheer coincidence.

Not long before Dr. Stephen Ambrose passed away in 2002, I hosted a small breakfast for him in my office to visit with several members of Congress. The noted historian, biographer of Dwight Eisenhower, was a neighbor to our good mutual friend from Bay St. Louis, Mississippi, Congressman Gene Taylor. Dr. Ambrose talked about his book, *Undaunted Courage,* the saga of the Lewis and Clark expedition, which had such bearing on Missouri's history and the nation's.

As he was preparing to leave after his fascinating and vivid presentation, I asked him, "Dr. Ambrose, what is it that makes America so unique and so great?" I noted that some believed it was a combination of the sturdy immigrants who brought so much to America, the pioneers who led our bold westward expansion, and our abundant natural resources.

Without hesitation, Dr. Ambrose replied, "Look at Russia—Russia has a hardy workforce, Russia has more natural resources than all of North America. But Russia never had a George Washington, a John Adams, a Thomas Jefferson, or a James Madison and the values that they established."

He was absolutely correct—our values set us apart, and we must be worthy of the founders who established them. If we confront the challenges of this century with courage and clear vision, I believe we will be.

How do we get there? It starts with leadership of solid character. A prime example—not that it will surprise you to hear me say it—is that of President Harry Truman. He made bold decisions, some of which were unpopular at the time, that have been borne out by history as the correct decisions. Truman biographer David McCullough writes of his "inner iron, his bedrock faith in the democratic process, his trust in the American people, and his belief that history was the final, all-important judge of performance."

McCullough goes on to quote columnist Mary McGrory's declaration that Truman was "unexpectedly wise when it counted," and he provides commentator Eric Sevareid's tribute that remembering Truman "reminds people what a man in that office ought to be like. It's character, just character. He stands like a rock in memory now." I had the privilege of knowing President Truman, and his strength of character came through loud and clear.

Along with values, America must also have leadership with vision. Our leaders must have the ability to map our trail into the future, past the obstacles and dangers that cause other countries to falter and often collapse. This leadership must include persuasive powers to bring together opposing views and shape constructive compromise. Some presidents have been great persuaders in their own times, such as John Kennedy, Ronald Reagan, and Bill Clinton. They led us to compromise and progress, and it usually happened after much vigorous debate.

Historian Barbara Tuchman's remarkable book, *The March of Folly*, lays out four examples of historic societal blunders that were committed by misguided majorities which could not be dissuaded and therefore marginalized those who disagreed. The first example she notes is the Trojan horse, which as history teaches was presented as a generous gift of tribute, but in actuality was concealing Greek soldiers who decimated Troy once they were inside its walls.

One of Tuchman's stipulations for inclusion in her book's catalogue of societal follies was active disregard of vocal contemporary opposition to the impending disaster. For the Trojans, this was Laocoon, who warned, *"A deadly fraud is this!"* And he wanted to jab a spear into the wooden horse to see whether it would reveal treachery or at least yield a painful cry. Alas, Laocoon's warnings were disregarded.

Today, as in ancient Troy, we have some in Washington who come at issues from extremes and ignore the loyal opposition. But a political strategy to govern without the loyal opposition and to disdain seeking middle ground is not a reflection of principles that yield results.

For Democrats, the leadership decision to place the highest priority on debating contentious health care proposals early in 2009 could provide a fifth example of folly for Tuchman's list. Why? Well, my father always told me to keep my eye on the ball. The health care debate got my party off track from seeking consensus and action on the two much more urgently pressing issues of war abroad and economic recession at home. With the health care battles, many Democrats took their eyes off the ball. We paid the price in November 2010 by losing control of the House.

Finally, we must have a strong military. This principle makes the others possible. Should conflicts occur, our military must be ready, whether it is force on force or combat with guerrillas in the most unforgiving conditions. I believe in the admonition of George Washington: "If you want peace, prepare for war."

That preparation must include harnessing and pioneering the latest technology. President Kennedy provided the perfect example of a far-reaching vision for scientific achievement when he called for sending a man to the moon and returning him safely to Earth. In his undelivered speech of April 1945, President Roosevelt noted that "science has brought all the different quarters of the globe so close together that it is impossible to isolate them from one another."

What then would President Roosevelt think about our era of cyberspace, our biological and medical research, our scientific explorations with all of their breathtaking possibilities and potential dangers? It is clear that technological leadership must remain a top priority for America, and it is up to our leaders to inspire us to make this a top priority. And I would like to think that our efforts over the years to add rigor to the professional military education system have cultivated the heavy-hitting thinkers with real-world experience and intellectual grounding who could make invaluable contributions to any project to develop a new strategy.

It is up to the president and Congress to lead the way. Our country has the talent to undertake this task and to do it well. In our third century, I know we will continue to cherish our rights, love our freedom, and celebrate America's greatness.

But there are enduring questions for every generation:

Will we work to protect it all?

Will we fight for it?

Will we sacrifice and even die for it?

These are the enduring questions, because there is an enduring truth: nothing, but nothing, costs nothing. Freedom is not free. But to echo President Roosevelt's unfinished speech of 1945, our only limitations to our realization of tomorrow are our doubts of today, so in his words, "let us move forward with strong and active faith."

We do know our history, and thus we know we have the capacity to summon that remarkable courage and faith cited by Mr. Roosevelt as we confront the dangers. We must be worthy of the founders in recognizing our opportunities and preserving our values.

In 1976, when I was the vice chairman of the Bicentennial Commission, I would speak about the farmer who was very patriotic and wanted to do something nice for the bicentennial, but a lot of people were in pageants and the choir was singing and he felt like he didn't have any special talent. He had an old beat-up pickup truck, and he got it out and painted it red, white, and blue. In the back of that old truck he placed a sign that said, "America. We ain't perfect, but we ain't done yet." And I think that's what we could say about America today.

We must, and we will, continue to strive to *achieve the honorable.* This is more than an admonition embedded in stone at a venerable military school in the American heartland. It is the American ideal.

As for me, my three sons have given us five beautiful and brilliant and practically perfect grandchildren. Ike serves in the U.S. Navy and he and his wife, Elena, are the parents of Alexander Boone Skelton and Conor Booth Skelton. Jim serves in the U.S. Army and he and his wife, Anita, have Sarah Elizabeth Skelton and Abigail Anding Skelton. And our youngest son, Page, the businessman, and his wife, Caroline, have Harry Page Skelton Jr. My sons are all men of honor and achievement, as well as luck for marrying wonderful, lovely, smart, and resourceful women. I brag that I handpicked my daughters-in-law. But the boys did show remarkable hereditary instincts in this regard, especially since Susie set such a sterling example of what a wife and mother should be.

I like to say that all three of our boys "smelled the smoke." If you're not familiar with the term, it dates to the use of specially trained horses that pulled water wagons to fires—it was said that the horses smelled the smoke and would charge without fear in the right direction. In the context of our three sons, it means setting goals and then heading straight for those goals with dedication.

And there is a new branch of the Skelton family, one that I am cultivating with great joy.

When I lost Susie in 2005, the sense of loss was profound. But sadness, while deep, does diminish over time, and much more frequently remembered are the joys of forty-four years of marriage and the pride in having such a wonderful wife and mother of three sons.

Love and the Lord work mysteriously, hand in hand. I was speaking about history to a student group at Lexington Middle School, and I was reintroduced to a hometown friend of Susie's and mine, school counselor Patty Martin. Patty and her husband, Lieutenant Colonel Robert Martin, came to Lexington in 1973 when he joined Wentworth Military Academy as a top administrator.

Patty also taught and served as a counselor at Wentworth before joining the staff of Lexington's public schools. She retired from her middle school counselor's job in 2009 after twenty-nine years with the Lexington school district, during which she was such a positive and cheerful and trusted influence in the lives of so many young people.

So our families were acquainted, and Susie and Patty had many mutual friends. Robert Martin died in 1997, and Patty had been a widow for more than a decade. We found nice chemistry upon getting reacquainted in my 2006 school visit, and we began keeping company, as the old folks used to say.

Patty and I thoroughly enjoyed one another's company and found we had many common interests, centered on a devotion to Lexington and to Missouri and to our children and grandchildren, which is a fine way to get started in a relationship.

Our first big date was a White House holiday event in 2006. The friendship evolved into deep affection. In August 2008, I gave Patty an engagement ring, and to my combined relief and delight, she accepted. We were married on August 29, 2009, with family members in attendance and my wonderful congressional colleague, the Reverend Emanuel Cleaver, officiating in his Kansas City church's chapel, assisted by Patty's former minister, Ron Page.

So a new branch of the Skeltons is growing, including the five children Patty raised and adored with her late husband and thirteen terrific grandchildren to add to my five. May the new branches grow and prosper, in love and long life, always with the blessings of a Lord who provides for us beyond all human understanding.

I am still close with a few of my House colleagues, particularly Gene Taylor. It's not as collegial after you leave as you might think. You're good friends while you're there, but as Kipling says, that's all shoved behind me. Most of those that have left Congress are back home pursuing their own lives, not close by to Missouri or Washington. And those that remain in Congress remain good friends, but you don't see them much. The Capitol Hill schedule hasn't changed for the better.

I did see a bunch of my former colleagues in March 2012. The Armed Services Committee displays portraits of former chairmen in its hearing room—not paid for by taxpayer dollars, I hasten to point out. Many members, past and present, turned out for the unveiling of my portrait, although I'm sure it was mostly to see the picture. The young artist, Gavin Glakas, did a superb job. I told him initially that I wanted to resemble a movie star like Clark Gable of *Gone with the Wind* fame, and Gavin remarked that he would be pleased to put a moustache on the painting. That ended that conversation.

And, exercising my right to petition my elected representative, I recently had breakfast with the congresswoman from the Fourth District of Missouri. I ran into Representative Hartzler at the airport and proposed a breakfast or lunch, and she seemed to be willing. She met me and Russ Orban, my law associate, for a very pleasant meal at the Army-Navy Club in Washington. I gave her some thoughts on some of the lessons I'd learned and things I wish I'd known when starting out in Congress, and particularly discussed the military travels that I had made. I stressed the importance of the Congressional Research Service and the Library of Congress, which I've used extensively, particularly during my early years in Congress.

As with so much of my life, most of my present and future circumstances spring from roots planted long ago in Missouri.

After graduating from law school, I asked two people to sign my application to become a member of the Missouri Bar—my lawyer father and the highly respected dean of the Lexington lawyers, Horace Blackwell. Horace Blackwell had a son, Menefee Blackwell, who was raised in Lexington and attended Wentworth Military Academy. Menefee went on to graduate from college and law school and began his practice in nearby Kansas City in 1939. Along came the war, and he went off to the Army, returning as a major and having earned the Silver Star. He founded a Kansas City law firm, which has grown to a national law firm with offices in Washington and across the country. It is with this firm, Husch Blackwell, that I am now a partner.

I also serve on a couple of corporate boards and was honored by President Obama with an appointment to a seat on the American Battle Monuments Commission. As you might imagine, with my love of military history and desire to honor the troops, this is a labor of love for me—and a great honor.

I also was privileged to become only the 170th American–and the first congressman– to be named an Honorary U.S. Marine. I'm not sure how it happened, or who suggested it, but on December 1, 2010, the Commandant of the Corps, General James Amos, welcomed me to the brotherhood. I suppose that if you live long enough, wonderful things–even very improbable things–will happen.

President Harry Truman would tell of the grave marker in Tombstone, Arizona, which read, "Here lies Jack Williams. He done his damnedest." In the years ahead, it is my sincere hope that someone in Missouri, or an American in uniform, might see this book, or read *Whispers of Warriors*, or perhaps see my name on the side of one of the buildings the military has named for me and, recalling the challenges of yesteryear, will say, "He done his damnedest."

I had originally intended to end this memoir on that note. But as the final words of the first draft were written, I received an unexpected telephone call.

It was from the superintendent of the U.S. Military Academy, informing me that I had been selected by the Association of Graduates to join such notables as generals Omar Bradley and Colin Powell, and presidents Ronald Reagan and George H. W. Bush, in receiving the Sylvanus Thayer Award, given to "an outstanding citizen whose service and accomplishments in the national interest exemplify the Military Academy motto, 'Duty, Honor, Country.'"

I have been privileged to receive a number of such awards through the years, but this one moved me deeply, because it meant that after eighty-one years on this earth, after Wentworth and polio, law school and prosecuting, practice law and running for Congress, fighting for the troops and getting upside down in a truck, reaching my professional dream and losing my seat, loving, losing, and loving again . . .

. . . after all that, finally, I was getting an appointment to West Point.

EPILOGUE

ON OCTOBER 18, 2012, a beautiful autumn Thursday in New York, the West Point Corps of Cadets stood at attention on the Plain, the parade ground at West Point. There, accompanied by my family, friends, many former staff, and the West Point faculty, I reviewed the corps as it passed in formation. Then I joined the superintendent, Lieutenant General David H. Huntoon Jr., in inspecting each company. The formal parade was just one of the activities surrounding the granting of the Thayer Award—but easily the most impressive.

Following the parade, the corps assembled for dinner in the vaulted gray stone cadet mess hall. There, beneath the platform from which Douglas MacArthur told the world that old soldiers never die, I spoke to the cadets who will be the Army's future leaders.

I told them of examples of great West Point graduates who had preceded them into the profession of arms, of Hector Polla and William Hoge and (to his surprise) Arch Barrett, who was there at a front table. I recommended that they study the Constitution, the art of war, and their military specialties. And I reminded them of the great value of taking care of their troops and their families, and the importance of listening to their sergeants.

But most of all, I thanked them—for their service to America and the kind honor they had been a part of granting to me that day. And I concluded:

> During the sunrise of my life, it was my dream to come to West Point. That did not happen. But now, as the sun dips toward the sunset, I am at West Point. No graduate with brand-new second lieutenant bars could be more thrilled than I. I will cherish this medal as if it were my diploma.

APPENDIXES · INDEX

APPENDIX A: MY STRONG RIGHT ARM

I am about to invite trouble, because the list of friends I have accumulated in life goes on and on and it's risky to single out anyone. We may not have the joy of seeing one another in person nearly enough, but they all know of my affection and appreciation.

The common denominator is that they stood by me through the roughest seas and the best of times—and they are real, in the sense that they keep me grounded in Missouri. So I'll go out on a limb and mention a few good friends.

Since childhood, one of my closest pals through grade school, high school, my fight with polio, and my own public service has been Don Savio, now retired as a bank president in Lexington. Another very close friend of long standing is Larry McMullen, my law school classmate, fraternity brother in Sigma Chi, and now a nationally known trial attorney practicing in Kansas City. My first-year law school roommate was Bob Devoy of Brookfield, now retired as a circuit judge. My longtime friend, attorney Bob Welling of Warrensburg, assumed the chairmanship of my congressional campaign committee when Jack Anderson of Harrisonville passed away. They are examples of friends who knew me "back when," and who won't sit still for any silliness from me.

Fellow Democrats Jim Mathewson of Sedalia and Harold Caskey of Butler followed me in their service in the Missouri senate, but their unflinching support and counsel from Jefferson City and in their sprawling districts strengthened me politically and personally during my years in Congress, when our elective territories overlapped.

Another pal from my Jefferson City days in the state senate was the skilled legislator Norman Lee Merrell, now deceased, who was nicknamed "Peaches," with whom I shared an apartment for several sessions. And there's current State Representative Joe Aull from Marshall, whose father, William Aull III, was an esteemed attorney and good friend, although I frequently found myself at the opposite table in court, and I always had my hands full at those times. Over the years, these Missouri legislators and many others worked with me on some of the best examples of state and federal cooperation.

I like to tell my many newspaper friends that I once worked in their field—in the sixth grade, when I delivered the *Lexington Intelligencer*. The *Intelligencer's* owner was a former Army major named A. W. Allen, a nice man who contended with constant breakdowns of the press that kept me waiting and then sent me scurrying to make my deliveries, sometimes as late as 11 P.M. on publication days.

Other Lexington newspapermen who were good friends over the years included publisher John Shea and his newsman and successor as publisher, Jim Shannon. Mr. Shannon gave me an early lesson in the role of the newspaperman when I was a green prosecutor—I tried to tell him what to put in his story, and he sharply reminded me that *he* was the reporter, not me, and it was *his role* to decide what was news, not mine.

My friends in the newspaper world include Betty Spaar of Odessa, a friend from our college days at the University of Missouri and a wonderful confidante who keeps me grounded. Betty is a second-generation newspaper publisher, with papers in Odessa and Oak Grove, and her sons and their families are building on the family publishing heritage. Betty also served as president of the Missouri Press Association, the statewide organization of weekly and daily newspapers. And among Betty's cub reporters who long ago covered my father and me in Lafayette County was high school student Doug Crews, who rose to become executive director of the Missouri Press Association and a nationally honored leader in publishing circles.

Another Missouri newspaper person I counted as a good friend and supporter was the late Mrs. William H. "Betty" Weldon of Jefferson City, publisher of the capital city's *News Tribune*. Betty Weldon was also nationally recognized as the owner of Callaway Hills, a sprawling and beautiful ranch north of Jefferson City with a long history of breeding champion horses. Although she was a strong Republican and once presented a champion horse to President Ronald Reagan as a personal gift, Betty Weldon and I saw eye-to-eye on many issues and she always supported my efforts.

Dalton Wright, publisher of the *Lebanon Daily Record*, receives double respect from me. In addition to keeping up a fine family heritage of providing the best media coverage in his community, he is a strong supporter of the military, not only to the thousands based at nearby Fort Leonard Wood but also through his own service in uniform as an accomplished pilot.

I also count many friends among the broadcast media, such as Maria Antonia Twyman, an accomplished journalist who anchors and reports on Kansas City television. Maria and her husband, Tim, have been good friends of the Skelton family through the years.

I made many good friends among colleagues during my time in elective office in Jefferson City and Washington. In the state senate there was Bill Cason, who served as president pro tempore and led the chamber while I served. Other veteran state legislators in those days before term limits imbued me with political lessons that still resonate—work hard, study the bills, show up, and above all, keep your word.

I was elected to the U.S. House in 1976 alongside a fair-haired youngster who had most recently served as a St. Louis city alderman. His name was Richard Gephardt, and of course he rose to become House majority leader and twice ran unsuccessfully for the Democratic presidential nomination. Dick was one of the most able legislators I have ever known, a man of his word. For eleven years, we carpooled together to work on Capitol Hill from our neighborhoods in the D.C. suburbs. Even though Dick retired from Congress, his top political aide, Joyce Aboussie, remains a key player in St. Louis political and civic circles—and she was a strong supporter of mine.

When Dick moved to a new neighborhood farther away, I started riding to work with Bill Emerson, a Republican congressman from southeast Missouri. Bill was one of the most likable men I ever met, and we became great friends. Just as Mike Boorda had started as an enlisted man and risen to CNO, Bill had begun his Capitol Hill life as a page and eventually became a congressman. After Bill died of cancer in June 1996, his widow, Jo Ann Emerson, was elected to succeed him, and she and I remain devoted friends and allies in the interest of what's best for Missouri, irrespective of party politics. She is also a leading voice of reason on the influential Appropriations Committee.

When I arrived in Washington, I quickly came to admire the brilliant Kansas City Democratic Congressman Richard "Dick" Bolling. Dick helped me join the House Armed Services Committee, for which I will forever be grateful. First elected in 1948, Dick Bolling was the unrivaled expert in rules of the chamber, and you wanted him on your side. Fortunately, he liked me, and we remained friends until his death.

The year I was first sworn into Congress, the legendary Thomas "Tip" O'Neill was sworn in as House Speaker, and we became great friends. Through my work on Armed Services, I became particularly close to several members. I helped my fellow Democrat, the late Les Aspin, win a hard-fought challenge to become committee chairman, and Les later served as President Clinton's secretary of defense.

The late Mississippi Congressman G. V. "Sonny" Montgomery was an icon on veterans' issues, and the Montgomery G.I. Bill is so appropriately named for him. Sonny was a conservative Democrat, and he was my great friend. Perhaps his best friend dating to their joint House service was former President George H. W. Bush. During Sonny's 2006 funeral, the elder former President Bush was to deliver the eulogy, but he was so overcome with emotion that he called on his wife, Barbara, to deliver remarks in tribute to Sonny. Such was the depth of friendships held by Sonny Montgomery, whose work means at least a down payment on the immeasurable debt we owe to our veterans.

Congressman Bill Nichols of Alabama was a leader in working for joint training and operations between the service branches, long before it became a mandated reality. The 1986 Goldwater-Nichols Act so appropriately bears Bill's name.

Another Mississippian, sea power expert Gene Taylor, was one of my closest friends on and off the committee. Although Gene was actually more conservative than me on many issues and was one of the most conservative Democrats in Congress, he and I were both among the members of our party who were swept away in the 2010 Republican wave.

Former Congressman Duncan Hunter of California, who served as our chairman when Republicans earlier controlled the House, collaborated closely with me to assure that the committee's work was bipartisan and productive. Duncan paid me a marvelous compliment once during a visit to Whiteman Air Force Base in Missouri, when he told reporters that he and I left partisanship at the door when it came to cooperation on matters of national security. In an interview for this book with my collaborator, Scott Charton, Duncan really captured the essence of why the Armed Services Committee worked on our mutual watches as the least partisan and therefore one of the most effective committees on Capitol Hill:

> As a result of being on the committee with Ike since 1981, I developed a close friendship—we are personal friends. Interestingly, in the business of legislation and politics, that enables you to have some tough partisan battles, and to then move past those battles, and when you have that sort of relationship and can work together on issues you concur on, it's wonderful.
>
> The relationship between Ike and myself was one of constantly finding common ground. The center of that common ground was the well-being of the armed forces of the United States.

Duncan Hunter Sr. is a true patriot and a dear friend—and I was also pleased to count his son, U.S. Marine veteran Duncan Hunter Jr. of California, as a very able congressional colleague and member of the Armed Services Committee during my chairmanship of the panel.

I have worked very effectively with House Speakers of both parties, including Tip O'Neill's Democratic successors Jim Wright, Tom Foley, and Nancy Pelosi, and Republicans Newt Gingrich and Dennis Hastert. One thing I don't believe in is savaging people just because they are members of the opposing party. Especially on matters of national security, politics must stop at the ballot box.

Newt Gingrich as Republican Speaker once paid me a huge compliment right in my district. He came in to campaign for my Republican opponent in 1996, but their Jefferson City news conference went down the drain when Newt acknowledged that he liked how I voted on most issues and that he would enthusiastically welcome me into the GOP if I'd consider a party switch. His heart clearly wasn't in seeing me ousted, but he was going through the motions as a party leader.

When it was time to go to conference committees with the Senate, no one proved a stronger or more gentlemanly partner across the Capitol on defense issues than former Republican Senator John Warner of Virginia. With his outstanding ranking, Democratic member Carl Levin of Michigan (who later became chairman under Democratic control), Senator Warner, and our various House Armed Services chairmen worked diligently with me as ranking House Democratic member to hammer out solutions.

I have particular affection for John Warner because when he was selected to receive the Patriot Award from the National Defense University, he insisted to the sponsors that I also receive the award, and I treasure that impressive American eagle sculpture as much for the generosity and courtesy of John Warner as for its own symbolism of our nation's honor.

I served in Washington alongside six presidents—Jimmy Carter, Ronald Reagan, George H. W. Bush, Bill Clinton, George W. Bush, and Barack Obama. Of these men, I must say Mr. Reagan was one of the most charming people I ever met. You couldn't help but like him. Once when Susie and I attended a White House event, Mr. Reagan startled us by including in his formal remarks the public recognition of our wedding anniversary. It came across as so warmly conversational, and only later did I obtain out of curiosity the notes from which Mr. Reagan the superb speaker based his comments:

> *By the way, I've learned a little secret. Today Ike and Susie Skelton celebrate their silver wedding anniversary—congratulations. It's fitting for us to begin this evening on a note of celebration.*

The president followed the script perfectly, and today those notes are framed in my Lexington home, along with a picture of Susie and me being welcomed so warmly to the White House by Mr. Reagan. And there is a hand-inscribed note on the picture: *"Congratulations Ike and Susie on the Silver—now go for the Gold. Ronald Reagan."*

We did make it to forty-four years of marriage when Susie passed away, and that silver anniversary was one of the most pleasurable highlights because of President Reagan's thoughtfulness.

At the time I left office in 2011, prior to the decennial census leading to redrawing of district boundaries, the Fourth District reached eastward from Kansas City's eastern suburbs along the curving Missouri River, past Lexington and Marshall, and on down to Jefferson City, our state capital. Then the Fourth swung south to encompass Fort Leonard Wood and nearby Lebanon and St. Robert. From there it extended back toward the west, along Interstate 44 to points just a few miles north of the Arkansas border. Then it jutted north around Springfield and reached westward to Missouri's border with Kansas, a scene of great bloodshed and anguish during the Civil War.

My congressional offices were in Blue Springs, just east of Kansas City; Sedalia, home of the Missouri State Fair, serving the southwestern portion of the district and a few miles from Whiteman Air Force Base; Jefferson City, near the geographical heart of our state; and Lebanon, anchor of the southeast corner of the district, just down I-44 from Fort Leonard Wood.

The Washington office was our home away from Missouri, though Bob Hagedorn, my fantastic chief of staff who first joined me in Washington in 1977 and was at my side until I left office in 2011, was headquartered in the district office at Blue Springs. Bob led what I considered to be the finest congressional staff anywhere, many of them serving with me for more than two decades. I want to particularly mention some of my longest-serving staff members—the former chief of staff, Jack Pollard, and Missouri district office administrators Berna Dean Nierman, Joy Seitz, Carol Scott, and Ann Kutcher.

In Washington, several staff members were with me for many years, including Deputy Chief of Staff Whitney Frost, who was in charge of my Capitol Hill office; Press Secretary Lara Battles; Legislative Director Dana O'Brien; and Missouri staffers Carol Johns, Melissa Richardson, and Arletta Garrett, as well as former staffers who were very important early in my tenure, Gary Edwards, Denise Auer, and Wahnita Corse.

I admire and appreciate them and others, for they were indeed the helpful faces and voices of the congressional office when I was working at the Capitol. All members of my staff understood that Missouri and Missourians always came first.

In the 1950s, I attended a dinner in Springfield, Missouri, headlined by then-Senator John F. Kennedy of Massachusetts. I will always remember Mr. Kennedy declaring at that event: "If you stay close to the people, the people will stay close to you."

Mr. Kennedy's words resonated with me, leaving a lasting impression and guiding me as I began my career of public service. Throughout my time in Congress, I worked hard at staying in touch with the people I represent. During my years in Congress, I made from 150 to more than 200 appearances every year in the Show-Me State, and in 2010, I was in the district for all or part of more than 200 days—nearly three-quarters of the year—that usually included three out of four weekends each month.

Each year, I spent a lot of time attending meetings and visiting farms, schools, community events, and businesses of all sizes. I was even invited to speak at Sunday services from time to time, though I could not match the graceful and moving sermons of my longtime Kansas City congressional colleague, the Reverend Emanuel Cleaver, who has long pastored a devoted congregation in his hometown.

I always appreciated visiting with Missourians, whose commonsense advice and guidance steadied me in Washington. In addition to listening to Missourians at home, I invited their letters, phone calls, and e-mails. In a democracy, citizens have a responsibility to communicate with their elected officials, so when issues of interest were being considered by Congress, I wanted to hear from my fellow Missourians. And to paraphrase President Truman, the people can keep your hat size in proper proportion.

A great illustration of this point came from the late Congressman Morris Udall, with whom I was privileged to serve early in my career. He was known for his sense of humor that kept things in perspective. One time in the House cloakroom, Udall told a story about his unsuccessful 1976 campaign for the Democratic presidential nomination.

It seems that Udall the White House hopeful walked into a barbershop and said, "Hello, I'm Mo Udall and I'm running for president." And one old fellow shot back, "Yeah, we were just laughing about that a few minutes ago."

So much for expanding hat sizes.

During my congressional service, when I was back home in Lexington, just after dawn on certain Sundays I rubbed the sleep from my eyes, adjusted my ball cap, and spooned my own apple butter onto hot biscuits when I visited the Ponderosa Sunday breakfast club for Lafayette County's elder statesmen and experts on sports, hunting, and current events. Lord knows, we all have our aches and pains, but they can seem a bit more insistent at that early hour! And, as my belt and the scale sometimes remind me, I take second place to no man in wielding a fork to enjoy the delicious treats of Missouri pie suppers, fish fries, county fairs, and country ham breakfasts.

Sure, my left arm remains underpowered and of little use, but my right arm has been lifted more times than I could count for handshakes while visiting with Missourians as a campaigner and as an elected official over a span of fifty-four years.

My stamina is a definite blessing, too. Actually, I'm blessed in so many ways because I am able. In my eighty-second year, I am in good general health and have plenty of energy, and with the Lord's help and the help of so many relatives and friends, I achieve what needs doing. Many of my fellow Warm Springs patients had it far worse, and I am humbled and grateful when I witness the determination of people whose physical challenges make mine seem minor indeed.

Nowhere is this more moving and humbling than when I meet our military servicemen and women, and our veterans of all ages, who shed their blood and stood in harm's way for our country. Many still carry scars—some scars are unseen on the outside but no less real—and in many cases they carry the life-long health consequences. They embody achievement of the honorable through quiet determination and self-sacrifice, and we are all in their debt.

In addition to a positive attitude, I am blessed by the caring, affection, and uncomplaining help of so many people. I think of my mother and how she helped me through those early days after I returned from Warm Springs as well as in later years. And then there were longtime family friends, including John Pollard, father of my now retired chief of staff Jack Pollard. There are my great Lexington friends Bill Cross, Wally Hulver, John Giorza, and Bob Warner. The late Lynn Rider of Lexington was my mentor through activities in the Masonic

Lodge, culminating with me becoming a 33rd Degree Mason. The late Margariet Jackson worked for the Skelton family from 1948 through 1977, helping to raise me as well as my sons. My late first cousin Arch Skelton practiced law in Missouri and Texas, and he was a very close friend and confidant.

In the complicated world of electoral politics, my friends and consultants Michael Rowan and David Doak provided wise counsel. Landon Rowland, a distinguished Kansas City business leader, is a trusted adviser and confidant. The late Tommy Walsh, a Lee's Summit attorney, was a great political ally with a friendship dating to our days at the University of Missouri. State representative Bill Ransdall of Waynesville was always a solid political adviser. Through the years, Kansas City attorney Harvey Kaplan, an accomplished trial lawyer, gave scores of speeches on my behalf.

Among my closest military advisers through the years were the late Chief of Naval Operations, Admiral Mike Boorda, who was always and remains a hero to me; the late Army General Maxwell Thurman; retired Air Force General Chuck Boyd; retired Army General John Abrams; retired Air Force General Jim McCarthy; retired Navy Admiral Ron Hays; and Air Force Lieutenant General Chris Miller.

My current Husch Blackwell associate, Russ Orban, joined me in 1978 and was with me for fifteen years both on my personal staff and small business staff as an expert in small business matters and taxation.

On the Armed Services Committee staff, I had invaluable assistance from former staff director Erin Conaton, who was subsequently undersecretary of the Air Force and later undersecretary of defense for Personnel and Readiness, and her successor, Paul Arcangeli. I must also pay tribute to several former Armed Services Committee staffers. Tommy Glakas and Jim Schweiter were formerly top staff assistants to me on the committee. And a former Armed Services Committee staff member, really a national treasure, is now-retired Dr. Archie Barrett. He was instrumental in crafting legislation requiring jointness within the military and improving professional military education. His wealth of historical knowledge and real-world experience, as a military veteran as well as a scholar, provided tremendous service to our nation.

All of these people—boyhood friends; classmates; neighbors; mentors; colleagues in the law, national security, and public life; supportive constituents and the dedicated congressional staffers who helped me serve them for thirty-four years—they were, and are, my strong right arm.

Appendix B: My National Security Book List

1. Constitution of the United States
2. *The Art of War*, Sun Tzu
3. *On War*, Carl von Clausewitz
4. *Masters of War: Classical Strategic Thought*, Michael I. Handel
5. *The Book of War*, John Keegan, ed.
6. *Fifteen Decisive Battles of the World: From Marathon to Waterloo*, Edward Shepherd Creasy
7. *Alexander the Great*, Peter Bamm
8. *Hannibal*, Sir Gavin de Beer
9. *The Face of Battle*, John Keegan
10. *Crucible of War: The Seven Years War and the Fate of Empire in British North America, 1754–1766*, Fred Anderson
11. *Daniel Boone: The Life and Legend of an American Pioneer*, John Mack Faragher
12. *Washington: An Abridgment in One Volume by Richard Harwell of the Seven-Volume George Washington by Douglas Southall Freeman*, Richard Barksdale Harwell
13. *Tecumseh: A Life*, John Sugden
14. *Undaunted Courage*, Stephen Ambrose
15. *Napoleon Bonaparte: An Intimate Biography*, Vincent Cronin
16. *The Military Maxims of Napoleon*, Napoleon Bonaparte
17. *Nelson: A Personal History*, Christopher Hibbert
18. *The Price of Admiralty: The Evolution of Naval Warfare*, John Keegan
19. *The Washing of the Spears: The Rise and Fall of the Zulu Nation*, Donald R. Morris
20. *Lee*, Douglas Southall Freeman
21. *Personal Memoirs of Ulysses S. Grant*, Ulysses S. Grant
22. *Gray Ghosts of the Confederacy: Guerrilla Warfare in the West, 1861–1865*, Richard S. Brownlee
23. *Battle Cry of Freedom: The Civil War Era*, James M. McPherson
24. *Son of the Morning Star*, Evan S. Connell
25. *A Message to Garcia*, Elbert Hubbard
26. *Yanks: The Epic Story of the American Army in World War I*, John Eisenhower

27. *Black Jack: The Life and Times of John J. Pershing,* Frank Everson Vandiver
28. *Churchill: A Biography,* Roy Jenkins
29. *A War to Be Won: Fighting the Second World War,* Williamson Murray and Allan R. Millett
30. *Reminiscences,* Douglas MacArthur
31. *Rise and Fall of the Third Reich,* William L. Shirer
32. *Combined Fleet Decoded: The Secret History of American Intelligence and the Japanese Navy in World War II,* John Prados
33. *Ghost Soldiers: The Forgotten Epic Story of World War II's Most Dramatic Mission,* Hampton Sides
34. *Guadalcanal: The Definitive Account of the Landmark Battle,* Richard Frank
35. *The Victors: Eisenhower and His Boys: The Men of World War II,* Stephen Ambrose
36. *Black Knights: The Story of the Tuskegee Airmen,* Lynn M. Homan and Thomas Reilly
37. *Franklin D. Roosevelt: A Rendezvous with Destiny,* Frank Freidel
38. *Women in the Military: An Unfinished Revolution,* Maj. Gen. Jeanne Holm, USAF (ret.)
39. *Defeat into Victory,* William Slim
40. *Truman,* David McCullough
41. *This Kind of War,* T. R. Fehrenbach
42. *Boyd: The Fighter Pilot Who Changed the Art of War,* Robert Coram
43. *We Were Soldiers Once . . . and Young,* Harold G. Moore and Joseph L. Galloway
44. *Gulf War: The Complete History,* Thomas G. Houlahan
45. *Warrior Politics: Why Leadership Demands a Pagan Ethos,* Robert D. Kaplan
46. *Yellow Smoke: The Future of Land Warfare for America's Military,* Maj. Gen. Robert H. Scales Jr.
47. *Supreme Command: Soldiers, Statesmen, and Leadership in Wartime,* Eliot Cohen
48. *From Vietnam to 9–11: On the Front Lines of National Security,* John P. Murtha, with John Plashal
49. *Making the Corps,* Thomas E. Ricks
50. *The American Way of War: A History of United States Military Strategy and Policy,* Russell F. Weigley

APPENDIX C: "TREE HONORS SKELTON'S WIFE," OCTOBER 21, 2005

WASHINGTON—The VIPs gone, the ceremony over, the gray clouds over the Capitol dome threatening more rain, 5-year-old Sarah Skelton wouldn't stop shoveling. It was, after all, her grandmother Susie's tree. Somebody needed to finish filling in all that dirt. And so Sarah shoveled, paying no heed to the dirt dropping on her black dress shoes or the pink ribbon skewing on her head.

Susie Skelton, the wife of U.S. Rep. Ike Skelton, died in August at age 69, after 44 years of marriage. Her twin passions—Congress and her family—met Thursday afternoon in a ceremony on the grounds of the U.S. Capitol, where a Norway maple was planted in her memory at the Capitol's base.

Several dozen friends, family and members of Congress of both parties attended the ceremony.

"I'm grateful for this tribute to Susie," Skelton said, fighting back tears.

The Skeltons, beloved in their hometown of Lexington, were equally regarded in Washington. Though Ike Skelton, as ranking Democrat on the House Armed Services Committee, is better known to the public, Susie Skelton was a devoted political partner and well known in her own right as a leader of the Congressional Spouses Club.

"To the members of the congressional club, Susie Skelton of Missouri was larger than life," said Vicki Tiahrt, president of the group.

Speakers at the ceremony spoke of her humor, openness and especially the close bond with Ike. House Minority Leader Nancy Pelosi of California noted that on official trips, Ike Skelton would send a postcard home every day.

"There was no separation," said U.S. Rep. Emanuel Cleaver of Kansas City. "There was no such thing as Susie and Ike. What we had were the Skeltons. The Bible says in marriage, the two shall become one. This is one marriage where that happened very clearly."

And all agreed that a tree was a fitting memorial to Susie Skelton.

"Like Susie, the roots must grow deep," said the Rev. Daniel Coughlin, the House chaplain. "And her colorful presence will enhance the story of the Capitol."

A memorial tree must be approved by the House speaker's office and the Senate Rules and Administration Committee. The Architect of the Capitol, which maintains the grounds, ensures that the tree's type and location is in keeping with the plan of Frederick Law Olmsted, the landscape architect who designed the grounds.

"The Norway maple is specified in the 1874 Olmsted plan," said Matthew Evans of the Architect of the Capitol's Office.

"What we are doing is taking the opportunity not only to provide a living memorial to Susie Skelton, but at the same time, we are reinstating a historic landscape at the Capitol."

At the conclusion of the ceremony, all were invited to shovel dirt around the tree's base. Members of Congress went first, then the other invited guests. And then there was just Sarah, who wouldn't stop shoveling as her grandmother Susie's tree loomed over her.

Story reprinted with the permission of the Kansas City Star.

Appendix D: Letter to the President regarding Iraq

March 18, 2003

The President
The White House
Washington, D.C. 20500

Dear Mr. President:

This is a critical week for our nation and for the world. As you prepare to make the most difficult decision of sending our troops into combat, the thoughts and prayers of all Americans are with you. My colleagues here in Congress have many different views on the wisdom of action in Iraq and the severity of its consequences. But we are united in our support for all the men and women who serve this nation.

There is no doubt that our forces will be victorious in any conflict, but there is great potential for a ragged ending to a war as we deal with the aftermath. I appreciate the efforts that members of your administration have made to keep me informed about plans for the administration and reconstruction of Iraq following military conflict. Your team has thought about many of the things that will need to be done.

Secretary Rumsfeld frequently talks about the list he keeps of things that could go wrong in an Iraq war. I have kept my own list— of things that could go wrong after the war is over. The list below is indicative of this broader list. My hope is that this will be helpful to members of your administration as you continue to plan for all possibilities. These are not complete scenarios but rather a series of possible problems that could occur in some combination.

Internal Divisions and External Influences in Iraq

- Without access to Iraq through Turkey, U.S. troops are not present in northern Iraq in large numbers. Turkey enters northern Iraq to establish a buffer zone and fighting breaks out between the Turks and Kurds. A significant U.S. military force is needed to separate the groups, complicating the governmental transition and international support.

- An uprising in Kirkuk leaves the Kurds in control of areas of the city and surrounding area. This triggers a large Turkish invasion to protect the Turkmen minority and to prevent Kurdish control of oil resources. Again this would require U.S. military resources with all the attending effects.
- In the event that Turkey crosses into Iraq, Iran may do the same, ostensibly to stem the refugee flows from southern Iraq and to protect Shi'a interests.
- Shi'a populations in the south rebel and undertake attacks against Sunnis. U.S. troops must step in to protect the Sunnis and restore peace. These tensions resurface during attempts to build a federal and representative government.
- Urban fighting in the south brings Shi'a into conflict with Sunnis. The resulting devastation causes a refugee crisis as Shi'a make for the Iranian border. The results of Saddam's policy of forced Arabization of areas like Kirkuk yield dangerous consequences. Groups like the Kurds flow back into these areas seeking to reclaim their former homes and land, sparking conflict with Iraqi Arabs.
- Attempts to fashion a federal government in Baghdad prove difficult. Iran is able to establish proxies for its influence among the Shi'a representatives. Once in Iraq, infighting breaks out among members of the former Iraqi opposition in exile. The United States is unable to transition the administration of Iraq effectively and has to remain in place, with significant military backing.
- The war involves lengthy urban combat, particularly in Baghdad. Most infrastructure is destroyed resulting in massive humanitarian problems. The emphasis on humanitarian aid distracts from efforts to establish a new government. Once established the government faces massive political pressure from the sustained humanitarian crisis.

Weapons of Mass Destruction

- Saddam uses biological and chemical weapons against advancing U.S. troops, but also inflicts substantial civilian casualties. Efforts to stabilize cities and to establish a government are complicated by the need to deal with the large number of dead and to decontaminate affected areas.
- Saddam uses biological and chemical weapons directly against civilian populations or against another Arab country and seeks to affix blame for civilian suffering to the United States. Over the period of occupation, this resentment complicates U.S. efforts to maintain support for reconstruction efforts.
- U.S. troops are unable to quickly find all of Saddam's capabilities, requiring a long, labor-intensive search and anxiety as to when the task is complete.

- Regional leaders, for money or to gain influence, retain caches of WMD and transfer some to terrorist groups.
- Saddam attacks Israel with missiles containing weapons of mass destruction. Israel retaliates. Arab countries, notably Saudi Arabia and Jordan, come under intense political pressure to withdraw their support from the U.S. war effort. U.S. forces are forced to reposition operational centers into Iraq and Kuwait, complicating reconstruction and transition efforts.

Oil Resources

- Saddam sabotages a significant number of wells before his defeat. Current estimates indicate he may already have wired up to 1,500 of these wells. The damage takes years to contain at great economic and environmental cost and removes a major source of reconstruction funding.
- Internal groups, such as the Kurds, seize oil-rich land before American troops reach the area, causing internal clashes over these resources. Militant Shi'as seize other wells in the South.

International Support

- The United States takes immediate control of Iraq's administration and of reconstruction. The United Nations can't agree on how involved to get given the divisions among the Security Council about the need for conflict. The lack of UN involvement in the administration makes the European Union and others less likely to give. This situation delays reconstruction and puts more of the cost on the United States and a smaller number of partners.
- U.S. reconstruction efforts that give U.S. corporations a great role at the expense of multilateral organizations and other participation—as was detailed in yesterday's *Wall Street Journal*—spur resentment and again limit the willingness of others to participate.

American Commitment

- Stabilization and reconstruction prove more difficult than expected. U.S. troop requirements approach 200,000—the figure General Shinseki has mentioned—for a sustained period. This puts pressure on troop rotations, reservists, their families, and employers and requires a dramatic increase in end-strength.
- Required funding reaches the figure suggested by a recent Council on Foreign Relations assessment—$20 billion annually for several years. During a period of economic difficulty, the American public calls for greater burden sharing.

It is my hope that none of these eventualities comes to pass. But as you and all military leaders know, good planning requires considering the range of possibilities. It also requires advance preparation of the American people. You have regularly outlined the reasons for why the United States must disarm Iraq. I urge you to do the same in explaining why we must stay with Iraq for the long haul, even with the economic and military burdens this will entail.

As always, I am willing to help in any way I can to make this case to my colleagues and the American people.

Sincerely,
Ike Skelton
Ranking Democrat

cc: Honorable Donald H. Rumsfeld
Honorable Paul D. Wolfowitz
Honorable Peter W. Rodman
Honorable Colin L. Powell
Honorable Richard L. Armitage
Honorable Condoleezza Rice

APPENDIX E: BROTHER BOONE'S MARRIAGE SERVICE

Used by J. T. Boone

The Wedding is the beginning of a new and beautiful life

I hold in my hands authority to unite in wedlock

Mr. _____

and

Miss _____

I presume there is no lawful reason why this man and woman should not be made husband and wife?

Marriage is a heaven-born institution, ordained of God, and intended to make and keep pure the home. Woman was God's first and best gift to man. She was not taken from his head to rule over him, nor from his feet to be trampled upon, but from his side that she might be his companion, and from near his heart that he might bestow upon her his affections.

"Husband, love your wife," is the injunction of God's Book. "Wife, reverence your husband," is also the injunction of the Holy Book. "Love is the golden link that binds two souls with but a single thought; two hearts that beat as one."

Trusting that you are thus united in spirit, if you will join right hands, we will hear your plighted faith. Do you each take the one you hold by your right hand to be your lawfully wedded and beloved companion? Do you? . . . I do. Do you? . . . I do . . . By authority invested in me as a Minister of the Gospel, by the laws of the State of Florida, and I trust, by the God of Heaven, I pronounce you husband and wife. What God hath joined together, let no man put asunder.

In olden times the ring was used by kings, potentates, and others to seal their legal documents. Today, it is used for the more modern and beautiful purpose of sealing the marriage vow. This is done by the groom, placing it upon the finger of the bride in the presence of witnesses, thereby by his actions, as well as by his words, declaring that he bestows upon her his all, especially all his affections.

Prayer . . . Our Father, we thank Thee that we are not left alone in this life, but that Thou hast given companions. We trust that in Thy sight, today these two are one. Grant, our Father, that they may be one in Christ Jesus. Bless them with Thy richest blessing in time, and prepare them unto that eternal life and joy at thine own right hand at last, we beg in Jesus' name. Amen.

I now have the pleasure of introducing to their friends,

Mr. and Mrs_____

READ

GO TO CHURCH
KEEP SWEET

INDEX